Studies in Modern History

General Editor: J. C. D. Clark, Joyce and Elizabeth Hall Distinguished Professor of British History, University of Kansas

Titles include:

James Mackintosh
VINDICIÆ GALLICÆ
Defence of the French Revolution: A Critical Edition

Robert J. Mayhew
LANDSCAPE, LITERATURE AND ENGLISH RELIGIOUS CULTURE, 1660–1800
Samuel Johnson and Languages of Natural Description

Jeremy C. Mitchell
THE ORGANIZATION OF OPINION
Open Voting in England, 1832-68

Paul Monod, Murray Pittock and Daniel Szechi (editors)
LOYALTY AND IDENTITY
Jacobites at Home and Abroad

Marjorie Morgan
NATIONAL IDENTITIES AND TRAVEL IN VICTORIAN BRITAIN

James Muldoon
EMPIRE AND ORDER
The Concept of Empire, 800–1800

F. D. Parsons
THOMAS HARE AND POLITICAL REPRESENTATION IN VICTORIAN BRITAIN

Julia Rudolph
WHIG POLITICAL THOUGHT AND THE GLORIOUS REVOLUTION
James Tyrrell and the Theory of Resistance

Lisa Steffen
TREASON AND NATIONAL IDENTITY
Defining a British State, 1608–1820

Lynne Taylor
BETWEEN RESISTANCE AND COLLABORATION
Popular Protest in Northern France, 1940–45

Joseph Tendler
OPPONENTS OF THE ANNALES SCHOOL

Anthony Waterman
POLITICAL ECONOMY AND CHRISTIAN THEOLOGY SINCE THE ENLIGHTENMENT
Essays in Intellectual History

Doron Zimmerman
THE JACOBITE MOVEMENT IN SCOTLAND AND IN EXILE, 1746–1759

Studies in Modern History
Series Standing Order ISBN 978-0-333-79328-2 (Hardback)
978-0-333-80346-2 (Paperback)
(outside North America only)

You can receive future titles in this series as they are published by placing a standing order. Please contact your bookseller or, in case of difficulty, write to us at the address below with your name and address, the title of the series and the ISBN quoted above.

Customer Services Department, Macmillan Distribution Ltd, Houndmills, Basingstoke, Hampshire RG21 6XS, England

---

Also by James B. Bell

A WAR OF RELIGION: Dissenters, Anglicans and the American Revolution

FROM ARCADE STREET TO MAIN STREET: A History of the Seeger Refrigerator Company: 1902–1984

THE IMPERIAL ORIGINS OF THE KING'S CHURCH IN EARLY AMERICA, 1607–1783

Empire, Religion and Revolution in Early Virginia, 1607–1786

By James B. Bell
Distinguished Fellow, Rothmere American Institute, University of Oxford

First published 2013 by
PALGRAVE MACMILLAN

Palgrave Macmillan in the UK is an imprint of Macmillan Publishers Limited, registered in England, company number 785998, of Houndmills, Basingstoke, Hampshire RG21 6XS.

Palgrave Macmillan in the US is a division of St Martin's Press LLC, 175 Fifth Avenue, New York, NY 10010.

Palgrave Macmillan is the global academic imprint of the above companies and has companies and representatives throughout the world.

Palgrave® and Macmillan® are registered trademarks in the United States, the United Kingdom, Europe and other countries.

ISBN 978–1–137–32791–8

This book is printed on paper suitable for recycling and made from fully managed and sustained forest sources. Logging, pulping and manufacturing processes are expected to conform to the environmental regulations of the country of origin.

A catalogue record for this book is available from the British Library.

A catalog record for this book is available from the Library of Congress.

In gratitude to colleagues and friends:

Jonathan C. D. Clark
William Appleton Coolidge
J. Martin Dodsworth
Sir John Huxtable Elliott
Simon Head
Bridget Hill
Christopher Hill
Judy Longworth
Sir Colin Lucas
James E. Mooney
John Pinfold
John Prest
Walter G. Seeger
Kevin Sharpe
John D. Walsh
Anne Whiteman

Contents

List of Tables

Acknowledgements

Inevitably, when the long assignment of researching, analysing, interpreting, describing, and writing a book is finished the author recalls and reflects on the many persons along the way that have contributed to the creative process and work. I am especially appreciative in distinctive ways to each of the persons remembered in the Dedication of the book. Over several years my research interests have been generously aided by my association as a Distinguished Fellow of the Rothermere American Institute at the University of Oxford. I am grateful to Dr Nigel Bowles the Executive Director for his sustaining interest and support.

A band of immensely talented and congenial librarians at several of the libraries of the University of Oxford have lightened my burdens at every step and aided my efforts and I welcome the opportunity to publicly acknowledge their help. At the Bodleian Library I have received prompt and courteous assistance from David Busby, Ernesto Gomez, Sally Matthews, and Calista Meinert, and the late Vera Ryhajlo; at the Vere Harmsworth Library, from Jane Rawson, Sophia FitzMaurice, Johanna O'Connor, Martin Sutcliffe, and Judy Warden; and at the Rhodes House Library from the knowledgeable John Pinfold and Lucy McCann. In the United States my research tasks have been reinforced by the help from the librarians and the collections of the Firestone Library at Princeton University, the Princeton Theological Seminary Library, and the Harvard College Library. At Balliol College, Oxford, I have received cheerful hospitality and thoughtful assistance from Judy Longworth and Ian Plummer during my regular visits to the college and Oxford.

The research and writing of this book was immeasurably aided by two simultaneous year-long visiting fellowships at the Princeton Theological Seminary and at Princeton University's Center for the Study of Religion. I am grateful for the kindness and support of President Iain R. Torrance and Vice-President Rosemary Mitchell at the Seminary, and to Jennifer Legath, Anita Kline, Professor Robert Wuthnow, and Professor Judith Weisenfeld, and the participants of the Religion in the Americas Workshop at the university.

On the occasion of my preliminary exploration of examining England's imperial civil and ecclesiastical policies that gave rise to its first two extra-territorial ventures I discussed the matter with my friend and colleague Professor J. Martin Dodsworth. He immediately, forcefully, and emphatically advised me that my efforts would be incomplete if I did not include England's Irish experience. His persuasive advice was embraced for further consideration and gave rise to the structure and comparative account of the book in hand.

Three readers of successive drafts of the book have offered constructive and helpful comments on the text. I do want to thank the Series Editor Professor J. C. D. Clark, Professor Jeremy Gregory, and Dr James E. Mooney for their wise, encouraging, and insightful interest in the course of the development of the work, contributions that have without reservation strengthened, refined, and enriched the book.

I would be remiss not to recognize Steve Barron for his contributions as the designer and administrator of my website, 'The Colonial American Clergy of the Church of England, 1607–1783'. It is a collection of biographical details relating to the men who were associated with the Church in Early America. The data has been a basic resource for my analysis, description, and interpretation of the men who were linked to the extension and experience of the church in seventeenth- and eighteenth-century Virginia.

Finally, I owe thanks to my family: to my wife Miriam and children James, Scott, and Vanessa, all of whom have lived with and heard about the book for longer than they probably care to acknowledge. They have been patient and supportive and I am grateful for that forbearance, encouragement, and kindness. They graciously never asked the question, 'when will it be finished?'

Terms and usage

Whenever reference is made in this book to the Church of England, or Anglican or English church, I mean the church and its organization and practices in England. Because the origins, educational and early religious experiences of many of the Virginia ministers occurred in the distant provinces of Scotland, Ireland, and Wales, they were required to submit in all matters to the jurisdiction of the bishop of London and the customs of the English church. Such sister institutions as the Episcopal Church in Scotland, the Church of Ireland, and the Church of England in Wales, differed in varying degrees from practices of the Anglican church.

Dates of the months and years are given here according to the New Style throughout the text; but when reference has been made to manuscript source materials in the footnotes, the Old Style system of dating has been maintained.

After 1619 all Virginians were parishioners of the Anglican Church – men and women, young and old, planters and merchants, yeoman farmers and artisans, servants and slaves, and dissenters. Professor John K. Nelson has admirably examined their relation to the parish in Anglican Virginia in *A Blessed Company: Parishes, Parsons, and Parishioners in Anglican Virginia, 1690–1776.*

The African slaves (the term 'Negro' reflects contemporary usage) who began to arrive in the colony about 1619 gradually became a major component of the parish tax base, and during the two or three decades before the War for Independence received attention from some ministers for catechetical instruction and baptism. In some churches galleries were built and reserved for the use of slaves and servants.

Native Americans, (the term 'Indian' reflects contemporary usage) despite the proclamations of the early proponents for colonization, were not exposed to systematic evangelization during the colonial era.

The experiences of women as parishioners during the seventeenth and eighteenth centuries signalled prevailing social and cultural practices. There were no female parsons and they did not have a role in the governance of the local or provincial church. In the course of the narrative for the book the word 'men' has been used interchangeably to describe ministers, clergymen, and parsons.

Rothermere American Institute
University of Oxford, 2012

Some Useful Dates

1583–1604	John Whitgift, Archbishop of Canterbury
1603–1625	James I and VI – King of England
1604–10	Richard Bancroft, Archbishop of Canterbury
	Hampton Court Conference
	The Canons of the Church
1604–07	Richard Vaughan, Bishop of London
1607	Settlement of Jamestown
1607–09	Thomas Ravis, Bishop of London
1610–11	George Abbot, Bishop of London
1611	The Authorized Version of the Bible
1611–33	George Abbot, Archbishop of Canterbury
1611–21	John King, Bishop of London
1620	Settlement of Plymouth Colony
1621–28	George Montaigne, Bishop of London
1624	Settlement of New Amsterdam
1625–49	Charles I, King of England
1628–33	William Laud, Bishop of London
1630	Settlement of Massachusetts Bay Colony
1633–40	Thomas Wentworth, Earl of Strafford, appointed lord deputy
1633–45	William Laud, Archbishop of Canterbury
1633–60	William Juxon, Bishop of London
1634	Settlement of Maryland
	Civil War in England
	Ordinance abolishing use of the Book of Common Prayer
	Ordinance for abolishing bishops and archbishops
1649	Charles I executed (30 January)
1649–60	Commonwealth in England
1653–58	Cromwell Lord Protector of the Commonwealth of England, Scotland and Ireland
1660–85	Restoration of Charles II, King of England (May)
1660–63	Gilbert Sheldon, Bishop of London
1661	Gilbert Sheldon, Archbishop of Canterbury
1662	Book of Common Prayer

1663–75	Humphrey Henchman, Bishop of London
	Henry Compton, Bishop of London
1676	Bacon's Rebellion
1685–88	James II, King of England
1688	Glorious Revolution
1689	William (1689–1702) and Mary (1689–94), King and Queen of England
	Toleration Act
1702–14	Anne, Queen of England
1702–13	Queen Anne's War
1707	Union of England and Scotland
1713	Treaty of Utrecht
1714–27	George I, King of England
1714–23	John Robinson, Bishop of London
1718	First large emigration from Ulster to the American colonies, again in 1729. Toleration Act exempts Protestant Dissenters from the Test Act
1723–48	Edmund Gibson, Bishop of London
1727–60	George II, King of England
1739–45	Great Awakening in the American Colonies
1748–61	Thomas Sherlock, Bishop of London
1754–63	French and Indian War
1755–69	Parson's Cause
1758–68	Thomas Secker, Archbishop of Canterbury
1760–1820	George III, King of England
1761–62	Thomas Hayter, Bishop of London
1762–64	Richard Osbaldeston, Bishop of London
1763	Treaty of Paris, English control over North America east of the Mississippi confirmed
1764–77	Richard Terrick, Bishop of London
1765–66	Stamp Act
1767	Townshend Acts
1770	Boston Massacre
1773	Tea Act
	Boston Tea Party
1774	Coercive Acts
	Continental Congress
1775	Lexington and Concord
	Battle of Bunker Hill
1776	British forces evacuate Boston
	Declaration of Independence

	Virginia State Constitution adopted
	Thomas Paine, *Common Sense*
1777	State financial support of clergy ends in Virginia
	Articles of Confederation adopted
1778–87	Robert Lowth, Bishop of London
1778	Treaty of Alliance with France
1780	First use of the name Protestant Episcopal Church by the former Church of England in Maryland
1781	British forces surrender at Yorktown, Virginia
1782	William White, *The Case of the Episcopal Churches in the United States Considered*
1783	Treaty of Paris
	Protestant Episcopal Church organized in Maryland
1784	Samuel Seabury of Connecticut is consecrated in Scotland the first bishop of the Protestant Episcopal Church in the United States
1785	The Episcopal Church is organized in Virginia, New Jersey, and South Carolina
	First General Convention of the Protestant Episcopal Church in the United States of America
	Virginia State Constitution enacted
	Virginia Statute for Religious Freedom enacted
	English Parliament enacts statute to allow for the consecration of American bishops by English prelates
1787	Anglican Church disestablished in Virginia
1788	Virginia ratifies United States Constitution
1789	Constitution of the United States of America approved
	General Convention of the Episcopal Church adopts for use a revised liturgy from that of the English church and a revised Book of Common Prayer

Prologue

The purpose of this book is to examine the ideas and forces during the last two decades of the reign of Queen Elizabeth I that gave rise to King James I's grant of a charter to the Virginia Company of London for England's first settlement in the western hemisphere.

An extensive debate at court over the establishment of a second English colony was shaped in part by the 70-year-old attempt by Henry VIII to subjugate Ireland and the Irish people. Following in the wake of Spain and Portugal's voyages of exploration and discovery, England was entering the early modern era of interest in extra-territorial ventures in the Old and New Worlds. Yet the nation's first two imperial projects differed significantly: Ireland represented the crown's efforts to replicate and impose the civil and ecclesiastical reforms of England on the Irish, while a colony in Virginia was not undertaken by the government but delegated by the crown as a commercial for-profit venture for the merchant adventurers of the London Company.

On the occasion of Henry VIII's reformation of the church in England as the Church of England authority over the church was wrested from the hands of the Bishop of Rome, the pope, and placed in the hands of the king. Parliament by statute declared the monarch the Supreme Head of the church. The institution became an essential element of the state in company with the military, the law, and civil officials and organization. A component of England's first attempts to form an overseas empire in Ireland and Virginia was the reformed Protestant Church of England under sharply contrasting circumstances. The chapters and pages ahead will note, describe, compare, and contrast the salient features of the English church in both territories.

The effort to extend the state church to Virginia and the later American colonies was never as systematic as the Spanish Roman

Catholic efforts in New Spain. The cross and flag were intertwined with Spanish national interests as Roman Catholic priests accompanied the voyages of exploration, discovery, and settlement. Under Spanish auspices the church was at a strong advantage because it was able to recruit and delegate for its overseas missionary activity members of the Dominican, Franciscan, Jesuit, and other orders. Henry VIII's dissolution of the monasteries removed a similar potential reservoir of personnel and talent to support English ecclesiastical efforts overseas. From the beginnings in Virginia the recruitment of ministers was a singular task. Funds needed to be provided to underwrite their travel expenses and annual salaries, and meet the costs of erecting and outfitting churches. These were essential obligations for the Virginia Company and later for the colony's legislature, the General Assembly, throughout the colonial era. After the Declaration of Independence and the disestablishment of the church in 1786 all financial expenses for churches became the responsibility of the local membership.

Virginia, the strongest representation of English imperial policy in the western hemisphere, was the first colony in America in which the church was established. Over nearly two centuries it became the province served by the largest number of ministers and churches during the colonial period. By the last quarter of the seventeenth century and after the extension of royal jurisdiction in the colonies, the church was extended to Maryland, Massachusetts, New York, and Pennsylvania. Unlike the other religious groups that appeared in the American colonies of the period it was the only church favoured by the English government, royal governors, and six legislatures. The situation inspired a dual effect that was at once welcomed by some provinces and opposed by others, especially in Boston after 1686. Beginning with one minister at Jamestown in 1607, Robert Hunt, ministerial ranks gradually increased and by 1783 1,289 men had been associated with the American church, of whom 534 clergymen served Virginia congregations. The first service of worship in the western hemisphere was held at Jamestown on 8 May 1607 under an awning tied to trees in the settlement, but by 1783 there were 249 church buildings in the colony and a further 243 distributed in the other twelve provinces.

The Virginia chronicle is linked to England's first venture in Ireland but contrasted in a significant manner from the structure of the Church of England and the reformed Church of Ireland. No archdioceses or dioceses were created with defined geographical boundaries in Virginia or elsewhere in America to organize and administer the church. No archbishops or bishops were appointed to supervise and guide the church in any of the provinces throughout the long colonial era. Unlike the Irish experience, there is no evidence that crown officials considered extending to Virginia or other American colonies a reformed Church of Virginia after the style of the institution established in Ireland.

The Virginia church and parsons were not exposed to the controversial confessional issues that occurred in the Church of Ireland during the seventeenth and eighteenth centuries. The controversies did not travel to the province, and if the men were inclined to put their thoughts to paper they were deterred by the lack of a printer and printing press in the province until about 1730. Virginia voices and pens were silent; they did not reprise or debate such topics as the formulation and legacy of the Irish Articles of 1615 and the dogmatic tenets.[1] There was no colonial author to complement Jonathan Swift's *Sentiments of a Church of England Man* (1708) or apologists in the conflict against heresy during the eighteenth century. Absent, too, is any notice in the colony of Bishop Benjamin Hoadley's sermon in 1717 stating that the gospels offered little or no evidence for any visible church authority, known as the Bangorian Controversy. The best known defence of orthodoxy in England was *The Analogy of Religion, Natural and Revealed* by the Bishop of Durham, Joseph Butler (1692–1752). Bishop George Berkeley's *Alciphon, or the Minute Philosopher* (1732), a thoroughgoing rebuttal of the popular case against revealed religion, had anticipated Butler. But the Church of Ireland had its own William Law (1686–1761): Philip Skelton (1707–87), a mystic and devoted pastor, published his *Proposals for the Revival of Christianity* ('1736) and *Deism Revealed* (1748). Dr John Clayton, a fellow of Trinity College in Dublin (1714–28), Bishop of Killala (1730–35), Cork (1735–45), and Clogher (1745–58), and friend of Dr Samuel Clarke (1675–1729) critically examined the *Scripture Doctrine of the Trinity* (1712), denied the doctrine of the Trinity in his essay on *Spirit* (1757), and reiterated his views in the third part of his *Vindication of the Old and New Testament* (1757).

The first Anglican services of worship in 1607 followed the ritual of the Book of Common Prayer but did not become a distinctive American institution in the footsteps of the Congregational church in Massachusetts and Connecticut, or the Presbyterian church in Pennsylvania or New Jersey. The religious group became an English–American body and not an American–English church or a Church of America with English ancestry. Without episcopal oversight in either Virginia or London until about 1680 the church was more akin to the structure of the Congregational and Presbyterian churches. It was a state church in England and Virginia and favoured throughout the American colonies by royal government, governors, and provincial legislation, but without the familiar ecclesiastical apparatus of England and Ireland.

The perspective of this book differs from my two earlier studies about the transfer, development, and experience of the Church of England in mainland America, *The Imperial Origins of the King's Church in Early America, 1607–1783* (London, 2004), and *A War of Religion: Dissenters, Anglicans, and the American Revolution* (London, 2008). In my first book I considered the role of civil and ecclesiastical officials in London and America in shaping and implementing the policies for the extension and governance of the provincial church during the seventeenth and eighteenth centuries. My second volume, *A War of Religion*, had a two-fold purpose: first, it examined the several ecclesiastical polity controversies between the church and its ministers and mainly Congregational critics during the decades from the 1680s to the 1770s which, in large measure, cast the Anglican group's colonial identity; second, it examined how the significant roles played by the radical political leaders John and Samuel Adams in Boston and John Wilkes in London shifted and transformed the discourse of longstanding religious and civil disputes during the 1760s and 1770s. This trio redirected the sharply focused debate from the realm of esoteric ecclesiastical argument to the domain of a fundamental political, civil, and constitutional issue. They were fearful of the authority of parliament to enhance and extend the political power of the English church, particularly in Massachusetts. They adroitly circumscribed the church's constitutional status in England, demonstrated that it was ripe for application in rhetorical complaint against imperial policies, and placed it as one of the causes of the American Revolution.

This book presents a different perspective from the publications of three prominent historians of early Virginia: the Reverend George Maclaren Brydon, and Professors John K. Nelson, and Rhys Isaac.[2] The works by Brydon and Nelson chronicle the history of the church in Virginia from divergent but complementary perspectives. On the one hand, Brydon's *Virginia's Mother Church* provides an under-structure for the institution's experience between 1607 and 1814 and is framed by the chronology of the reigns of successive English monarchs and the colony's royal governors. On the other hand, Nelson's *A Blessed Company* leaves no stone unturned in the investigation and analysis of the essential elements and factors that gave rise to the establishment and accounts of the parishes of the province. Isaac's book, *A Transformation of Virginia, 1740–1790* is not a church history but an engaging social history of the colony and state over half-a-century. His chronicle of the problems of the church and college of the period focuses without perspective on the explosive character of two long-simmering issues over the payment of the parsons' salaries and the management of the college. The Parson's Cause and the college faculty's dispute with the Board of Visitors deserves and demands a full representation for a true understanding.

It may be argued that Virginia's seventeenth century ended with the death of James Blair in 1743 and that for the remainder of the colonial era the church and college were thrust into new circumstances. Blair guided and controlled the destiny of the church as the commissary of the Bishop of London and founder and president of the College of William and Mary for more than fifty years. The church and the college were, probably unknowingly, entering a gradually changing new age. Establishment of the church, and a royal charter for the college, did not insulate either institution from criticism or represent a burst of support. Neither body was protected by the authority of a bishop or a civil official. Ultimate responsibility for the church was scattered, it did not rest entirely with the House of Burgesses, or the local vestry, or the local parson. Yet each played a vital role in its experience. In 1777 the legislature acted to terminate the state's responsibility for payment of the clergymen's stipends, and nine years later to disestablish the church.

The account of the church in America and Virginia is divided into three distinct periods. The first phase ranges over the decades between its founding in 1607 until the 1680s and the English government's innovative new imperial policies for governing and administering the American colonies. The second era begins about 1689 with the English parliament's passage of the Toleration Act, granting rights to religious groups to organize, build chapels and churches, and conduct services of worship. Without reservation, the Toleration Act contributed to reshaping religious culture in England and America. The final phase of the story begins with the emerging colonial critical rhetoric on imperial policies in the 1760s, shaped in part by the Declaration of Independence, the formation of the new republic's civil institutions, and the church's disestablishment. The sudden and complete withdrawal of favoured imperial administration, leadership, and financial support diminished the church's status and membership. The civil and ecclesiastical apparatus of empire was terminated, leaving a legacy of a weak and impaired church.

The architecture of this book is in three parts. Part I examines the background of England's early imperial efforts in Ireland and the proposal late in Elizabeth I's reign, led by Walter Raleigh and Richard

Hakluyt, to establish a second colony in the western hemisphere. It was not a whimsical or politically unsophisticated plan: the establishment of an English settlement in America was intended to counteract Spain's further imperial expansionist efforts in North America – a political and territorial buffer zone against the possible advance of Catholic Spain from its imperial outposts in Florida.

In step with Elizabeth I's grant of a charter to the merchant adventurers of the East India Company in 1600 to undertake trade and commerce in Asia, James I granted a charter in 1606 to the members of the Virginia Company of London for a settlement in America. The charter represented a new direction for imperial affairs, a policy that subsequently influenced not only settlement of Virginia during the seventeenth century but also the first colonies in New England. The novel plan for settling Virginia drew on the precedent and practices of the English merchant trading companies on the European continent and in the Near East since at least the later fifteenth century. The new responsibility for undertaking and administering an overseas province shifted the burden from the crown to the shareholders and officers of the Virginia Company of London (1606, 1609). The innovative format became the procedure for the later colonies established in New England at Plymouth (1620) and at Salem and Boston in Massachusetts Bay (1629).

The crown's imperial policy for Virginia differed sharply from Tudor policy in Ireland. The course of action in Virginia was undertaken outwith the system of England's civil, military, and ecclesiastical establishment. In Ireland, English officials transplanted the familiar apparatus of the church, including the creation of archdioceses, dioceses, cathedrals, and the appointment of archbishops and bishops. Laws enacted by the Virginia legislature established and governed the church in the province between 1619 and 1786. A 1619 statute provided for church services in the parishes and defined the duties of ministers in accordance with the 1603 Canon Law that governed the church at home. Over the next 25 years, additional legislation refined the governance of the church and assigned further duties for the vestry – uniquely Virginian obligations that differed from the practices in England. It remains puzzling that the church's first steps overseas were initiated without the review and approval of officials in England – say, the Archbishop of Canterbury (the titular head of the Anglican Church, a chief officer of state, and a member of the Privy Council). In addition, the account of England's second extra-territorial venture is silent with regard to any discussions at court by ecclesiastical officials for the creation and establishment of a reformed Church of Virginia after the manner of the Church of Ireland.

The statutes enacted by the General Assembly on behalf of the church were not intended to illuminate the nature of provincial worship services, or the placement of altars, pulpits, and baptismal fonts in the buildings. Nor do the laws or any other collateral resources offer or inform us about the forms and frequency of worship practices, the use of the Book of Common Prayer, or the version of the Bible that was used: was it the Geneva, the Bishops', or the King James edition? We are compelled to inquire, what was the seating arrangement for the congregation, were benches or pews the common practice? Did men and women sit together during the services or were the sexes segregated by an aisle? When did the singing of hymns begin? While historians may offer a suggestive reconstruction of the worship experience it must remain speculative owing to the lack of documents and diaries that illustrate New England congregational life.

After the default of the Virginia Company's operations in 1624 the charter was revoked and the colony became a royal territorial jurisdiction. Governors were appointed and empowered to provide a degree of oversight over the church. Part II of the book considers the major components of the extension, establishment, and development of the Anglican Church in seventeenth-century Virginia. The absence of any oversight from ecclesiastical officials in London for more than 70 years provided an opportunity for laymen to step forward and assert leadership over local church affairs. Vested by statute with certain religious and civil duties, the parish vestry, along with the provincial courts, became the centre of power in the local community and churches were controlled by laymen with little influence from the incumbent minister. The provocatively innovative American turn meant that the superintending of affairs of the congregation was in the hands of an elected corps of leading parishioners and not, after the English manner, dominated by a single individual or corporate patron with possible oversight by a diocesan bishop or his deputy. This was a significant turn of events that would chart a new course and destiny for the church in Virginia.

The Reformation of the English church undertaken during the reigns of Henry VIII and Elizabeth I was not accomplished with voices speaking in unison. During the sixteenth and seventeenth centuries several groups contended under the large umbrella of the Church in England, including traditional-Anglican, Anglican–Puritan, Puritan, Presbyterian, and Nonconformist. They did not fit neatly into one coherent liturgical or theological mould. These divisions of the church at home extended to, and were represented by ministers in, seventeenth-century Virginia.

We have statistical knowledge of the number of churches built and the number of parsons who served the Virginia church during the seventeenth century, but little is known about the practices of worship and biographical details of the ministers. It is a circumstance that contrasts sharply with the many New England Congregational clergymen of the era who left a trail of substantial information regarding their lives and careers. Our understanding of the New England ministries is enhanced by the manuscripts or printed materials that they bequeathed to posterity, including sermons, journals, and correspondence: resources that aid the reconstruction and description of their careers and the religious history and culture of the communities they served. Details of many of the Virginia men are limited to their names and approximate dates and places of service. We do have a few biographical clues regarding their origins, parentage, education, and professional careers in the colony or earlier in England or Scotland. A similar situation was not uncommon among the men who served as ministers of the Church of Ireland during the sixteenth century. Our understanding of the period is largely limited to the prelates of the several dioceses.

We do, at least, know the names and approximated dates of service of the 159 men who served the seventeenth-century Virginia congregations. They were probably all English natives, and many had attended Oxford or Cambridge universities. The financial affairs of the church were initially the responsibility of the Virginia Company of London. After 1619 the obligation was transferred to the provincial legislature that provided the means for funds to be raised and the construction and maintenance of church buildings and property, and provide for the payment of the clergymen's salaries.

An effort is undertaken to identify complaints against clergy and the terms of discipline. Because there was not a printer in the Virginia colony until about 1730 there are few traces of printed contributions from the pens of the seventeenth- and early eighteenth-century clergymen. New England had a printing press from 1639 forward. By the time that Virginia had a press New England and the Middle Colonies had published 3,883 items. Without a bishop to conduct visitations at parishes or summon a convocation of the ministers the first recorded gathering of the ministers in Virginia did not occur until 1686. At that time Governor Francis Lord Howard of Effingham summoned the men, presumably to inspect their licences from the Bishop of London to officiate in the colony and to discuss other unknown issues.

Little is known about the books that were owned and used by colonial Virginia ministers in their professional work or personal lives. Because the ministers were representatives of a learned professional class and their books were a source of inspiration and instruction for duties, an analysis is presented of the only two inventories of their libraries extant. This indicates that the two libraries represented different perspectives on theological and ecclesiastical polity and reflect in part the differing educational backgrounds and theological outlooks of seventeenth-century parsons. One book collection represents the acquisitive and intellectual interests of a university-educated English clergyman, while the other is an example of the knowledgeable bent of a Nonconformist minister who was not a university graduate.

Part III considers four overarching topics that relate to the church's imperial experience across the seventeenth and eighteenth centuries. The new interest in imperial administration aroused by the English government's Council of Trade and Plantations in the 1670s, 1680s, and 1690s provided structure and guided the course of England's presence in Virginia and the other early American colonies until 1776. The accession of King William and Queen Mary, and then Queen Anne, brought new royal support for the overseas church and the College of William and Mary, chartered in 1693. Favoured and sustained by their English connections and associations, both church and college encountered severe consequences as public objections to imperial policies were voiced in the run-up and aftermath of the War for Independence.

The fortunes of the church were transformed by the War for Independence at the expense of nearly a century of attention and influence of English policy and leadership. The unravelling of the imperial administration and the lack of popular support for the established Virginia church and the College of William and Mary after the Declaration of Independence all reflected popular anti-English political opinion. The situation had been shaped by the rise of the authority and power of the provincial legislature. The state of the church was a consequence of the English government's policy of 'Salutary Neglect'. The transfer of the church to colonial Virginia was incomplete and it lacked the familiar hierarchical structure of the homeland. Though it was at worship a traditional Episcopal church, there was no prelate to ordain candidates for the ministry, to provide the sacrament of confirmation to members, or to consecrate churches, churchyards, and cemeteries.

The College of William and Mary was founded in 1693 under strong Anglican influence and auspices in London but floundered with the church because of the lack of popular financial support throughout the eighteenth century. It was also caught in a sustained battle between the faculty and the members of the Board of Visitors who sought to dominate institutional policy and affairs.

The long path to the Americanization of the English church crossed an important threshold in 1777 when the Virginia legislature terminated the payment of ministers' salaries. An uncertain new era dawned for the church with its disestablishment in 1786, an event followed by years of litigation over the status of glebes and parsonages. A post-Revolutionary War church emerged that was financially independent and required the voluntary support of its members to maintain it. The church in Virginia, as elsewhere in the new United States, faced the additional task of undertaking reconstitution and reconstruction.

Rising popular criticism and hostile rhetoric by colonial leaders about English trade and tax policies following parliament's passage of the Stamp Act in 1765 began the gradual erosion of the status of the provincial church. Because of its English heritage and link, the church was vulnerable; although the principles of the English law were not discarded the church's position was not secure. Loyalty to, and membership of, an Anglican Church could easily be transferred to some other religious group perhaps more aligned with Patriot sentiments, notably the Presbyterian or Congregational. Anti-English political opinions in the colonies were sharp, persistent, and popular, escalating and coalescing during the run-up to the Declaration of Independence in 1776.

Despite the Patriot leanings of a majority of the 120 active Anglican clergymen in 1776, supporting the American cause, the destiny of the church as institution was in jeopardy in Virginia and elsewhere in America. Not one layman, in Virginia or in any other place in America, raised his voice or gripped his pen to declare or defend the interests of the Anglican Church. In the absence of an articulate prelate or a band of prominent and respected members, the church's interests were unheard in the colonial cities, towns, and countryside. After nearly 170 years in Virginia, the place of the English church in the new state was in question, and peril; exposed for structural modification. In 1777 all financial obligations – the payment of the parson's salary and the construction and maintenance of church buildings – were quickly terminated and transferred from public funds appropriated by the legislature to become the responsibility of the local congregation's vestry. Churches were closed, the ranks of parsons diminished, members fled to join other religious groups such as the Presbyterian, and many vestry members resigned their posts. In 1786 the church was disestablished by the legislature with relative ease, and a heritage of 167 years dissolved. The new age required the colonial church to reconstitute and reconstruct itself to subsist on the voluntary contributions of members, a responsibility of the local vestries. The Episcopal church in Virginia would not recover its eighteenth-century position until after the Civil War and the 'Gilded Age' of the 1870s and afterwards.

The experience of the remnant of the colonial English church during the period after the War for Independence has been overlooked in the accounts of the democratization of American religious groups during the late eighteenth and early nineteenth centuries.[3] It is a puzzling situation because, arguably, in order to survive, the church was required to transform itself from an extension of the English church under the supervision of the Bishop of London in each colony to a distinctive American body in each new state and the nation. No other religious group shared the experience of the English church. England lost the war and 71 Loyalist parsons fled to exile in England or the Canadian maritime provinces. Without reservation, the ranks of the ministers and members of the church in 1782 were severely reduced: the institution was wounded, though not mortally. Interestingly, not all English cultural keystones suffered a similar fate as the church: the use of the law and language continued at large, and the works of Chaucer, Shakespeare, Milton, Newton, and Locke were discussed and taught without interruption at Harvard and Yale.

For the vestige of the colonial church in Virginia and elsewhere the complex and difficult question was simply, how could the religious group be reorganized and reconstituted under the new civil circumstances in each state and nationally? The leader's role was claimed and executed by the well-connected 34-year-old William White of Philadelphia, an able and politically sagacious minister of Christ Church.[4] He was not a bishop but he acted like one, and deftly orchestrated an interstate drive to reorder the church state by state and nationally. A graduate of the College of Philadelphia, he served as the Chaplain of Congress during the years it sat in the city (1777–85, 1789–1801) and was a long-time friend of Benjamin Franklin's.[5] White's skilful and diplomatic efforts were embodied in an essay he published in 1782, *The Case of the Episcopal Churches*. He reminded the reader that 'A prejudice has prevailed with many that the Episcopal Churches cannot exist than under the dominion of Great Britain. A church government that would contain the constituent principles of the Church of England, and yet be independent of foreign jurisdiction or influence, would remove that anxiety, which at present hangs heavy on the minds of many sincere persons'.[6]

The Philadelphia parson declared to his audience that in general the members of the church were supportive of the governments formed in each state, and admitted that 'inconsistent with the duties resulting from this allegiance, would be the subjection to any spiritual jurisdiction connected with the temporal authority of a foreign state'.[7] White emphasized that the colonial connection with the Bishop of London had been dissolved with the Revolution.[8] In addition he stated that 'the ecclesiastical power over the greater number of the churches, formerly subsisting in some legislative bodies on the continent, is also abrogated by the Revolution'.[9]

White's essay set the course and the agenda for the establishment of the Protestant Episcopal Church in the United States of America in each state and for the nation. There was no prospect for a retreat from his cogently argued position. He had boldly embraced the institution at its moment of need to be reorganized, reconstituted, and led into a new age of Americanization and democratization.[10] Notable was the arrangement for the clergy and laity to share power equally and meet every three years, a feature that may have been induced by the debates over several decades in New England between Anglican writers and numerous Nonconformist critics. The scheme contrasted with the practices in England where the deliberative and final authority over ecclesiastical affairs rested in the hands of the bishops and the Convocation of the Clergy.[11]

It would be interesting to know the names of the persons, if any, with whom White consulted before the publication of his essay. Did he share his ideas in advance with his friend and parishioner Benjamin Franklin, or discuss details with his brother-in-law Robert Morris, the financier of the American Revolution? When it came time in 1785 to undertake an approach to English officials over the prospects for the consecration of American bishops he turned to and sought the assistance of such political luminaries as the Virginian Richard Henry Lee, the president of the Congress, John Jay, a seasoned diplomat and Secretary for Foreign Correspondence for the Congress, and John Adams, the minister to Great Britain, to aid the arrangement for the Church of England to consecrate the American bishops without swearing allegiance to the crown and parliament.[12]

Part I

1
England's Early Imperial Interests: Ireland and Virginia

The origin of the establishment of England's first colony in the western hemisphere at Jamestown, Virginia, in 1607 is intimately linked to the nation's long historical interest and extra-territorial venture in Ireland. For nearly a thousand years before the reigns of the first two Tudors, Henry VII and Henry VIII, in the fifteenth and sixteenth centuries, Ireland had been a land of notice for English monarchs. It was an attraction that began about 684 A.D. when an expeditionary force under the ealdorman Berht was sent to the Celtic Isle by the Northumbrian King Ecgfrith. England's early historian Bede recorded that Berht 'wretchedly devastated a harmless race that had always been most friendly to the English and his hostile bands spared neither churches nor monasteries. The islanders resisted force by force so far as they were able, imploring the merciful aid of God and invoking His vengeance with unceasing imprecations'.[1] Five hundred years later, in 1155, Henry II requested authorization from the newly elected Pope Adrian IV to invade Ireland.[2] Henry II acknowledged that the kingdom of Ireland belonged to the dominion of the church and could not, therefore, be subjected to any new ruler without the pope's approval. Born Nicholas Breakspear and the only native-English pope, Adrian IV issued the Papal Bull *Laudabiliter* that granted authority to Henry to invade Ireland for the purpose of bringing its church under a closer association with the Roman Church, and conduct a general reform of governance and society throughout the land.[3] It is a grant made in and for a world that preceded the emergence of strong nation states, one that was organized and governed by regional families holding claim to land in a defined geographical area. The authenticity of *Laudabiliter* is one of the great questions of history, but 860 years ago the instrument launched English overlordship on to Ireland. It is notable that decisions of Pope Alexander III confirmed

Henry's claim, as did those made by his successor, Pope Lucius III, and that Henry VIII's proclamation of the Crown of Ireland Act of 1542 was predicated on this document.[4]

Tudor King Henry VIII and his chief minister Thomas Cromwell forcefully applied the civil and ecclesiastical reforms established in England to Ireland. Seventy years later, at the dawn of the seventeenth century, the Stuart King James I under different circumstances, in an action that was to change drastically the course of imperial policy, granted a charter for a settlement in the western hemisphere to the Merchant Adventurers of the Virginia Company of London, and a colony was founded at Jamestown, Virginia in 1607.

The origin of a proposal to establish a colony in the New World lies in the last twenty years of the reign of Queen Elizabeth I. It was not an impulsive or whimsical idea but was grounded in the new knowledge of the region drawn from the recent Spanish and Portuguese voyages of exploration and settlement. A long debate flourished at court during the late reign of Elizabeth regarding the prospects for a second colony to be established in the western hemisphere that would act as a buffer to Spain's presence and unknown intentions in the area. Spain's perceived ambitions raised political and diplomatic alarms for the nation, signals that were proclaimed by Sir Humphrey Gilbert (1539–83), his half-brother, Walter Raleigh (1554?–1618), and the geographer Richard Hakluyt the Younger (1552 or 1553–1616).[5]

It is probable that knowledgeable advisors at Elizabeth's court were not of one mind regarding another overseas colony. Many questions must have been raised regarding how the new overseas circumstances would affect and transform England's national and international position. A primary concern must have been how England's half-century of military and administrative experience in Ireland could shape the founding and development of a second colony. Presumably a range of alternatives were offered and debated by rival court factions. Perhaps one strongly supported continuing the forceful Irish military policy of subjugation of the population while another group advocated a less confrontational course.

Gathering, distilling, and broadcasting for an English audience the details of the recent international voyages, Hakluyt was a passionate student of the history of geography and a highly placed churchman. Single-mindedly, he collected, edited, and published narratives of the trailblazing mariners. His tracts were influential among highly placed courtiers and contributed substantially to shaping England's national interests as an emerging political, commercial, and sea power. Raleigh and Hakluyt were the ideological advocates at the Queen's court for an English imperial policy designed to foil Spanish ambitions and counter Spain's settlements in Florida and elsewhere. It was in England's interest to establish a presence in North America. The problem for England in the mid-1580s, as understood by Hakluyt and Raleigh, was that Spain blocked the path to North America. In fact, the whole American continent was closed by Spain to English settlers, goods, and religion. Thus, Hakluyt's bold national policy risked war with Spain.[6]

For England's national interests colonization was strategically vital: occupation of North America could command the Newfoundland fishing banks and the Spanish homeward route from the Indies.[7] War against Spain was necessary in part as a religious act, to bring salvation to thousands, if not millions, of Native Americans who had been subjugated to popery and Spanish cruelty.[8] Because of Spanish oppression, Hakluyt assumed that the Native Americans – 'a poor and harmless people created of God' – would offer willing allies against Spain. To minister to the conversion of the natives Hakluyt proposed settling the colonies with clergymen underemployed and restless at home.[9] His comprehensive vision for England's overseas settlements also recognized that the national church was an element of the expansion of the empire.[10] Raleigh and Hakluyt's intention was to replace the Spanish Empire with an English empire.[11] They advocated a national policy that offered something to all sections of the community: underemployed Puritan ministers within the Church of England eager to extend true religion, City merchants and county manufacturers, discontented younger sons of the landed class, all, it seemed, had something to gain.

Accounts of the recent overseas voyages of exploration and discovery prompted Raleigh, Hakluyt, and Captain John Smith to plead with the government to counter the influence of Spain in the western hemisphere. While it was incumbent for England to shape a policy that would counter Catholic Iberian influence in the New World, the distance from the homeland, coupled with the memory of the Irish experience, may have reduced enthusiasm for expansion overseas. For two generations the champions for a second colony persistently tried but failed to convince successive governments of its expediency and viability. Their grand imperial design encountered little interest: not Elizabeth, nor James I, nor Charles I had any use for a new imperial policy. In fact neither James I nor Charles I ever sent a ship across the Atlantic. But to many merchants and government ministers, and to a large group in the House of Commons over the years, the strategy was compelling. Rather than a department or agency of the English government undertaking and implementing the extension and development of an overseas settlement, a new policy was introduced that drastically revised the system for English overseas expansion and settlement.

A new imperial policy emerged in 1600 that provided a framework for England's seventeenth-century extra-territorial interest. Beginning as early as 1407 merchants in London and other major ports engaged in trade exporting cloth to the Netherlands, originally to Bruges and, by 1446, to Antwerp.[12] Depots were established in several continental cities and flourished throughout the sixteenth and seventeenth centuries. Merchant adventurers were risking their money in speculative commercial opportunities in Europe[13] and their great innovation, the new channel for overseas expansion and development, was the London merchant adventurer companies, to whom the opportunities for commercial colonial ventures were delegated. In contrast to the long Irish experience, the English government was not responsible for providing civil and ecclesiastical personnel to undertake the establishment, administration, and development of the American colony. It was the Virginia Company's burden to govern the settlement, dispatch military forces to protect it, quell opposition from Native Americans, and maintain a steady, regular flow of ships to support the outpost 3700 miles distant from London.

Elizabeth inaugurated the model for the new system on 31 December 1600 when she granted a charter to the merchant adventurers of the East India Company.[14] The company was formed initially for pursuing trade with the East Indies, but ended up trading mainly with the Indian sub-continent and China. The company acted as the primary agent for colonization. The Queen's grant of the charter to the company set a precedent for settlement in America for the next three decades. Elizabeth's successor, James I, granted a charter to the merchant adventurers of the Virginia Company of London in 1606, and the company undertook the colonization at Jamestown under Captain John Smith in 1607. A comparable charter was granted by the crown to the Somer Isles Company in 1615 as a commercial venture to operate the English colony of the Somer Isles, also known as Bermuda. Two decades later James I granted charters for the New England settlements established by the Plymouth Company (1620), and the Dorchester Company (1627), and his brother, Charles I, followed with a charter to the Massachusetts Bay Company (1629) at Salem and in Boston. Later, individual proprietors such as Charles Calvert in Maryland (1634) and William Penn (1680) in Pennsylvania received charters and grants of land to undertake their proposed colonies.

King James I's decision in 1606 to delegate to the Virginia Company of London the responsibility to undertake an English settlement liberated the crown from the expense of governing and supplying a far distant territory. The king did not apply in America the forceful and comprehensive program of governance applied in Ireland in the 1530s and 1540s and embraced by Elizabeth throughout her 45-year reign. James recognized that Ireland had not proved to be the source of a steady stream of revenue for the English crown over 70 years, and he saw that it was necessary to control the ever-increasing expense of maintaining a civil, military, and ecclesiastical establishment in the country. Ireland had been a costly project for the government, and a drain of funds between 1534 and 1572 with expenditures of more than £1,300,000. The revenues extracted did not offset the expenses, nor did their collection diminish violence or increase civil order.[15]

Unlike Pope Adrian's IV's determination that Henry II should attempt to encourage a closer association between the Celtic church and the church of Rome, there was no design to draw the peoples of America into a link with the English church or the Archbishop of Canterbury. Relentlessly promoted by Raleigh and Hakluyt, the Virginia colony differed significantly in structure and authority from the firmly administered and controlled state enterprise that was Ireland. Virginia's founding was shaped by the commercial, economic reforms that were a concomitant of the religious reformation and marked the politics and church in Europe and England during the sixteenth and seventeenth centuries.[16] The policies, procedures, and administration of England in Ireland were emphatically not a template for the settlement of Virginia: the crown and its associated bureaucracy faced contrasts in every aspect of the culture and politics of the two early colonies.

The account of England's imperial forays to Ireland and America is defined by complicated characteristics of culture, peoples, geography, and church. The reformed Church of England under the aegis of Henry VIII was the institution extended in full form to Ireland and in a partial and abbreviated manner to the first English colony in America: the cross followed the crown and flag to the outermost edges of the emerging empire. The church that appeared in both colonies represented one aspect of a nation in search of an imperial policy in a changing world. In both civil and ecclesiastical affairs the chronicle represents a national quest that remained tentative and unresolved for successive monarchs and governments until at least the second decade of the eighteenth-century. Henry VIII's vigorous interest in Ireland was a policy that displayed a full exercise of the power of the national government, whereas the venture in Virginia was an enterprise that captured the imagination and application of a merchant adventurers' company seeking commercial profit.

Both the Church of Ireland and the English Church in Virginia were legatees of the ecclesiastical revolution led by Henry VIII, Thomas Cromwell, and Thomas Cranmer, the Archbishop of Canterbury. The institutions were imperial expressions rather than indications of missionary enterprise by a modern-day evangelist of the status of St Patrick, St. Alban, or the medieval St Dunstan. Theirs is a chronicle of political and religious institutions of the Old World transformed by the ideas of the age of reformation. It must be underscored that the effort to extend the English Reformation to Ireland in the sixteenth century was in the hands of civil rather than ecclesiastical officials, the church was *de facto* an agency of the State. Yet the reformed Church of Ireland does not indicate any influence or participation in the task by successive archbishops of Canterbury during the period between 1541 and 1633: Thomas Cranmer (1533–55), Reginald Pole (1556–58), Matthew Parker (1559–75), Edmund Grindal (1576–83), John Whitgift (1584–1604), Richard Bancroft (1604–10), and George Abbot (1611–33).[17] The Irish and Virginia churches were linked by a common monarch, a common language, and the use of the Book of Common Prayer. Absent was a broadly formulated and applicable imperial policy for the governance of the two colonies. The king's Irish venture continued without significant modification during the reigns of his successors and children Edward VI (1547–53), Catholic Queen Mary (1553–58), and Elizabeth I (1558–1603).

Bishops were appointed to diocesan jurisdictions, and their names and years of service are known; however, other basic details about the Church of Ireland and its practices are elusive. We may ask how frequently were services of worship held, weekly, monthly, quarterly, or occasionally? Were services held in existing pre-Reformation churches, or in the houses of local members? By decade, how many men served the church during the sixteenth century in each diocese?[18] Were the men primarily English-born and educated at Cambridge or Oxford? Were any sixteenth-century Irish natives ordained by the prelates to the ministry, if so, in which dioceses and how many? Were the sacraments of baptism, marriage, and communion observed regularly, quarterly, or annually in the churches? How were the ministers paid and how much in cash or provisions? What was the range of their salaries, say, high, low, average, and median?[19] In common with the extension of the Anglican Church to Virginia in the seventeenth century, few details survive regarding the experience of the Church of Ireland during the previous century. There are few if any answers to these questions. A more complete understanding of the extension of the reformed Church of Ireland during the sixteenth and seventeenth centuries is needed and would be enhanced with the compilation of biographical and professional details similar to the resources available for the Anglican Church in England and America of the period.[20]

The new national Church of Ireland adopted the use of existing pre-reformation church buildings that were formerly used by the Catholic Church. It was not necessary for Irish imperial officials to develop plans and secure funds to construct new buildings. Yet only a few Irish priests are known to have shifted their allegiance from the Catholic to the reformed church. It was possible to recruit additional clergymen from England to fill pulpits. However, unlike the Spanish, Portuguese, and French, the English had no religious orders that could be enlisted to assist the extension of their national church in the western hemisphere: to undertake and accompany the voyages of discovery, serve the first settlers, and evangelize the natives. No English prelate, such as the primate of the Church of England, was summoned by the crown and instructed to raise and organize a group of clergymen to be sent as missionaries to Ireland or Virginia.

Unlike Ireland, Virginia had no church buildings, abbeys, friaries, or chantries to be commandeered by the colonists and used for worship services. The General Assembly's establishment of the church in 1619 provided for services in the parishes and defined the duties of ministers in accordance with the 1603 Canon Law that governed the Church of England. Over the next 25 years, additional legislation refined and defined the governance of the church and assigned further duties for the vestry, obligations that differed from the practice in England. Contrasting with the situation at home and in Ireland the apparatus for the church was not initiated with a plan or oversight from English ecclesiastical officials. King Henry's extension of the Anglican Church to Ireland as the reformed Church of Ireland did not recur in Virginia. No archbishops or bishops were appointed to supervise the small band of ministers, and the land was not shaped and defined by archdiocesan and diocesan territories as it was in England and Ireland.

Men educated at Cambridge and Oxford colleges served congregations in both colonies, but the number is uncertain. After more than four decades of petitions to English officials by Irish leaders for the establishment of a college in Dublin the crown finally granted a charter for Trinity College in 1592. Several of the original founders and early faculty members had been educated at the Cambridge colleges. Puritan ideas and intellectual influences among Cambridge scholars and students particularly influenced the Irish church life and provided an indelible academic and theological link for the new Dublin institution. Immediately the college assembled a strong faculty and implemented an academic programme that became a reservoir of talent and leadership for the Church of Ireland. By the late 1590s and first two decades of the seventeenth century Trinity College graduates began to fill pulpits and provide capable leadership for the Church of Ireland. Among the distinguished graduates were James Ussher (1581–1656), Archbishop of Armagh and Primate of all Ireland, William King (1650–1724), Archbishop of Dublin, Jonathan Swift (1667–1745), the satirist, essayist, political pamphleteer and Dean of St Patrick's Cathedral in Dublin, and George Berkeley (1685–1753), Bishop of Cloyne, the celebrated eighteenth-century philosopher.

Collegiate circumstances in Virginia differed markedly. An effort was undertaken about 1620 by leaders in the colony and in London to establish a college, a proposal that languished and was delayed and not accomplished until 1693 when a royal charter was granted by the crown for the College of William and Mary. A founding principle of the institution was to educate colonial students for the ministry, but it was not until about 1735 that a stream of men partially or entirely educated at the college began to serve local churches. However, the colonial institution never enjoyed the level of academic achievement among the faculty and students of its Irish counterpart. Oxford and Cambridge universities were the primary sources for ministers in the seventeenth century, supplemented in the 1680s, 1690s, and later by alumni of Scottish colleges.

Little is known about the men who served as ministers of congregations of the church in Ireland between 1536 and 1600 or in Virginia from 1607 to about 1680. Lacking is a surviving cache of manuscript or printed sermons, journals, diaries, or correspondence that describes or recalls the men's personal experiences or the religious culture of their communities. Missing, too, are details regarding the nature of worship services conducted and the popular availability and use of the Book of Common Prayer. But some evidence indicates that the theological, liturgical, and ceremonial divisions of the English church during the sixteenth and seventeenth centuries were represented among the ranks of parsons and congregants of seventeenth-century Virginia. It remains unclear how many congregations flourished at any time during the sixteenth century in Ireland, and it is not known how many Catholic clergymen conformed to the reformed church after its establishment in 1541 by parliament. Our lack of information extends to the bishops appointed by Henry VIII, Edward VI, and Elizabeth who may have ordained native-born Irishmen to serve posts, and their number. Because nearly all of the bishops appointed by the crown to Irish diocesan posts between 1536 and 1600 had been educated at Cambridge and Oxford it is probable that men enlisted for church service were educated at the ancient English universities.

The calibre of civil leadership of the two early colonies contrasted markedly. On the one hand the Irish officials were generally drawn from among the highest-ranked English army officers or from among experienced and trusted members of the royal household, whereas the Virginia royal appointees were uniformly without such experience and influential connections. During the period that the Virginia Company of London administered the colony, between 1606 and 1624, the leadership of the province was drawn from men with experience as second- or third-tier military officers.

Problems of imperial policy and governance in Virginia were not an urgent issue for leaders of the English Revolution. Royal Governor Sir William Berkeley, a favourite of Charles I during his service in the royal household, was appointed governor in 1641. He served in the first instance until 1652 when the Cromwell government replaced him with three successive appointments over the next eight years: Richard Bennett (1652–53), Edward Digges (1655–56), and Samuel Matthews (1656–60). On his accession to the throne in 1660 Charles II reappointed Berkeley to the governorship (1660–77).

In Virginia the governors were the link for communication with London officials, not through a key court administrator but at a considerably lower level of government bureaucracy. Beginning in the 1670s and continuing to 1776, the colonial executive's link to London was through the Secretary of the Board of Trade and Plantations at Whitehall. The Board was an emerging agency of the state charged by the Privy Council with overseeing the implementation of imperial policies, and it was the channel for communications with the colonial governors. Among the strong chief officers who served in Virginia during the seventeenth and eighteenth centuries were Sir William Berkeley, Francis, Lord Howard of Effingham, Sir Edmund Andros, Francis Nicholson, Alexander Spotswood, Robert Dinwiddie, and Francis Fauquier.

England's colonial military experience in Virginia contrasted sharply with the ingrained and enduring Irish encounters during the sixteenth and seventeenth centuries. Absent in the American province were the frequent rebellions and bloody encounters between chieftains in Ireland and the armies of Henry VIII, Elizabeth, Oliver Cromwell, and William III. There were no battles and massacres on the Virginia landscape to match the confrontations at Raithlin Island (1576), Drogheda, Wexford, and Waterford (1649), or the Desmond Rebellions (1569–73, 1579–83), the Battle of the Boyne (1690), or the Nine Years' War (1594–1603). English military forces appeared in Virginia twice: in 1676 in response to Governor Sir William Berkeley's request for assistance to quell Bacon's Rebellion, and in 1781 when Lord Charles Cornwallis led the English army at the siege of Yorktown, the last battle of the War for Independence.

2
The Virginia Company of London and England's Second Colonial Venture: Virginia, 1606–24

The settlement of Virginia in the early seventeenth century contrasted sharply with England's experience in Ireland during the previous century. Settlement of Virginia was not in the hands of the English government's civil, military, and ecclesiastical officials, as occurred in Ireland, but was delegated by James I to merchant adventurers, to the officials and private shareholders of the Virginia Company of London. The colony was launched without the familiar English civil, military, and ecclesiastical personnel and leadership which had been applied in Ireland. The responsibility for the civil administration, law-making, defence of the colony, provision of the regular ships of supply, and services of the Anglican Church fell to the officials of the Virginia Company. The company was responsible for the recruitment of settlers, and for providing governance, administration, laws, and religious worship in accordance with the Anglican Church. Ireland was not an imperial model for Virginia.

In 1606 King James granted the Virginia Company a charter for the lands in America between Cape Fear in North Carolina and the Hudson Bay in what is today Canada. The initial settlement of Virginia was financed by the company's shareholders, and was founded in 1607 by 108 English persons. The pristine New World landscape was untouched by the foundations and profiles of houses, buildings, forts, and churches common to the towns and countryside of Ireland and England. The ranks of the initial English colonists were gradually increased in subsequent decades by persons of diverse social and national origins, including arrivals from Scotland, Ireland, France, Africa, and elsewhere.

In Virginia and elsewhere along the Atlantic coast the past and present of the Native Americans was a curiously blank slate, unknown and unwritten. Their cultural heritage could not be recaptured from the pages of ecclesiastical, civil, or military registers but has gradually been uncovered by consideration of oral traditions, artefacts, and evidence mined from archaeological and anthropological sources. In retrospect the policies of Tudor and early Stuart governments were predicated on a design and policy to subjugate both the Irish and Native Americans.

The procedures for establishing the first three colonies in America, Virginia (1606), Plymouth (1620), and the Massachusetts Bay (1629) represented a significant policy shift for the English government in the early seventeenth century. In a manner similar to that of the successful ventures on the Continent, the crown delegated the responsibilities for overseas colonization to merchant adventurer commercial trading companies: the Virginia Company of London, the Plymouth Company, which was one of two Virginia Companies formed by London and Plymouth merchants, and the New England Company (1620).[1] The Plymouth Company (South Virginia) had jurisdiction up to the region of New York. The Plymouth Company (North Virginia) made explorations along the Maine coast in 1607, but abandoned its venture soon after. The report of Captain John Smith in 1614 of rich cod fisheries off the Maine coast revived interest in the Plymouth Company, which obtained a new charter under grant from the Council for New England (1620).[2] Despite several applications the pilgrims of the New Plymouth Colony were never able to obtain a charter from the crown. The colony's right to exist as a self-governing state rested always on the Mayflower Compact, buttressed by the Pierce Patent of 1621 until that was supplemented by the Bradford Patent in 1630.[3]

The Dorchester Company (1624–26) was organized as a joint-stock company by a group of Dorsetshire men who planted a colony of some fifty farmers on Cape Ann (Gloucester) in northeast Massachusetts. After a trial period of three years the settlement was abandoned. Some thirty members settled in Salem and the rest returned to England.[4] The Massachusetts Bay Company (1628) was an outgrowth of the New England Company and the Dorchester Company formed by a leading group of English Puritans.[5] A charter was obtained from King Charles I in 1629 and a fleet of seventeen ships carrying some 1,000 men and women with their families arrived at Salem the next year, founded Boston, and began their settlements. The transfer of both charter and company to America in effect gave the new colony a political structure that was incorporated into American institutions.

Unlike the first Virginia charter, the New England charters do not refer to the Church of England, the state church, or to a formula that the religion of the settlements should accord to the doctrines of the Church of

England.[6] The Massachusetts Bay Company's charter describes a purpose of the colony as to 'win and unite the natives to the knowledge and obedience of the only true God and Saviour of Mankind and the Christian faith'.[7] The Plymouth charter of 1620 granted to the New England Company declares that the settlers should 'live together in the Feare and true Worship of Almighty God, Christian Peace, and civil Quietness'.[8]

The settlements at Plymouth and Massachusetts Bay were each led by remarkably able and charismatic leaders, William Bradford and John Winthrop respectively. Winthrop, the first governor of the Massachusetts colony, embraced the notion that all nations had a covenant with God. In a profound sense he may be identified as a seer after the manner of an Old Testament prophet. He asserteded that because England had violated its religious covenant, the Puritans within the church had to leave the country. His opinion reflected the belief that the reformed Church of England had fallen from grace by accepting Catholic rituals. Winthrop eloquently proclaimed in his sermon 'A Model of Christian Charity', most likely given in England in 1630 before the group's departure for New England, that the new community in America would be a 'city upon a hill', watched by the world:

> For we must consider that we shall be as a city upon a hill. The eyes of all people are upon us. So that if we shall deal falsely with our God in this work we have undertaken ... we shall be made a story and a by-word throughout the world. We shall open the mouths of enemies to speak evil of the ways of God ... We shall shame the faces of many of God's worthy servants, and cause their prayers to be turned into curses upon us til we be consumed out of the good and whither we are a-going.[9]

In contrast to the situation in Virginia and Plymouth, the Massachusetts church included numerous inspired religious leaders during the colony's beginning and throughout the colonial era, including John Cotton, Richard Mather, and Francis Higginson.

William Bradford's account *Of Plymouth Plantation* was not shaped in the style nor with the purpose of Winthrop's sermon, but his work joins Winthrop's journal of twenty years in providing an illuminating account of the issues, disappointments, and accomplishments of the colony's early years.[10]

Richard Hakluyt, the celebrated geographer and Anglican minister, was one of the chief promoters of the petition to James I for patents for the colonization of Virginia, and was named in the charters granted by the King to the Company in 1606 and 1609.[11] In return he was named chaplain to the first fleet of ships that was sent by the Company to Virginia in December 1606 (probably an honorific title awarded for his persistent support and services on behalf of the English policy for colonization, because he was not in the party). Appointed in his place was the Reverend Robert Hunt, vicar of Heathfield in Sussex, who conducted the first English church services at Jamestown in May 1607. Unlike the experience of the earlier Spanish, Portuguese, and French settlements in the western hemisphere, there were no English religious orders that could be summoned to accompany the flag and the early waves of colonists to Virginia.

The extension of the English church to Virginia differed sharply from the procedures applied in Ireland. It was in the hands of Virginia Company officials to recruit and financially support ministers serving the settlements in the early years of the colony. There was no effort undertaken by London civil and ecclesiastical officials to create a reformed Church of Virginia with the familiar diocesan apparatus and episcopal leadership common to the Church of Ireland and the Church of England. Absent, too, was an existing pre-Reformation institution that could serve as foundation for the transplanted church. There were no ranks of prelates or pastors on hand to recruit and conform to the church, or monasteries to be suppressed and monastic wealth to be redistributed to prominent provincial families.

Sparsely settled, the province was served by few ministers. The controversial and factional theological and liturgical voices of the church at home were present in seventeenth-century Virginia. The handful of clergy on hand was not compelled by temperament or need to formulate a Virginia draft of confession of faith after the manner of the Thirty-Nine Articles. Presumably the articles of the Church of England were embraced without reservation and were sufficient should a question or dispute surface among the clergy or laity regarding doctrine or practice.

The first group of Virginia settlers was a diverse body, recruited by the officials of the Virginia Company, in sharp contrast to the relative religious and cultural homogeneity of the initial inhabitants of the later Plymouth and Massachusetts colonies. The passengers were required by the King and Privy Council to give an Oath of Supremacy and Allegiance before sailing on a vessel bound for the colony,[12] but they were not a band that shared a common religious or moral vision. The Plymouth and Massachusetts Bay colonists were assembled under separate banners with a particular religious plan but there was no such adhesive formula that gathered and motivated the Virginia participants.

Virginia was not a settlement that embodied a movement galvanized by differences and hopelessness over ecclesiastical polity or practices within the Anglican Church, nor was it shaped by a grand imperial design from civil officials at Whitehall, or an evangelistic impulse of the archbishop of Canterbury, bishop of London, or any other church or state official. Instead, the extension of the colony and church overseas was linked to the political strategy of Richard Hakluyt and his associates who campaigned during the last years of the Elizabethan era and the first years of the reign of King James to obtain royal approval and a charter for the establishment of a settlement.[13] A document entitled 'A Justification for Planting Virginia' briefly stated the rationale and legitimacy of England's effort to foil Spanish influence and power in the region.[14] In addition, the instructions for the colony of Virginia, issued at the time of the Letters Patent of King James I to the merchant adventurers on 10 April 1606, declared that the religion of the settlement should be 'according to the doctrine and rights professed and established in England'.[15] Recognizing that the primary purpose of the Virginia Company and its shareholders was commercial, we are left to speculate on what would have been the course of the first English colony in America if it had been driven by a clear religious and moral vision coupled with charismatic civil and ecclesiastical leadership for a generation or more.

The early years of Virginia were a struggle, marked by widespread sickness and death and by a modest stream of new settlers. The condition of the province was precarious and its future uncertain. In 1609 the company was reorganized, given a new charter, and its council was provided with increased authority. The arrival of Sir Thomas Gates as lieutenant governor of the colony in 1610 brought the introduction of a new code of statutes relating to religious affairs and moral discipline. Later the acts were known as 'Dale's Laws' after Sir Thomas Dale who was in control of the province from May to August 1611 and again during the years between 1614 and 1616.[16] The stern military laws of the Netherlands, where both Gates and Dale had served, were reflected in the new legislation, although the code of laws also embodied some of the religious ideals of the company's charter. Even though the statutes were not rigorously enforced, they serve as a reminder that strict, rigid legislation on religious matters was found in Anglican Virginia as well as in Puritan New England.

Following the example of the Dale Laws the company required the governors and clergy to maintain religious and moral discipline and order in the parishes or face punitive consequences. A Proclamation issued by Governor Sir Samuel Argall, 10 May 1618, called for every person to attend church on Sundays and holidays or 'lye neck & heels on the Corps du Guard the night following & be a slave the week following 2d offence a month 3d a year & a day'.[17] The next year the General Assembly adopted legislation requiring clergy and churchwardens to be aware of scandalous behaviour in their parishes, exercising against the violators such punishments as warnings, suspension, and excommunication.[18] Furthermore, the ministers were required to meet quarterly at St Michael's Day (September), Nativity time (December), Annunciation (March), and midsummer (June), at Jamestown, near the governor's residence, to review the list of offenders and charges against persons in the colony, and present their recommendations for discipline to the governor.[19]

In step with England's imperial leadership in Ireland during the sixteenth century, the early Virginia officials had considerable military experience. The men were charged and commissioned by the company to provide governance, order, and discipline over a disparate community. After 1609, and for the rest of the century, their ranks included Thomas West, Lord De La Warr, Thomas Gates, Thomas Dale, Samuel Argall, George Yeardley, Captain John Harvie, Francis Wyatt, William Berkeley, Lord Howard of Effingham, Edmund Andros, and Francis Nicholson. In turn each man placed a stamp on the unfolding civil and ecclesiastical experience of the province. Perhaps it represented to London officials the provincial leaders' fulfilment of duties to enhance and promote their careers rather than a push on behalf of a religious group.

Hardship was the prevailing circumstance faced by settlers during their first two years. In addition to illness and death, conflicts and disorder among the settlers reflected the unruliness and diversity of persons recruited for the colony. Contemporaries attributed the turmoil to the novelty of the transplantation of custom without the sanction of law, and the routine that church and state should cooperate closely to restrain wickedness and promote righteousness.

In 1606 Gates had been listed first among those persons who petitioned James for a charter to settle Virginia, and he invested £2,000 in the Virginia Company. In 1610 he and his friend and colleague Thomas Dale, both of whom were in Dutch military service, obtained permission from army officials to leave their assignments and pursue their investment and political interest in Virginia. Under the new charter, issued in 1609, Thomas West, Lord De La Warr, was appointed governor and Gates governor *ad interim* until De La Warr arrived in the colony. Arriving at Jamestown on 23 May 1610 Gates found a scene of desolation, over the winter the colony had endured what was called a starving time; the 500 settlers alive in the fall of 1609 had been reduced to 60.

An experienced military officer, Gates is remembered for bringing a sense of discipline and order to the community. He promulgated, on 24 May 1610, a strict code of 'Lawes, Divine, Morall, and Martiall' for the colony based on his elaborate instructions from the Virginia Company.[20] A large section of the laws emphasized regulated military duty to maintain the peace and provide defence against the possible attacks of the Native Americans. Another section addressed procedures for handling civil and criminal complaints.

The origins of 'Dale's Laws' may be linked to Gates's and Dale's army experience.[21] In the course of his military career Dale had made powerful friends and patrons, including Sir Francis Vere (commander of the English troops in the Netherlands), Sir Thomas Gates, Henry Wriothesley, the third Earl of Southampton (later treasurer of the Virginia Company), and Sir Robert Cecil, the principal secretary to James I and a proponent of overseas settlements. He arrived in Jamestown in early June 1611.

The laws were extremely harsh: for instance, the penalty for profaning God's word or denouncing the Christian faith was death.[22] Any expression of disrespect to the minister was punished with a public confession before the congregation and whipping. In addition, religious uniformity was insured by requiring all residents to give an acceptable account of their orthodoxy to a clergyman.[23] The statutes directed colonists to prepare themselves at home with private prayer for attendance at public worship.[24] They were to attend morning worship, afternoon catechism instruction, and evening prayers every Sunday and meet twice each workday for services.[25] On Wednesdays they were to hear the week's second sermon. The penalty for not attending Sunday services was for the first offence loss of a week's provision and allowance, for the second, whipping, and for the third, death.[26] The death penalty was imposed for major crimes and certain sexual wrongs, and also for conduct that led the colony to the threshold of disaster, such as robbing stores, trading with the Native Americans, and price-gouging. The parish minister was charged with maintaining a register of the christenings, marriages, and burials in the parish according to Henry VIII's Injunction of 1547 and Canon 70.[27]

Until he returned to England in 1615 Gates ruled the province with a firm hand, but the Gates and Dale Laws were the measure for law and order in the colony for nearly a decade. We have no evidentiary record of how widespread, rigorously, or frequently the laws were cited and applied. Nor do we have any gauge of their impact and effectiveness on the daily and weekly religious and moral life of the community. Gates's successors governed more leniently.

Captain Sir Samuel Argall (1580–1624) succeeded Gates, bringing to the new colony military experience and navigational training gained in continental warfare. In 1609 he received command of an expedition to America under Sir Thomas Smythe, a relative who was director of the Virginia Company. Argall departed from the recent pattern and considered public worship as a means of fostering social welfare within the community. He eliminated the death penalty for failure to attend worship, while maintaining that all persons were to attend church on Sundays.

Sir George Yeardley served a military apprenticeship under Captain Thomas Gates in the Netherlands and sailed for Virginia with Gates in 1609 on board the *Deliverance*. He was shipwrecked in the Bermudas but eventually reached Virginia in 1610. In April 1616 he became deputy governor of the colony, acting for the designated governor, Thomas West, Lord De La Warr, who spent most of his time in England. Yeardley relaxed the exceedingly severe system of government adopted by Dale, although at the same time he showed firmness in his dealings with the Indians. Under his leadership the colony seems to have prospered for the first time. He returned to England in 1617 and soon afterwards married Temperance West. Now highly experienced in Virginia affairs, he attended meetings and conferred with the officers of the Virginia Company who controlled the colony. Plans were laid for major reforms in Virginia to encourage more rapid settlement, abandonment of the former military-style rule, creation of civil government, and expansion of the policy adopted in 1616 to end the company's monopoly on landholding and to award estates to individuals.[28] On 18 November 1618, Yeardley was appointed governor in his own right for a three-year term. He arrived in Jamestown on 18 April 1619, as Argall's successor. The Virginia Company instructed him, on 28 November 1618, to set out a glebe for each minister of 100 acres.[29] It was intended that the glebe would generate an income for the parson of about £200 sterling per year.[30] There were at the time only two ordained ministers residing in the colony, together with two others who were acting as clergymen but who were not ordained.[31]

On 8 November 1621 Yeardley was succeeded by Sir Francis Wyatt. When, in early 1626, Wyatt retired from office, Charles I appointed Yeardley his successor, and he held the reins of government from 17 May until his death on 10 November 1627. During his three administrations important events in the life of the colony took place. The 'first representative assembly in the western hemisphere' met at Jamestown on 30 July 1619. In 1620 a Dutch man-of-war landed twenty Negro slaves for sale, the first brought into the English colonies, while in the last year of his governorship a thousand new emigrants from England arrived.

Despite the acknowledgement in the patent granted by James I to the Virginia Company that the Church of England was to be the religion of the American settlement, the officials of the company in London and the colony delayed establishing the Church of England for twelve years after the province's settlement in 1607. Why might this be? The published records of the company are silent on the matter, but there are several factors that may have contributed to the situation. Perhaps the initial band of settlers represented the same diversity of religious opinion that occurred in England, some persons embracing Anglican and others either Puritan or Nonconformist practices. If so it was a situation that officials of the commercial venture may have tolerated in hopes of encouraging an essential and continuing stream of new migrants to the colony. Alternatively, the lack of commercial success of the colony, difficulties administering the distant territory, and the exposure of settlers to sickness and death, may have diminished the sense of urgency to establish the Anglican Church during the years of lacklustre failure of the venture. It is possible that the Company's officials were bowing to political pressure and the need to give a new sense of purpose to the Virginia adventure when they eventually determined that it was important to fulfil a key intention of James's patent for the American settlement, the establishment of the Anglican Church.

Our speculation regarding the situation continues: What forces were at work in the colony and London that prompted the adoption and revision of statutes that governed the church during the province's first century? Was the legislation during the first two decades in response to directives of the Virginia Company? Or perhaps it was imposed after the province became a royal colony in 1624 by civil officials in Whitehall? How did the legislators formulate the statutes; did they have at hand published law books to serve as models for the statutes, or a copy of the Constitutions and Canons of Ecclesiastical Laws for the church as a guide for shaping the contents of the laws relating to the church? What was the role of the successive governors of the colony in aiding the church's interest with the legislature?

Following the initiatives of the early Virginia governors, the House of Burgesses in 1619 and in years afterwards enacted statutes that established and maintained the church in the colony, providing for the creation of parishes, the construction of churches, and the payment in tobacco of the annual stipends for the ministers, providing for its basic structure and system of financial maintenance for the remainder of the colonial period.[32] Every minister was to receive a fixed income and a glebe. The company was to recruit six tenants for every glebe to cultivate and harvest crops for support of the minister and themselves. Yet, despite the company's encouragement, the church was not a complete or vigorous institution. There was no episcopal hierarchy – no resident or visiting bishop to ordain men, bestow confirmation rites on members, consecrate churches or churchyards, or render supervision over the clergy and parish practices. No dioceses had been created and no archdeacons or deans had been designated to offer administrative oversight within defined territorial areas. The distance from London and the slowness of communication impeded administration of church affairs in the sparsely settled colony, regardless of the urgency or complexity of matters. Inevitably these conditions marked and shaped the experience of the young church, giving rise to a sense of quasi-independence in the handful of parsons and lay-persons who controlled local church affairs. These two distinguishing characteristics gave form to the institution for the remainder of the colonial era, during the Revolutionary War, and afterwards, as it passed through a period of reorganization and reconstitution.

The General Assembly which met in the church at Jamestown on 30 July 1619 enacted fifty statutes to replace the 'Lawes Divine, Morall and Martiall'.[33] It established the church in the province, declaring that 'all ministers to read divine services and exercise their ministerial function according to the Ecclesiastical Laws' and order of the Church of England.[34] In addition, a provision of Gates's Law was reaffirmed, that the ministers were to present to the Secretary of Estates in March of each year an account of all christenings, marriages, and burials that had occurred during the previous twelve months.[35] The procedure was in adherence with Henry VIII's Injunctions of 1547 and Canon 70 of the English church.[36]

Some laws prohibited idleness, gaming, drunkenness, and excess in apparel, and one ordered all persons to frequent divine service and sermons in the forenoon and afternoon of the Sabbath.[37] Clergymen were responsible for enforcing attendance, with the fine of three shillings for each transgression going to the church rather than the state. Servants who wilfully neglected their master's command to attend church were to be whipped. But the Assembly did not ban profanations of the Lord's Day.

Francis Wyatt succeeded Yeardley as governor in October 1621. By his marriage in 1618 to Margaret Sandys, granddaughter of Edwin Sandys, Archbishop of York, he became connected with the faction in the Virginia Company headed by his wife's uncle, Sir Edwin Sandys. In 1620 Wyatt became a shareholder in the company and the next year Henry Wriothesley proposed him for governorship of the colony.[38] He reached Virginia in October 1621, accompanied by his brother, the Reverend Hawte Wyatt, who later became rector of the church in Jamestown.[39]

In 1624, the assembly directed every plantation to reserve a house or room solely for worship and made unexcused absence from Sunday service finable by one pound of tobacco for the first violation and fifty pounds for a month's absence.[40] In addition, the body approved the establishment of 22 March as a Holy Day in the colony as an official remembrance of the 1621/22 Henrico Massacre.[41]

The English church, on the eve of the colonization of Virginia, lay in the crosswinds of the aftermath of King Henry VIII's 1547 reformation of the institution.[42] For more than half-a-century the church and its leaders continued to undertake the transformation of devotional habits of worshippers from the routine of the medieval church to the practices of the post-Reformation era.[43] The impact of the division and dissension within the church at home was manifest in the first three English colonies in America.[44] The settlers in Virginia, Plymouth, and Massachusetts Bay represented three differing faces of the ecclesiastical and civil affairs of England. In the first Virginian settlement the traditional Anglican style, though probably with some variation, was the practice; in New England the church in the Plymouth colony was aligned with the Puritan separatist faction, whereas the church in the Massachusetts Bay colony represented Puritans who hoped to remain within the Church of England while pressing the institution to purify and reform its faith and practices. Each group embraced differing ideas and interpretations of theology, liturgical practices, the Bible, and the history of the Christian church: opinions that reinforced the separation of the religious communities.[45]

3
Virginia and Royal Jurisdiction: Laws, Governors, and Church: 1624–60

Governing a sparsely settled colony 3700 miles away from Whitehall proved financially difficult for the Virginia Company. In 1624, after nearly twenty years of seeking commercial profit from the Virginia venture, the London Company was bankrupt. King James revoked the company's charter and the province became a royal jurisdiction.[1] Gradually, over several decades, the governor and legislature implemented statutes for the conduct of civil, ecclesiastical, and commercial affairs; Virginia slowly enjoyed greater stability and growth.[2] But the real catalysts in the eventual prosperity of the province were the black slaves who began to arrive in 1619, and who could be exploited in the lucrative cultivation of tobacco.

Under royal authority the king appointed the governor and council, while qualified citizenry elected the burgesses. During the second half of the seventeenth century the council and burgesses gradually developed into a two-house legislature, known as the General Assembly. The General Assembly eventually enjoyed considerable power over the affairs of the province and rigorously guarded its power against encroachments from the governor or crown. The House of Burgesses was representative of the sentiments and interests of the farmers and planters of the tidewater region. From 1624, leadership of civil affairs was in the hands of a series of royal governors.

Under the aegis of the troubled Virginia Company, in 1619 the House of Burgesses enacted a statute that established the Church of England in the colony. The basis for the legislation is found in the Canons of the Church of England, but it is not known whether the deliberations were informed by a copy of the *Constitution and Canons of Ecclesiastical Law 1604* in the hands of one or more leaders or residents.[3] Our first evidence of a copy of the *Canons* is noted in the inventory of John Goodbourne's

(1605–35) library that accompanied him on his voyage to the colony. Regretably, he died at sea en-route to the colony but the books survived,[4] though Goodbourne's brother requested that the books be returned to England for probate proceedings. It is possible that Governor Thomas Gates and local officials were relying solely on personal recollections of the Canon Law for application in the 1610 orders.

Additional legislation relating to the established church in Virginia was enacted by the General Assembly between 1625 and 1680. It represents a series of efforts to address ecclesiastical policy shortcomings that became apparent through experience. The legislature attempted to fill the legal and administrative vacuum in the administration of the overseas church, which in England would have been undertaken partly by a diocesan bishop and partly by parliament. There was no bishop in Virginia, and no prelate in England was charged with supervising the extension and development of the overseas church and clergy. Successive London governments did not recognize the need to administer or extend the state church in the New World. This situation persisted until the late 1670s and 1680s, when the Council of Trade and Plantations eventually adopted and implemented several ecclesiastical policies as part of a larger effort to bring order and control to imperial administration. Viewed in hindsight, it is clear that these delays and belated attempts to impose metropolitan policies shaped Virginian practices in church administration.

In Virginia, unlike England, the church was actively under the authority and supervision of civil officials. The General Assembly controlled church affairs such as creating and dividing parishes in each county, approving the funding and construction of church buildings and parsonages, and approving the purchase or exchange of glebe lands. These unconventional powers were underscored by the colony's occasional recruitment of ministers who had not received episcopal ordination at the hands of a prelate in England, Scotland, or Ireland. In 1679, this situation created tension between public officials and the Bishop of London, Henry Compton, over the American church and parsons, which erupted in heated conflict and controversy.

I have not found any evidence that legislation affecting the Virginia church was dispatched to civil and ecclesiastical officials in London for review, comments, revision, and approval during the period between the implementation of Dale's Laws in 1610 and the granting of jurisdiction over the American church to the Bishop of London, Henry Compton, in 1679. It remains puzzling why the Archbishop of Canterbury, George Abbot, did not request to review the early statutes on church and moral affairs. He was not unfamiliar with current interest in overseas voyages of discovery and settlement. In 1599 he published a popular poem entitled *A Briefe Description of the Whole World* that commented on such themes as geography, politics, and trade; it passed through six editions before his death.[5] Perhaps it was this publication that brought him to the attention of the founders of the Virginia Company of London. He was probably personally acquainted with authors on the subject, such as Raleigh, Richard Hakluyt (whose *The Principal Navigations, Voiages and Discoveries of the English Nation* provided almost everything known about the early voyages to America) and the cartographer Captain John Smith (1580–1631), an original settler of Jamestown and a prolific writer. Abbot was a Puritan and a member of the Virginia Company of London, but his effectiveness as a civil and church leader had been challenged and restricted by several church leaders, notably William Laud, following his misfortune of killing a gamekeeper during a hunting expedition. Abbot's critics asserted that a homicide by a prelate under Canon Law made the archbishop incapable of exercising jurisdiction. The tragic accident shadowed the archbishop to his grave, interrupted his duties, and terminated his efforts on behalf of the Virginia church.

Abbot's rival at the court of Charles I, and successor as Archbishop of Canterbury, William Laud, paid close attention to the church's interests at the outer edges of the kingdom, in Scotland and Ireland, but displayed only fleeting interest in the affairs of England's first American colony. There was a brief flurry of interest in Virginian religious affairs from London civil and ecclesiastical officials in the summer of 1628. Laud, a confidant of King Charles I, was appointed by the monarch as Bishop of London in June 1627 and installed in office in July 1628. Because of his ecclesiastical position, Laud became a member of the Privy Council and began attending its meetings on 14 July 1628, soon after his installation.[6] His hand is apparent in the instructions issued on 6 August by the Privy Council to Captain John Harvie on his appointment as Governor of Virginia. The second of 22 instructions presented to Harvie noted:

> That in the first place you be carefull Almightie God may be duly and dayly served, both by your selfe and all the people under Charge, which may draw down a blessing upon all your Endeavours. And let everie Congregacion that hath an able Minister build for him a Convenient Parsonage house; to which for his better maintenance, and over and above the usual Pencion, you shall lay 200 acres of Glebe land for the clearing and inclosing of that Ground everie of

his Parishioners for three yeares, shall give some daies labours of themselves and theire Servants. And see that you have an especial Care that the Glebe land be sett as neare to his Parsonage house as may be, and that it be of the best contioned land. Suffer noe Innovacion in matters of Religion, and be careful to appoint sufficient and conformable Ministers to each Congregacion that may Catechise and instruct them in the grounds and principles of Religion.[7]

Hugh Trevor-Roper writes that until Laud came to power in the late 1620s the English government took little interest in the souls of American colonists. Official documents paid lip service to the Church of England, the Virginia Company's charters made no reference to religious orthodoxy, and when the *Mayflower* pilgrims applied for leave to settle, the authorities discreetly avoided enquiring into their religious beliefs. Even in 1629, no insistence upon religious conformity was included in the Massachusetts Bay Company's charter. The plantations were so far away that they were unlikely to infect the mother country with heresy, and they might be regarded as a valuable safety-valve for the discharge of critical opinions[8].

At the session of the General Assembly of February–March 1631/32, a complete revision of all the enactments and orders of former sessions of the legislature was undertaken and the first code of laws of the colony was put into effect. The code of 1632 constitutes the first body of laws governing the church in Virginia.[9] The Church was to be uniformly established throughout the colony according to the *Constitutions and Canons of Ecclesiastical Law of 1604*. As noted in the previous orders and legislation, the services of Morning and Evening Prayer according to the Book of Common Prayer were to be observed each Sunday. A sermon was to be delivered every Sunday and the minister was to catechize every Sunday before Evening Prayer on church doctrine and polity. But because there was not a prelate in the colony it did not lead to confirmation, as was the practice in England. Communion was to be administered by the minister three times a year, of which Easter was to be one.

A fee of one shilling was to be imposed on persons who did not attend the Sunday service.[10] No man was to disparage a minister and his ministry, under pain of severe censure of the Governor and council.[11] The ministers and at least one churchwarden of every parish were to attend the annual meeting of the midsummer quarter courts at James City to present the register of the previous year's baptisms, marriages, and burials in the parish.[12] The minister was required to have a license from civil authorities to perform a marriage.[13] The assembly also set a schedule of fees to be paid to the minister: for performing a marriage, two shillings, for the churching of a woman, and a burial, one shilling each.[14] The minister's salary was to be paid in tobacco.[15]

In England, an Order of the King in Council was issued at Whitehall on 1 October 1633 and endorsed by Archbishop of Canterbury Laud which granted to the Bishop of London the responsibility for supervising the English church's European congregations at Hamburg and Delpht, both centres of activity for English merchant traders.[16] The following year, an Act of Charles I and the Privy Council granted to Archbishop Laud, Thomas Lord Coventry, Lord Keeper, Richard Neyle, Archbishop of York, Richard Earl of Portland, Lord High Treasurer, Henry Earl of Manchester, and seven others a commission for the 'government of all persons within the colonies and plantations beyond the seas, according to the laws and constitutions there, and to constitute Courts as well as Ecclesiastical as Civil, for determining causes'.[17] The commission was intended to address the settlers of New England and not the colonists of Virginia. Archbishop Laud and the king were familiar with the numbers of non-Anglican individuals transported to New England each year, who were out of reach of traditional English ecclesiastical authority. The purpose of the commission was to allow only persons who conformed to the discipline and ceremonies of the Anglican Church to emigrate to New England.[18] Oliver M. Dickerson has written that the commission was not applied and came to an end when parliament seized control of the English government.[19] Perhaps London officials considered American affairs too far distant for close attention, or possibly, as Hugh Trevor-Roper has suggested, the colony was nothing more than a place to send unwanted persons.[20]

Sir William Berkeley (1605–77) purchased the office of governor of Virginia from the incumbent Sir Francis Wyatt in August 1641. A graduate of St Edmund Hall in Oxford in 1626, he was appointed to the privy chamber of King Charles I in 1632, an association that allowed him to form valuable social and political connections.[21] Arriving at Jamestown in March 1641/42 Berkeley received the reins of government from Wyatt on 8 March.[22] He inherited a troubled colony, with a sharply divided General Assembly.

It is unclear how and why the General Assembly was prompted to revisit the requirements of Sunday worship services in the colony in 1641. Perhaps the nudge came from the staunchly Anglican Governor Berkeley. In any event the legislature addressed the problem of Sunday services and weekly catechetical instruction being irregularly observed. Established law required that each congregation was to hold two services on Sunday and undertake weekly catechetical instruction. To correct the situation the General Assembly, on 11 January 1641/42, enacted a law which reaffirmed that the requirement that ministers should be 'preaching in the forenoon and catechizing in the afternoon of every Sunday be revived and stand in force, and in case any minister do fail to do so, that he forfeit 500 pounds of tobacco to be disposed of by the Vestry for the use of the parish.[23] At the time, the population of the colony was about 10,442, and while there were 23 parishes established by the General Assembly, only six churches were reconstructed, with six clergymen serving in the colony. Undoubtedly, the calibre and performance of the men serving the congregations raised some concerns and initiated the General Assembly's concern with the state of church services. At Hungar's Parish, William Cotton was in frequent legal dispute with the vestry over his salary, while his assistant, Nathaniel Eaton, a former and discredited schoolmaster in Cambridge, Massachusetts, Thomas Hampton of James City, Thomas Harrison of Elizabeth River, and John Rosier of York, Hungar's and Cople parishes, were all demonstrating strong Puritan, rather than traditional Anglican leanings.

At the next session of the General Assembly, in March 1642/43, a general revision of the laws of the colony was undertaken. Significant alterations to the 1632 laws were made, particularly that a vestry be established in each parish. The vestries were granted specific responsibility for making levies and assessments on qualified residents for repairs to the church building.[24] The vestry was also to elect two or more churchwardens each year. The primary duty of the minister and churchwardens of each parish was to convene annually with the commissioners of each county court, in the nature of a 'visitation according to the order and constitutions of the Church of England, which is there usually held every year after Christmas'.[25] In addition to the monthly reporting of the number of births, marriages, and burials that had occurred in the parish to the commissioners of each county court, the church wardens were to provide, on an annual basis, the same details at the visitation. At such sessions the churchwardens were also required to report on the income and expenses of the parish.[26]

The legislature meeting at Jamestown in early March 1642/43 introduced and enacted statutes that further defined the establishment and structure of the church in the colony. The vestry alone was to have the power 'to elect and make choice of their ministers', and to recommend to the Governor their candidate for admittance to the post.[27] It was a departure from the traditional procedure practised in England, which granted to the patron or bishop the right to admit a parson to a parish post, and it became a disputed issue in Virginia during the colonial period. Granting such lay authority on the appointment of ministers may have been simply owing to the lack of episcopal supervision in the colony; if it was a calculated political strategy it was designed to establish lay control over provincial church affairs. The royal governor was granted the right to elect and admit a minister in the James City parish. In any event, the long shadow of lay authority was firmly cast over the Virginia church for the remainder of the colonial era. By default, the inaction of church officials in London gave a strong congregational character to the church that would prevail until the outbreak of the War for Independence.

A decade later, the General Assembly's meeting on 26 April 1652 repealed the statutes of the 1642 session concerning church government. The royally appointed Governor Berkeley had been removed from office by Cromwell's government and the Directory of Worship was approved for use at worship services in the place of the Book of Common Prayer. New legislation declared:

> That all matters concerninge Vestrye, Theire agreement with the ministers, touchinge church wardens, [the] poore, and other things Conercinge the parishes or parrish Respectively be Referred to theire owne orderinge and disposal from time to time, they shall thinke ffitt, That Register Bookes be kept by theire appointment of all Christening, Burialls, and Marriages.[28]

Four years later, the General Assembly was addressing the constant shortage of ministers to serve the congregations. At the time there were 12 men serving provincial congregations.[29] At least two of the men were Puritans and serving on the Eastern Shore, John Rosier (1604–60) at Accomack Parish, a graduate of Gonville and Caius College in Cambridge, and Francis Doughty (1616–69) at Hungar's Parish. He had been ordained as a deacon in the Church of England, but practised his ministry as a Puritan in Massachusetts, a Dutch Reformed minister in New York, and an Anglican in Virginia.[30] On 1 December 1656 the legislature adopted a resolution and enacted a statute that declared the following:

> Whereas many congregations in this colony are destitute of ministers whereby religion and devotion cannot but suffer much impairment and decay, which want of the destitute congregations ought to be supplied by all means to be used. As also to invite and encourage ministers to repair hither and merchants to bring them in. Bee it therefore enacted for the reasons aforesaid, that what person or persons soever

shall at his or their proper cost and charge transport a sufficient minister into this colony without agreement made with him shall receive for satisfaction of their or their said charges of him the said minister or they that shall entertaine him for their minister, twenty pounds sterling by bill of exchange or two thousand pounds of tobacco, and also for what money shall be disbursed for them beside their transportation to be allowed for.[31]

The restoration of Charles II and his government to power in England in 1660 provided a new opportunity for colonial and London officials to review and address civil and church affairs in Virginia.[32] Right away the interests and needs of the church were viewed from differing perspectives by two parties, one publicly and the other in secret. On the one hand, in 1661 and 1662, the General Assembly reviewed and revised the laws relating to the church's establishment and enacted since 1619.[33] Previous legislation was reaffirmed, but several important modifications were made. The duties and the number of members of vestries was firmly fixed. An attempt was made to secure clergy stipends at £80 sterling per year, tied to the market value of 13,333 pounds of tobacco and to be supplemented by the usual perquisites and the use of a glebe. Fees for performing marriages were set at 200 pounds of tobacco or 20 shillings. Seeking again to curb the appointment of non-Anglican ministers to parish posts, the assembly reasserted lay and legal authority over the affairs of the church and required all clergymen to present to the governor a certificate of their ordination by a bishop of the Church of England before being allowed to serve a congregation or to officiate in Virginia. In addition, the General Assembly reviewed and supported the need for the construction of church buildings and chapels, the need to recruit ministers, lay out glebes, and define the responsibilities of the vestries. Furthermore, the parishes were required to provide the essential ornaments for a church, including a great Bible, two folio copies of the Book of Common Prayer for the use of the minister and the clerk, a communion plate, a pulpit cloth and cushion, and so forth.[34]

In 1660/61, the church in the colony comprised 54 parishes created by the General Assembly since 1607, eight church buildings, and ten ministers, one of whom did not hold a post.[35] The population of the province was estimated at 27,020, rising to about 35,309 in 1670. There was one parson to serve every 3,002 inhabitants in 1660. At least four of the ten ministers are known to have held Puritan tendencies.

On 23 March 1660/61, the General Assembly again turned its attention to the shortage of ministers in the colony and petitioned for clergymen who had attended either Oxford or Cambridge.[36] The session turned to Philip Mallory, a graduate of St Mary's Hall in Oxford, minister of the church at Jamestown and also serving as chaplain to the Assembly in 1658 and 1659/60, to undertake a mission to London to urge Bishop Gilbert Sheldon to plead with Charles II to send to the colony additional ministers and establish a bishop. We do not know if he was able to accomplish his task before he died in London sometime after 23 July 1661.[37]

Nearly coinciding with Mallory's appearance in England, Roger Green, a graduate of St Catharine's College, Cambridge, settled at the West Parish in Nansemond County between 1653 and 1671 and, in 1661, crafted a letter to Bishop of London Sheldon under the pen name 'R.G.' reporting on the state of the church in Virginia. Why he wrote to the London prelate rather than to the head of the Church, the Archbishop of Canterbury William Juxon, is unclear. Perhaps he believed that the London prelate would be more receptive to his plea. In any event, the letter was published in London the following year under the title *Virginia's Cure*. Green's words pointedly declared that after more than half-a-century the church was struggling with several deficiencies; some parishes did not have church buildings or glebes and only about one-fifth of the congregations had ministers. He noted that at churches with an incumbent there was usually only one service on Sunday and sometimes not at all if the weather was either too hot or too cold.[38] He also suggested that to aid the settlement and administration of the colony it was necessary to build towns and schools in each county.[39] Green also advanced a novel idea for the establishment of a special fellowship programme at Cambridge and Oxford that would require a minister to serve a set term of service in Virginia.[40] Despite its identifying the significant shortcomings of the church, Green's tract was primarily raising the question that should have been addressed more than a half-a-century earlier: how was the distant established colonial church institution to be administered, developed, and staffed? While officials in the province and London were without a historical precedent or strategy to address the matter clearly, the issue needed to be resolved. Yet, another 15 years would elapse before the situation was addressed.

Part II

4
Churches and Worship

For more than half a century after King Henry VIII's 1536 reformation of the English church, its leaders were obliged to manage the transformation of devotional habits of worshippers from the routine of the medieval church to the practices of the post-Reformation era.[1] During this period the church was wracked by division and controversy. Partisans disagreed violently as they embraced differing forms of Christian worship and life, Catholic and Protestant – a situation that contributed to the drive for American colonization in the seventeenth century.[2]

Unlike Ireland, Virginia had no pre-Reformation church buildings available for services of worship and equipped with the necessary furniture of altars, pulpits, and fonts; it was a virgin countryside. After 1619, it became the responsibility of Virginia's House of Burgesses to approve and appropriate funds for the construction of church buildings. Between 1607 and 1680 churches were of simple and basic design but from 1680, and for the next century, the exterior and interior church architecture and detail became more attractive and refined.

For London officials at Whitehall and in the church, administering a transatlantic settlement was a novel effort, without a national template or formula. But historical records reveal that for the first 80 years of the Virginia colony's existence, the provincial church was little more than an uncertified step-child or orphan of the mother church. The institution was extended and established in the New World without any vestige of the ecclesiastical structure, support, and supervision familiar in the villages, towns, and cities at home. The tide did not turn for church affairs until the 1670s, 1680s, and 1690s, when the Council of Trade and Plantations considered and implemented strong policies of imperial administration.[3]

Our knowledge of the seventeenth-century experience of the church and its founding and development is hampered by the sparsity of surviving details.[4] Only anecdotal evidence provides us with a glimpse of the experience of Virginia churches during the first years of the province. We have only a handful of clues regarding the size, shape, and design of church buildings, for instance. In England the churches of the late sixteenth and early seventeenth centuries had served as Catholic churches before the Reformation and were refitted for the Protestant practices of the reformed church during the successive archbishoprics of Thomas Cranmer and Matthew Parker.[5]

Perhaps the elements of a Virginia congregation's experience were shaped entirely by the minister or a handful of members. Chapter 7 discusses and describes clergymen in the colony who represented several factions, within and without the church in England. Barbette Levy's analysis of early Puritanism in Virginia identifies the most significant strongholds of such sentiments in the region as south of the James River and on the eastern shore.[6]

Worship

However, regardless of the location or theological complexion of the congregations, or the shades of Anglicanism or Puritanism practised, we do not know the usual routine of worship: were the offices and sacraments of the Book of Common Prayer rigorously observed, or exercised with moderate or extensive modification? Were Morning and Evening Prayer read only on Sunday or daily?[7] How often was the sacrament of Holy Communion celebrated – weekly, monthly, quarterly, or less?[8] Were baptisms, marriages, and burials regularly performed? How frequently was the office of the Churching of Women performed? Is there any extant evidence that describes the private devotions of clergymen or church members? Given the sparsity of the historical records of ministers and churches during the seventeenth century, what, if anything, can we glean from the sources regarding the pastoral duties of the ministers and the observation of the liturgical calendar?[9] Nor do we know the manner or extent of the spiritualization of the family in Virginia during the seventeenth century.[10]

It would be interesting to know the level of acceptance and practice of the Church of England Canons of 1604 in Virginia. In particular, did the design of churches include a stone font for baptisms and a decent communion table, as required by Canons 81 and 82 respectively?[11] Were there any attempts to introduce Laudian ceremonial practices at worship services in the colony during the late 1620s, 1630s, and 1640s?

We may ask whether an altar was usually placed against the east walls of the buildings.[12] Was it covered in some kind of fabric such as linen or velvet? Was the table or altar surrounded in part or completely by a rail? Was a screen erected between the altar or table and the congregation? Were any changes introduced in the seventeenth century that echoed transformations in England?[13] Did the successive bands of clergymen bring with them the most recent style and application for altars to reflect contemporary English usage? Were communion tables placed either in the chancel, nave, or at the base of the pulpits?[14] Were there desks and pulpits for the use of the ministers?[15] In a letter seeking a New England Puritan minister for a Virginia congregation I have found one reference to a church in 1642 which was equipped with a desk and pulpit.[16] Were candles and books placed on either the altars or communion tables? What was the interior furniture? Were there benches or pews or both for the congregation? Did the churches have the essential plate and vessels for use in the communion service? What was the dress of the ministers during services? Did they wear a surplice?

Church design and construction

The first description of religious services in Virginia appears in Captain John Smith's published writings. He noted that in the community's early years the settlers, except for guards, assembled twice daily for common prayer and gathered every Sunday under an awning or old tent for two sermons.[17] According to Smith, the minister that accompanied the first settlers, Robert Hunt, celebrated a service of communion on 21 June 1607, presumably under similar circumstances.[18] Soon afterwards a modest building was constructed at Jamestown, but it was destroyed by fire during the winter of extreme frost in 1607.[19] Smith recounts that as spring approached in 1608 the colonists began to rebuild the town.[20] Sometime later another church building was constructed, about 64 feet in length and 24 feet wide.[21] The building was still standing when Governor Thomas West, Lord De la Warr, arrived at Jamestown in 1610 and oversaw repairs to it. The Instructions, Orders and Constitutions issued by the Virginia Company to Sir Thomas Gates in May 1609 required that the Church of England be observed in the colony and that a church must be built.[22]

When Thomas Dale arrived in the colony in 1611, Smith reported that there was also a church built at Henrico, which included a parsonage and glebe of 100 acres for the new minister, Alexander Whitaker. According to a letter Dale sent to the Virginia Council in London in May of that year, the chancel of the church was constructed of wood from cedar trees, as were the pulpit, the pews, and the window frames. The communion table was crafted from black walnut, while the baptismal font was carved from wood. The chancel and interior walls were decorated with different types of native flowers. In a steeple at the west end of the church were suspended two bells which summoned the community at ten o'clock in the morning and four in the afternoon. But this building was in such disrepair by the time of Dale's arrival in the province that it was found to be in danger of collapsing.[23] Historian Philip A. Bruce reports that when Governor Samuel Argall reached Jamestown in 1617, the church was in such ruin that worship services were held in a storehouse.[24] When Governor Yeardley arrived at Jamestown two years later he found a church building in use that was about 50 feet in length and 20 in width, but the church at Henrico had fallen into disrepair.[25] By 1656 only eight of the 52 parishes had a church building, and the General Assembly passed legislation in an attempt to correct the situation.[26]

Perhaps during the first years after settlement worship services were held in the house of the minister or of members of the congregation, or in a public building. It is unlikely that earlier churches were modelled in the cruciform manner of English buildings of the late sixteenth and early seventeenth centuries, which had served as Catholic churches before the Reformation.[27] While the General Assembly enacted legislation for the construction of church buildings, the first description of a seventeenth-century church does not occur until the 1680s.[28] It is not known whether the first churches in the new communities were built on a standard model that was duplicated at several sites. Nor do we know whether the design of a building was in the hands of local civil or church officials or was dictated by a committee of the House of Burgesses. It is possible, although no evidence has appeared to confirm the matter, that the handful of Puritan ministers who migrated to Virginia from Massachusetts and took up posts in the 1630s, 1640s, and 1650s, may have proposed suggestions for the design of churches. Our understanding of the first century of worship in the Bay colony is fashioned by Horton Davies' careful analysis and description of the only surviving seventeenth-century New England meeting-house, at Hingham.[29]

Dell Upton concludes that by the end of the seventeenth century many parishes were building their second or even third churches; surviving churches, which date mostly from the 1730s onwards, are third- and even fourth-generation buildings.[30] Professor Upton has provided a valuable account of the historical architecture and structure of Virginia church buildings by decade, of the number of parishes created and churches built, and the materials of construction for the seventeenth century, as noted in Tables 4.1, 4.2, and 4.3.[31]

Table 4.1 Number of parishes created in Virginia during the seventeenth century, by decade

Decade	Number
1607–19	9
1620–29	4
1630–39	8
1640–49	16
1650–59	17
1660–69	9
1670–79	4
1680–89	4
1690–99	0
Total	71[1]

[1] In contrast to the construction of churches in Virginia between 1629 and 1642, 40 meeting-houses were built in New England – 29 in Massachusetts, six in Connecticut and Long Island, and four towns replaced their meeting-house with a second building. From 1643 to 1660, 41 meeting-houses were built in the region, 29 were for new congregations and 12 were replacements of older structures – 27 in Massachusetts, six in Connecticut, four on Long Island, three in New Hampshire, and one in Maine. By 1660 there were at least 80 meeting-houses in the New England colonies. Between 1661 and 1700 122 meetinghouses were built, 52 were new, 58 were second buildings, 11 were third, and one was fourth – 70 in Massachusetts, 37 in Connecticut, five in Maine, five on Long Island, three in New Hampshire, and two in Rhode Island. (Horton Davies, *The Worship of the American Puritans, 1629–1730* (New York, 1990): 235–7; Peter Benes, *Meeting Houses of Early New England* (Amherst, 2012): 289–99.)

Source: Upton, *Holy Things and Profane*: 8.

Table 4.1 indicates the number of parishes which the civil authorities created in each decade. These parishes provided a local social structure for the community after the English pattern, but the number of parishes does not correlate with the number of known church buildings in each era.[32] Construction of a church would follow when the number of settlers in a parish warranted it. By 1629 there were 13 established parishes in the province, with an estimated population of around 2,500, but only four churches had been built. If the population was evenly distributed there would have been a church for every 625 persons.

In 1660, after more than fifty years of settlement, the estimated population of Virginia was 27,020. During that period the General Assembly approved the creation of 54 parishes, but only eight churches were built and it is unclear whether any of the buildings were replacements for earlier structures. If we accept that there were eight active churches in

Table 4.2   Number of churches built in Virginia
in the seventeenth century, by decade

Decade	Number
1607–19	4
1620–29	0
1630–39	1
1640–49	1
1650–59	2
1660–69	8
1670–79	3
1680–89	5
1690–99	4
Total	28

Source: Upton, *Holy Things and Profane*: 12.

the colony and the population was distributed evenly then there was one church for every 3,375 residents.

In 1699 the situation may have changed to a degree because there were 71 parishes and a provincial population of 58,040. We know that 28 churches had been built in the colony since 1607, but again we do not know how many of these were replacement buildings. If we follow our population statistics, the 28 churches each represented a congregation of about 2,073.

Table 4.2 shows that after about 1650 the number of churches constructed did not keep pace with the increased population. In 1624 the population was about 1,227, in 1661 about 25,000, and in 1699 about 58,040.[33]

Captain John Smith notes that the Jamestown fire in the cold winter of 1607 destroyed the first building and a second church became so dilapidated by 1611 that it had to be replaced.[34] A church, a parsonage and a glebe were available for Alexander Whitaker when he arrived at Henrico in 1611,[35] but we know nothing further about the buildings. Table 4.3 shows the types of church buildings constructed in the province between 1607 and 1700. Among the 29 known churches, 18 were of frame construction, six brick, two of some other materials, and three of unknown construction.

Books for the Minister and Congregation

We do not have evidence of the use of the Bible in church and private devotions. Professor David S. Katz has noted that between 1560

Table 4.3 Type of construction of churches built in Virginia during
the seventeenth century, by decade

Decade	Brick	Frame	Other	Unknown
1607–19	0	3	0	0
1620–29	0	0	0	0
1630–39	0	1	0	0
1640–49	0	1	0	0
1650–59	0	2	0	0
1660–69[1]	1	7	1	1
1670–79	0	2	0	1
1680–89	3	2	0	0
1690–99	2	0	1	1
Total	6	18	2	3

[1]Hening, *Statutes at Large*, 21 February, 1631/32, I: 160–1. The law required
church buildings to be replaced only when the original structure was beyond
repair. It is unclear how many of the churches built during the decade
between 1660 and 1669 were replacements or new buildings.
Source: Upton, *Holy Things and Profane*: 13.

and 1644 over 140 editions of the Geneva Bible or New Testament were
printed.[36] But no surviving evidence exists to confirm or demonstrate
the regularity and extent of its use in services of worship or private
devotions of individuals in Virginia.[37]

In fact, there is no evidence to indicate which version of the English
Bible was commonly available and used in Virginia. Was it the popular Geneva Bible, first fully published in England in 1576 and in more
than 90 editions by 1603? This was a popular publication, used by
such luminaries as William Shakespeare, Richard Hooker, John Donne,
John Bunyan, and Walter Raleigh. Did the first Anglican minister at
Jamestown, Richard Hunt, take a Bible with him on the voyage for
his personal use? It is reasonable to speculate that Hunt took a Bible
with him from England for official and devotional use. Did Captain
John Smith or other members of the original settlement bring a Bible to
America? The pages of history are silent on whether Governor Thomas
De La Ware or his successors in office, including William Berkeley and
Francis Lord Howard of Effingham, carried a Bible to America in par-
tial fulfilment of their royal instructions to supervise the church in the
colony, and if so which edition.

We know that the Geneva Bible was taken to America on the
Mayflower in 1620 and used by many English dissenters.[38] But per-
haps in Virginia the first Bible used in the settlement was the Bishops'
Bible, published in 1568 in response to the Calvinism of the Geneva

Bible, which offended the high-church party of the Church of England, to which almost all of its bishops subscribed. Even though, in 1566, Archbishop of Canterbury Matthew Parker and Bishop of London Edmund Grindal endorsed the reprinting of the Geneva Bible because 'It shall nothing hinder, but rather do much good, to have diversity of translations and readings',[39] many of the prelates objected to the Geneva Bible and its association with Presbyterianism, which sought to replace government of the church by bishops with government by lay elders. The bishops were aware that the Great Bible of 1539, which was then legally authorized for use in Anglican worship, was deficient in text. Archbishop Parker was the leading figure in replacing the objectionable Geneva translation with a text of the prelates' approval, which became known as the Bishops' Bible.[40] The Bishops' Bible, or its New Testament, went through over 50 editions, while the Geneva Bible was reprinted in more than 90 editions before 1603.

When the King James Bible was published in 1611 it soon replaced the Bishops' Bible as the standard scripture of the Church of England. But it is not clear how quickly it came to be used in Virginia. Furthermore, because many of the ministers in the colony were aligned with the Puritan party within the divided Anglican Church, it is possible that they used the Geneva Bible. Because Archbishop of Canterbury George Abbot and other influential officers and members of the Virginia Company of London were Puritans, did the company send copies of the Geneva, Bishops', or James I Bible to the colony for use in services? We do not know. The first indication of the Virginia Company sending religious books to the colony does not occur until 1619.[41]

The lack of printed materials for the clergymen and church members may reflect the company's modest interest in such matters, or the lack of a coherent religious policy. The published records of the Virginia Company indicate only one occasion where religious books were purchased and sent to the colony.[42] Included in the shipment were two church Bibles, two Books of Common Prayer, three books 'for the practice of piety', and three books 'of the playne man's path ways'.[43] Were the Bibles and Books of Common Prayer fulfilling the requirement under Canon 80 of the Ecclesiastical Laws that 'a great Bible and Book of Common Prayer' be in each church, or were the volumes replacements of earlier works?[44]

The clergymen who arrived in Virginia between 1607 and 1662 were required to use the 1604 edition of the Book of Common Prayer,[45] which contained few changes over the version promulgated for use by Queen Elizabeth I in the Act of Uniformity.[46]

Judith Maltby has raised the question 'How common was common prayer?' She notes that between the date of its initial publication in England in 1549, and 1642, 290 editions of the Book of Common Prayer appeared,[47] and estimates that perhaps half-a-million copies were in circulation before the English Civil War.[48] But she acknowledges that the evidence of availability of the book in private or clerical hands is unavailable because estate inventories of such persons are rare.[49] We do not know how common it was for Virginia colonists to own a copy of the Book of Common Prayer and use it at Sunday services and in private devotions. Sometimes the early Prayer Book was prefixed to the Bible and included the Orders of Morning and Evening Prayer, the Litany, the Collects throughout the Year, and occasionally the Order of Communion,[50] so ownership of a Bible implied access to a portion, if not all, of the offices of the Book of Common Prayer.[51]

The Book of Common Prayer was not without its critics: Calvinists considered it 'saturated with popery', and the Puritans wished to purify divine service from all the abominations it authorized. The Independents or Nonconformists, later the Congregationalists, rejected the English church and its bishops, priests, and sacraments. Each congregation formed an independent unity and elected its own minister, whose office was limited to prayer and preaching.

But how common was it for a provincial member of a congregation to own a Book of Common Prayer, a Bible, or both volumes?[52] According to Christopher Hill,

> the Bible played a large part in moulding English nationalism, in asserting the supremacy of the English language in a society which from the eleventh to the fourteenth century had been dominated by French-speaking Normans. The translation of the Bible into English coincided in time with the spread of the new invention of printing.[53]

It seems probable that at least a few persons venturing from England to Virginia owned a prayer book and Bible. While the ownership of a religious book may reasonably imply that a person knew how to read, it may also have been held for its intrinsic devotional value. It is possible that many congregants participating in worship services did not need a prayer book because they recalled from memory Archbishop of Canterbury Thomas Cranmer's rhythmic usage of the Elizabethan language for the offices.

But the question of ownership of a prayer book or a Bible raises a significant ancillary query: what was the level of literacy in early seventeenth-century Virginia? Perhaps it followed the pattern of literacy in England during the Tudor and Stuart periods, shown in a study by David Cressy.[54] Based on his examination of differing types of documents he concluded that in 1640 around 70 per cent of the male population in England and 90 per cent of the women were not literate.[55] He noted, too, that women were almost universally unable to write their own name for most of the sixteenth and seventeenth centuries.[56] In contrast, in 1660 New England, Kenneth Lockridge found that just 39 per cent of the men and 69 per cent of the women making wills were unable to write their names.[57] Unfortunately we are unable to draw on similar studies for an estimate of the literacy rate among Virginia men and women.

The two immensely popular English devotional works sent to the province by the Virginia Company are noteworthy. Bishop of Bangor Lewis Bayly (d. 1631) wrote the Protestant classic *The Practice of Piety, Directing A Christian How to Walk that He May Please God*. The date of the first edition is unknown but the second appeared in 1612 and offered meditations and prayers for daily life. The manual, of more than 800 pages' extent, was instruction in some of the fundamental faith, and polemic against Roman Catholic errors. The seventeenth edition was published in 1618 and dedicated to Prince Charles, Prince of Wales; the fortieth edition was published in 1687. Bayly's carefully hewed book represented the perspective of a conformist Calvinist with appreciation of the Puritan ideas current within the Anglican Church.

Arthur Dent's work, *The Plain Mans Path-Way to Heaven*, first published in London in 1601, was another popular classic.[58] A graduate of Christ's College, Cambridge in 1576, Dent was probably influenced by the Puritan fellows, including William Perkins. Dent was recognized as a distinguished preacher and minister who refused to bow to Bishop of London John Aylmer's directives to wear a surplice. *The Plain Mans Path-Way* was dedicated to Sir Julius Caesar (1558–1636), judge, and reached a twenty-fifth edition by 1640. The book profoundly influenced the writings of John Bunyan and Richard Baxter.

The profile and analysis of churches and services in seventeenth-century Virginia has raised more questions than it has been possible to answer, inevitably circumscribed and restrained by the lack of historical records. First-hand details regarding the style and construction of the exterior and interior of church buildings, and the format of regular worship, have been lost. Perhaps worship services in the colony were held in rudimentary public buildings, churches, or the houses of congregants and closely followed the procedures of an English village church, observing the offices of the Book of Common Prayer. It is reasonable to speculate that the churches followed such a pattern, except that, for at least the first 80 years, many ministers represented divergent theological positions and practices. Some of the men may have adhered to the positions of the traditional Anglican, or Anglican-Puritan parties in the Church of England, or may have expressed opinions similar to separating Puritans or Nonconformists familiar in the homeland. The situation is a recapitulation of the theme developed by historian Peter Laslett for a sixteenth-century English village.[59]

5
A Social Profile Of Virginia's Ministers, 1607–1700

In contrast to England's ecclesiastical beginnings in Ireland, our knowledge regarding the development of the Anglican Church in seventeenth-century Virginia is fragmentary and anecdotal. Virginia differed from Ireland because the Anglican church encountered no network of congregations or existing corps of clergymen. What we do know rests in large measure on only two important sources, statutes enacted by the House of Burgesses in 1619 and later years, which established and governed the church in the colony, and biographical details of the ministers. We know the names of the 159 ministers who served congregations between 1607 and 1700 and limited details regarding their social origins, collegiate educational experience, place and date of their ordination, and place and range of years served in parishes in England and Virginia.[1] Ninety-five of the ministers (60 per cent) arrived in the province between 1606 and 1680, with the remaining 64 arriving between 1681 and 1700. The increased number of men arriving in the colony during the last two decades of the century reflects the new supervisory authority delegated to Bishop of London Henry Compton over American church affairs.

More than a century would pass after the establishment of the church in the colony before native Virginians entered the ministry and occupied pulpits. During the province's first 75 years the church was served by English natives, who were mostly educated at one or other of the two English universities. After about 1685, Scottish Episcopal ministers began to settle in the colony, and they were followed in the next century by graduates of Trinity College, Dublin, ordained in the Church of Ireland. Each of these groups came from different cultural, linguistic, educational, and religious backgrounds, and this diversity would continue to characterize the Anglican Church in the colony for the remainder of the early American era.

As well as diverse backgrounds, education, experience, and talents, the men also represented and displayed in their ministries the differing factions and tensions within the Church of England. Some of the ministers were Anglican Puritans, others strongly Puritan, and a handful Nonconformists. The multiplicity of religious outlook and practice among the clergy was not limited to the first or second generation of settlement in Virginia, but continued until the 1680s, when Bishop of London Henry Compton was authorized by the Council of Trade and Plantations to implement stronger and more uniform administrative supervision over the American church.

In Ireland, the sixteenth-century efforts of Tudor and early Stuart governments to anglicize the church rested on the willingness of the parochial clergy and congregations to conform to the Book of Common Prayer and liturgical practices of the English church. But an overwhelming majority of ministers and laity objected to the innovations of the Henrician reformation and firmly resisted the policy. Absent for comparative purposes are the names and number of men who served as ministers of the Church of Ireland during the early years, between 1536 and 1600.[2] Virginia differed from Ireland because it was without a network of congregations and a corps of clergymen.

Regardless of the period of the ministers' arrival, questions arise about their origins, education, and theological and liturgical viewpoints and practices.[3] Were they all natives of England? How many of the men were educated at Cambridge or Oxford, and which colleges within the two universities did they attend? How many of the ministers had attended the Puritan-influenced colleges at the universities? How long did they serve? Do we have evidence of their ordinations? Did they return to England after a few years or remain in Virginia until the end of their lives?

From the earliest years, colonial officials at Jamestown informed London leaders of the need for ministers. Table 5.1 shows the number of ministers active in the colony at the beginning of each decade during the seventeenth century. An analysis of the number of men who appeared in Virginia and their length of service to congregations provides an informative profile. Table 5.1 indicates that some men only served for one or two years before succumbing to illness and death, while others served a few years, and a handful of ministers served two or more decades. After about 1650, several parsons held posts for more than 20 or 30 years and in a few instances for more than 40 or 50 years.

Table 5.1 The number of clergymen who arrived and years served, by decade

Decade	Number of Men	Years Served
1600–09	1	1
1610–19	9	two men served 1 year; two served 3 years; one served 4 years; two served 6 years; one served 10 years; and one served 13 years.
		A total of 45 'man years', an average of 5 years per person.
1620–29	15	four men served 1 year; five served 2 years; two served 3 years; one man each served 4, and 9 years, two men served 7 years.
		A total of 54 'man years', an average of 2.77 years per person.
1630–39	9	two men served 4 years; three men each 1 year, two men each served 2 years; one man each served for 7 and 14 years.
		A total of 36 'man years', an average of 4 years per person.
1640–49	9	three men served 1 year; one man each served 3, 9, 13, and 19 years.
		A total of 67 'man years', an average of 7.55 years per person.
1650–59	21	three men served 1 year; two served 3 years; five served 4 years; 4 served 5 years; two served 6 years; and one man each served 18, 20, 23, and 38 years.
		A total of 162 'man years', an average of 7.71 years per person.
1660–69	12	two men served 1 year; four served 2 years; two served 3 years; and one man each served 13, 14, 30, and 39 years.
		A total of 112 'man years', an average of 9.33 years per person.
1670–79	19	six men served 1 year; two served 3 years; one man each served 5, 6, 7, 8, 10, 12, 16, 32, and unknown years.
		A total of 108 'man years', an average of 5.68 years per person.
1680–89	33	eight men served 1 year; three served 2 years; two served 3 years; two served 4 years; one served 5 years; four served 7 years; one man each served 5, 6, 10, 15, 20, 27, 38, and 58 years.

		A total of 241 'man years', an average of 7.30 years per person.
1690–99	31	six men served 1 year; two served 2 years; three served 3 years; two served 4 years; two served 5 years; four served 7 years; two served 8 years; one man each served 6, 13, 14, 19, 21, 25, 28, 31, and 46 years.
		A total of 313 'man years', an average of 10.09 years per person.

The entire group of 159 men gave in total 1,137 man years of service, an average of 7.15 years per clergyman. In each decade between 30 and 46 per cent of the ministers died.

Horton Davies notes that the ratio of congregation to ministers was much smaller in New England than in Virginia. In 1650 Massachusetts there was a minister for every 415 people, while in 1649 Virginia there was one clergyman to serve 3,359 persons.[4]

The colony was ravaged by hardship, turmoil, sickness, and death between 1607 and 1624. But the population gradually increased over the century, particularly after 1640: in 1610 there were 350 persons; in 1620, 2,200; 1630, 2,500; 1640, 10,042; 1650, 18,731; 1660, 27,020; 1670, 35,309; 1680, 43,596; and in 1700, 58,560.[5] In 1630, the Negro population numbered 50 persons; in 1640, 150; 1650, 405; 1660, 950; 1670, 2,000; 1680, 3,000; 1690, 9,345; and in 1700, 16,390.[6]

Between 1607 and 1624, it was the Virginia Company's responsibility to advance the Church of England in the province and to recruit, transport, and financially support the ministers. The requirement was not uncommon, all royal charters granted to late-sixteenth- and seventeenth-century explorers, merchant adventurers, and colonial proprietors included obligations to propagate and support the polity, doctrine, and traditions of the national church.[7]

But for at least eighty years, until about 1685, the recruitment of ministers to serve the colony remained an *ad hoc* administrative process, without a link to a bishop, archdeacon, or dean in England who was officially responsible for supervising the extension and development of the church overseas. It was not until 1677 that the Bishop of London, Henry Compton, was vested by the crown with the authority to administer American church affairs.[8] Until then, employment of ministers rested on the efforts of the leadership of individual congregations and the personal inclinations of clergymen in England.

Another quarter century would pass before a missionary society was founded, the Society for the Propagation of the Gospel in Foreign Parts, for the purpose of recruiting and financially maintaining men to serve congregations in the northern, middle, and southern provinces. During the Virginia Company's existence, several members probably aided in the recruitment of clergymen, including George Abbot, John King, Matthew Sutcliff, Richard Hakluyt, and the third Earl of Southampton, Henry Wriothesley (1573–1624).[9] Each held positions that allowed them to tap into a network of potential recruits. Abbot was the Master of University College, Oxford, Dean of Winchester Cathedral and later Archbishop of Canterbury (1611–33), while Sutcliffe was Dean of Exeter Cathedral (1588–1629) and a founder of Chelsea College.[10] Both of these leaders were sympathetic Calvinists and strident critics of the papacy and Catholic Spain.[11] It seems likely that any clergymen selected for a Virginia assignment would hold similar ecclesiastical opinions.[12] Captain Edward-Maria Wingfield, first president of the Council of Virginia, claimed that he enlisted the colony's first clergymen, Robert Hunt, a graduate of Magdalene Hall, Oxford, who was a Puritan and 'a man not any waie to be touched with the rebellious humors of a popish spirit, not blemished with the least suspicion of a factious Scismatik'.[13]

What attracted men to the colony in the seventeenth century and prompted them to leave their familiar surroundings, family, and friends in England? Were they unable to obtain a post at home? Were they attracted by the prospects and excitement of an overseas adventure? Were the men recruited by a Virginia Company official or by a resident in the colony? How were the Puritan and Nonconformist ministers in New England induced to move to posts in Virginia in the 1620s, 1630s, and 1640s? We can only speculate about the men's motives and interests because there are no surviving manuscripts, letters, journals, or sermons that recount their experiences.

There are several possible answers to the questions. A few of the men may have travelled to Virginia with the understanding that it would be a three- or four-year odyssey in a strange place. Perhaps after attending college or university they were testing their vocation for the church during a brief sojourn in the colony because they could conduct the offices of Morning and Evening Prayer but were not allowed to perform the sacrament. Other persons may have been compelled to respond to an inner voice that urged them to serve the new English settlements and seek to convert the heathen Native Americans. While another group of men, in addition to their professional interests, may also have been persuaded by the opportunity to obtain grants of land and improve their financial status (see Table 5.2). After some time in the colony a few men may have married a woman from a local family and decided to remain in the province. And, despite the men's long- or short-term plans, some met with illness and died after a brief residency in Virginia.

Table 5.2 Seventeenth-century Anglican clergymen identified as acquiring land through grants by the Virginia Company, provincial official policy, or personal purchase

John Banister (1650–92)	1,970 acres
Richard (Francis) Bolton	50 acres
James Bowker (1665–1703)	526 acres as noted on 1704 Quit Rent Rolls
Ralph Bowker (1671–17xx)	330 acres as noted on 1704 Quit Rent Rolls
Robert Bracewell (1611–68)	In 1668 owned a 300-acre plantation on Blackwater River
Richard Bucke	750 acres, 100 acres glebe
William Cotton (16xx–ca.1646)	Owned land
Robert Dunster (16xx–56)	Owned a dwelling plantation, Isle of Wight 1651–56
John Farnifold (1635–1702)	By his last will gave 100 acres for a free school
Stephen Fouace (16xx–17xx)	Residing in Virginia 1690–1702, listed on Quit Rent Rolls 1704, 750 acres
Roger Green (1614–73)	Received a land grant
Thomas Hampton (1609–16xx)	700 acres in Nansemond County. Patented to Elizabeth Webb in 1705 because it had escheated
Willis Heyley (1591–16xx)	250 acres, Mulberry Island, 1635
Richard Jones	950 acres, Martin Brandon Parish in 1650 and 1,500 acres in 1655
George Keith (1585–16xx)	Arrived in Virginia 1617. Owned 100 acres Elizabeth City. On Feb. 26 1634/35 he was granted 850 acres in Charles River County (York) also due him 50 acres for his own on arrival in Virginia 50 for his wife Martha, 50 for his son John, and 700 acres for transporting 14 persons to the colony
Philip Mallory (1617–61)	Owned a plantation
Lazarus Martin (16xx–16xx)	Granted the two plantations of the Neckofland and the College for his care

Table 5.2   (Continued)

Samuel Maycocke (1594–1622)	Peraley's Hundred; 1,000 acres in Charles City and the common land; settled at Flower Dew Hundred
George Robertson (1662–1739)	2,300 acres but how accumulated is unknown
Samuel Sanford (1669–1710)	Served Accomac Parish 1694–1702, 3,250 acres on Quit Rent Rolls 1704
John Shepard (1646–82)	Bequeathed a tract of land to parish, the number of acres unknown
James Stockton (1588–1628)	50 acres as of Sept. 8 1627
Thomas Vicaris (16xx–96)	Owned land in King and Queen County, patented April 10 1678
George White (1661–16xx)	Owned land, amount is unknown.

See sources for each individual in E. G. Swem, *Virginia Historical Index* (Roanoke,1934–36. 2 vols).

Owing, no doubt, in large part to the absence of episcopal oversight, the early church in Virginia included a wide range of interests and experience among the men who served. The situation reflected the newness of the province and the religious conditions at home in England during the period. Among the 159 men who served churches in the seventeenth century at least two were not ordained, a handful had previously held posts in New England and may have been ordained in England by a Puritan bishop but had embraced the religious tenets of the Massachusetts Bay colony, and, by the end of the century a few of the men were Presbyterians. Although a small group, the men represented a remarkable number of the factions and tensions within the church at home.

Only one clergyman arrived in the new colony between 1600 and 1609, while the highest number arrived during the last two decades of the seventeenth century, from 1680 to 1689, and 1690 to 1699 – 33 and 31 persons respectively. For the century as a whole, the average number of clergymen migrating to the province per decade was 15.9, a number that was exceeded during the 1650s, 1670s, 1680s, and 1690s. Table 5.3 indicates that between 1607 and 1629 25 men arrived in Virginia to serve a congregation. At first glance, the number seems more than adequate to serve the young, sparsely settled colony. But the inhabitants had been wracked with illness, death, and the devastating 1622 Good Friday Massacre at the hands of the Native Americans. Among the band

Table 5.3   The number of clergymen serving the
established church, by decade of arrival

1600–09	1
1610–19	9
1620–29	15
1630–39	9
1640–49	9
1650–59	21
1660–69	12
1670–79	19
1680–89	33
1690–99	31
TOTAL	159

of 25, seven served for around one year, six for two years, two for three
years, two for four years (but these men were not ordained), two each
for six and seven years, and one each for nine, ten, and 13 years. During
the next two decades only 18 clergymen arrived in the colony, and for
the following 30 years the number increased to 52. Between 1680 and
1699, 64 men came to the province.

The earliest ministers in the colony were associated with the Puritan faction within the Church of England. Perhaps to ward off the
sharp religious divisions experienced in England, the Council of the
Virginia Company issued an Instruction to the Governor and Council of
Virginia on 24 July 1621 stating that all religious services in the colony
should be:

> according to the usual form and discipline of the Church of England
> and carefully avoiding all factions and needless novelties tending
> only to the disturbance of peace and unity, and that such ministers
> as have been or shall be sent from time to time may be respected and
> maintained according to the orders made in that behalf.[14]

However, England's new colony was not religiously homogeneous; as
early as the 1620s a large number of Puritans settled on its eastern shore.
For the next half century several Puritan clergymen with experience in
New England arrived to lead congregations, until many Puritans were
exiled to Maryland by Governor Berkeley in 1649.[15] But the arrival of a
stream of Puritan ministers, beginning in the late 1620s and 1630s, may
have prompted Governor William Berkeley to urge the 1642/43 Assembly to enact a statute requiring that all ministers conform to the orders

Table 5.4   The number of clergymen by decade of
migration to Virginia for whom records indicate
that they attended either a university or college in
England, Scotland, or Massachusetts

1590–99	1
1600–09	1
1610–19	6
1620–29	9
1630–39	4
1640–49	6
1650–59	9
1660–69	4
1670–79	11
1680–89	15
1690–99	19
TOTAL	87

and constitutions of the Church of England.[16] We know that among
the 159 Virginia clergymen who served congregations between 1607
and 1700, at least 24, or 15 per cent, followed the religious practices
of Nonconformists, Puritans, Independents, or Presbyterians.[17]

At least 87 of the 159 men attended college, but it should be acknowledged that the records of collegiate matriculates of the period are
incomplete; therefore, the number is unreliable.[18] Based on the resources
available we know that the largest number of men (71) attended either
Cambridge (35) or Oxford University (36), while another 12 attended
one of the four Scottish colleges, one man was educated at Leyden
University in Holland, and one at Harvard College in Massachusetts.

The colleges attended at Cambridge and Oxford indicate that an overwhelming number of the men were students of colleges with strong Puritan leanings. Harry Culverwell Porter has comprehensively examined
and described the religious controversies that enveloped Cambridge
University during the sixteenth and seventeenth centuries.[19] Debates
raged in the 1540s and 1550s regarding the theological and liturgical nature of the Holy Communion, the design of the altar, and sale
of pre-Reformation missals, silver basins, copes, and other vestments.[20]
No college or its fellows and heads were insulated from the Puritans
and their challenges to religious and institutional authority and practice. Upholding the interests of the Anglican party was John Whitgift,
Master of Trinity College, while Thomas Cartwright, the Lady Margaret
Professor of Divinity, defended the Puritan position.[21] The Puritans did
not scrupulously use the Book of Common Prayer or conform to the

regulations about vestments and ceremonies.[22] Emmanuel College exiles to New England included Thomas Hooker, John Cotton, and Thomas Shepard. The 'Great Migration' across the Atlantic to New England between 1632 and 1642 was the climax to the history of the Elizabethan and Jacobean separatism.[23] Nicholas Tyacke writes that the character of divinity at Oxford until the reign of Charles I was militantly protestant, generally Calvinist, in the sense of adhering to the Reformed theology of grace, and strongly evangelical. This tradition was established in the later sixteenth century.[24]

During the years that the Virginia Company of London administered the colony (1607–24) 19 men arrived in the province and served congregations.[25] Among the universities they attended were Cambridge, eight; Oxford, four; King's College in Aberdeen, one; the colleges, if any, of the other six men are unknown.[26] Between 1630 and 1659, an era of civil and ecclesiastical turbulence in England, 39 clergymen migrated to Virginia. Representation from Cambridge and Oxford remained in balance with nine and nine ministers respectively and one graduate of King's College in Aberdeen. Following the Restoration of the English crown and church in 1660, 31 men arrived in the colony and served congregations during the next 20 years. The group had been educated at Cambridge (seven), Oxford (eight), and the new Harvard College in Cambridge, Massachusetts (one).

After 1676 the Council of Trade and Plantations undertook a comprehensive review of imperial administration in the provinces and implemented significant changes in policy.[27] During the next two decades provincial and proprietary charters were revoked and replaced with royal charters in Massachusetts, New York, Pennsylvania, and Maryland. Governors were withdrawn from service and new royal officials appointed in their place, and the English church became a vital element of the council's imperial administration and anglicization policies. In England, political events led to the 'Glorious Revolution'; King James II fled the country and was replaced by the Dutch William of Orange and his wife Mary.

Affairs in Scotland were no less confrontational, with significant consequences for the subsequent history of the church in America, particularly in Virginia. After the Reformation the Church of Scotland was exposed to the conflicts between the Presbyterian and Episcopal parties. Control of the church shifted from one group to the other through the years until the Scottish parliament outlawed the Scottish Episcopal Church in 1689. For about a century it was illegal for Episcopalians to gather in a group of more than five persons for worship. The effect of the statute was to immediately deprive Episcopal clergymen of their pulpits and livings. Without a church or income, many of the men sought relief and opportunity in the English church. Coincidentally, the turn of events in Scotland occurred during a period when Bishop of London Henry Compton was searching for recruits to serve colonial parishes, primarily in Virginia and Maryland. Beginning in the 1680s, and for the remainder of the colonial era, many men raised and ordained in the Scottish Episcopal Church found parish appointments in America, particularly in Virginia.

Between 1680 and 1699 the predominance of ministers who had attended Cambridge and Oxford continued, with 12 from each university. But it was also a period with sharply increased representation from the colleges in Scotland, including Aberdeen, with two; Edinburgh, five; Glasgow, two; and St Andrews, one. In addition, one man had attended the University of Leyden in Holland.

The search for details regarding the ordination of the men has been aided by The Clergy of the Church of England Database, which represents a compilation of more than 130,000 men ordained in the church between 1540 and 1835.[28] Among the 159 men that served congregations of the established church in the Virginia colony during the seventeenth century, only 31 (19.5 per cent) are noted in the registers as being ordained ministers of the Church of England. The number seems surprisingly low and requires further explanation and speculation. In the first instance, none the less, it must be noted that 123 men do not appear in the database at this time. The Ordination Registers for men ordained in the Scottish Episcopal Church are not readily accessible.[29]

The churchmanship of the individual seventeenth-century Virginia clergyman is difficult to classify because of the lack of such biographical details. It is not possible to group them precisely in one group or another of the spectrum of Anglican churchmanship of the day, as either traditional Anglicans, Puritans within the English Church, Presbyterians, or Nonconformists. Another segment, the total number unknown, was not ordained. It is a situation that invites challenging questions, such as: how Anglican was the seventeenth-century Virginia church? Is it possible to measure this?

Between 1600 and 1609 only one minister arrived in the colony, Robert Hunt, a graduate of Magdalene Hall, Oxford, and he was ordained.[30] For the period between 1610 and 1619, nine men arrived in the colony and served as ministers of congregations but we know of only one person who was ordained.[31] During the decade from 1620 to 1629 the colony's churches were served by 15 men, of whom ordination of ten is unknown, three were ordained by English prelates, and it is

Table 5.5 [1]Universities and colleges attended by seventeenth-century Virginia ministers

Scotland	12
Aberdeen	5
Edinburgh	5
Glasgow	1
St Andrews	1
England	72
Cambridge	35
Christ's	2
Clare	2
Corpus Christi	2
Emmanuel	1
Gonville & Caius	3
Jesus	5
King's	1
Magdalene	3
Pembroke	1
St Catharine's	3
St John's	3
Sidney Sussex	3
Trinity	5
Trinity Hall	1
Oxford	36
Brasenose	5
Broadgates Hall	1
Christ Church	3
Corpus Christi	2
Exeter	1
Hart Hall	4
Magdalen	3
Magdalen Hall	4
Merton	3
New	1
New Inn Hall	1
Pembroke	2
Queens	1
St Edmund Hall	3
St Mary's Hall	1
Wadham	1
Other	2
Holland	
Leyden	1
Massachusetts	
Harvard	1
TOTAL	86

[1]See Appendix III for a list of the men and the colleges attended.

Table 5.6   The number of men for whom
evidence of ordination exists, by decade

1590–99	1
1600–09	1
1610–19	5
1620–29	4
1630–39	3
1640–49	2
1650–59	–
1660–69	4
1670–79	3
1680–89	6
1690–99	5
TOTAL	34

likely that one man received the rites at the hands of a bishop of the Scottish Episcopal Church.[32]

The profile of the number of men serving congregations in the colony did not change during the three decades between 1630 and 1660. Among the nine men who arrived in the province between 1630 and 1639 only two men are known to have been ordained, while for the years from 1640 to 1649, 16 men filled parish posts but only two have been identified as ordained Anglican ministers. During the years between 1650 and 1659 only one of the 21 men who arrived in Virginia and served congregations is known to have been ordained.[33]

In the first decade after the 1660 Restoration of the Church of England and of Charles II to the throne, 12 men arrived in Virginia and served as ministers of congregations. Only one man was ordained, Morgan Godwyn, a graduate of Christ Church, Oxford. William Tompson, a 1656 graduate of Harvard College in Cambridge, Massachusetts, was a Congregational minister serving churches at Springfield, Massachusetts, New London, and Mystic, Connecticut, before migrating to Virginia to serve the Southwark and Lawne's Creek parishes.

This pattern continued during the years from 1670 through 1679. In the course of the decade 19 men arrived in Virginia and served established churches. Only three are known to have been ordained: John Banister, a graduate of Magdalen College, Oxford and a distinguished horticulturalist, Rowland Jones, a graduate of Merton College, Oxford, and Nathaniel Pendleton of Corpus Christi College, Cambridge.[34]

During the 1680s more ministers migrated to Virginia than during the previous 20 years. It is possible to detect the new interest by the Council of Trade and Plantations on behalf of the provincial church. Between 1680 and 1689, 33 men arrived in the colony and served parishes. But of the group we know of the ordination of only four men and the conforming to the church by Michael Zyperius, a Dutch Reformed Church clergyman. The process by which he conformed to the Church of England remains unclear because there was no bishop present in the colony to either perform a ceremony or to approve the matter. But it seems likely that more men must have been ordained than the available resources indicate. Bishop of London Henry Compton took a keen interest in the responsibilities delegated to him by the Council of Trade and Plantations and the crown for supervision of American church affairs.[35] It is unlikely that a prelate who takes such interest in licensing the men to serve colonial churches would have approved a man for a post who was not ordained.[36] Compton was suspended from office between 1686 and 1689, and only four men travelled to Virginia during that period.[37]

The final decade of the seventeenth century witnessed 31 men arriving in Virginia to serve congregations. We know for certain that five of them were ordained, and it is likely that the one-third of the group who were natives of Scotland had been ordained in the Scottish Episcopal Church before it was outlawed in 1689. The needs of the colonial church over the decade were met in part by Scots who had been turned out of their churches and found no prospects in their homeland.

It would be informative to present for the reader and researcher a comparative analysis of the data for the social origins of the ministers of the Church of Ireland and Virginia's Anglican Church during the seventeenth century. But such a project is impeded by the lack of a compilation of the careers of the Irish ministers similar to the Clergy of the Church of England Database and the Clergy of the Church of England in Colonial America, 1607–1783 Database.[38] A biographical profile of the Irish clergymen during the sixteenth, seventeenth, and eighteenth centuries would complement these studies and offer answers to questions such as: Where were the men born, in Ireland, England, or elsewhere? Were they educated at one of the colleges at Oxford or Cambridge or at Trinity College Dublin? What was the name of the bishop who ordained them and the date and place of the ceremony? Do we know the parishes the men served and the years of their appointments? Did any of the men publish sermons, religious books, history, poetry, or other works?

A comparison between the Virginia ministers and their colleagues in the seventeenth-century Massachusetts and Connecticut colonies is marked more by contrasting community and religious practices than similarities. Virginia, unlike Massachusetts and Connecticut, was not founded, developed, and governed by a profound theocratic vision held by its leaders and colonists, a vision that was supported and advanced by able civil and ecclesiastical leadership. First generation New England ministers were primarily educated at the key Puritan colleges in Cambridge University, and their ranks were subsequently strengthened and increased by graduates from Harvard College, founded in 1636. The initial corps of ministers shared an adherence to the principles, doctrines, and practices of Puritan theology.

The establishment of Harvard College provided the New England clergymen with an opportunity to gather annually at commencement season to discuss matters of common interest. But in Virginia, the College of William and Mary was not founded until 1693 and it did not become a centre for meetings of the ministers. Furthermore, the establishment of a printing press in Cambridge, Massachusetts, in 1638 provided an opportunity for clergymen to broadcast their theological ideas, sermons, and other religious works to a wider audience than their congregations, while Virginia was without a printing press until about 1730.

During the seventeenth century, the 159 men who served provincial congregations were mostly educated at the two English universities, 36 at Oxford and 35 at Cambridge. But the ministers did not embrace a common theological point of view, and the lack of available biographical details does not inform us of whether they were taught, heard, or knew the significant Anglican and Puritan thinkers and leaders of their days at Oxford or Cambridge. Despite the varying length of service of the men, we are unable to measure the character and careers of their ministry in the manner of historian David D. Hall's analysis and description of the careers and influence of Massachusetts and Connecticut Congregational clergymen in *The Faithful Shepherd*.[39]

6
Salaries and Discipline of Seventeenth-Century Ministers

The salaries and fees due to parsons for regular and special services were set by the legislature. The men were paid in tobacco, the colony's chief crop, but the value of the commodity varied from parish to parish depending on the quality and current market value. However, the review and discipline of clergymen who were alleged to have been errant in their conduct was not fixed by law or precedent. The absence of personnel and procedures for hearing such complaints meant that the administration of timely justice was varied, complicated, and difficult.

For 75 years or more after the founding of Jamestown the ministers who arrived in Virginia to serve congregations were not recruited and sent to the colony under the jurisdiction of any prelate or Anglican society. In every instance the men's presence in the colony represented a distinctively individual and unknown personal preference. Among the 159 ministers of congregations during the colony's first century we know the nationality of 117 of the men. England was the birth place of 97 (61 per cent) of the men, Scotland, 15 (9 per cent), Ireland, three; the origins of the remaining 42 (26.4 per cent of the ministers) is unknown.[1] Given that it is highly probable that the birthplace of many if not most of the 56 unknown men was England, if the percentages for the men whose national origins are known are applied to the unknown group the distribution would be: England, 41, Scotland, 14 and Ireland, one.

Biographical details are sparse for the clergymen, although based on the evidence at hand a summary profile can be constructed regarding their social origins, education, ordination, and experience. But the basic question remains, what kind of men were they? Unlike the portraits of pulpit and civil leaders of the period in Massachusetts, such as John Cotton, and Richard and Increase Mather, no likeness survives to offer a depiction of any of the 159 Virginia parsons of the period. We do

73

not know the physical characteristics, height, weight, or colour of the hair and eyes for any of the men. Furthermore, our knowledge of books owned by them is limited to two estate inventories, one of 1635, and the other of 1695.[2] We are without any particulars of the titles of books owned by the larger group of ministers on such subjects as theology, Biblical criticism, liturgy, or history.

Across the decades of the seventeenth century the gradually increasing number of Anglican clergymen in the colony shared in common an individual sense of purpose rather than a bond of corporate collegiality. There was no organizational apparatus for the church, as there was in England: no prelate, no diocese, no regularly scheduled episcopal visitations of parishes, no conventions of the clergy, and no special ecclesiastical ceremonies that would summon and assemble the men. Nearly 80 years elapsed before the first meetings of the ministers took place in 1685, and this was not under the supervision of an ecclesiastical official but under the civil leadership of Governor Francis Lord Howard of Effingham.[3] In addition, there was no provincial college that could serve as a vibrant intellectual centre in the province and would attract men to the annual commencement proceedings for informal discussions of personal and professional matters. In contrast, the New England Congregational ministers arranged a meeting at Harvard College at the time of graduation rites each year.

Missing, too, are accounts of the men's response to the novelty of the provincial scene, there are no historical records that offer an indication of their reaction to the New World, whether they regretted coming to Virginia, encountered moments of disappointment and discouragement, or longed to return to England. We do know that year after year they lived in relatively remote places, without any network of intellectual activity and discussion, or institutional identity. Probably the minister was the most highly educated person in his neighbourhood, and one of a few who were literate. We might ask with whom they talked or shared a meal? Were there ever exchanges of conversation, with neighbours say, on political affairs in the colony or in England, or discussions on historical, literary, or theological subjects? Were the ministers somehow able to survive and flourish in isolated rural surroundings encouraged and supported only by the import and nature of their calling and duties?

In contrast to Henry VIII's efforts to anglicize the ancient church in Ireland, the situation in Virginia was not in the hands of either state or church officials, but was the obligation of the officers of the Virginia Company of London. The charter granted by the crown to the company delegated the authority and responsibility for providing church services and practices as exercised in England.[4] Administering a transatlantic settlement 3,500 miles distant from the metropolitan capital was a novel national experience, and therefore without a strategy from experience. Officials at Whitehall and in the Anglican Church were without a compass or programme for extending and establishing the church in Virginia.

The first years for the company's settlers were precarious and unstable. Of the 775 persons sent to Virginia between 1607 and 1609, there were fewer than 100 survivors in 1609. This body increased by 150 in that year.[5] During the first decade of the settlement seven ministers are known to have arrived and resided in the colony. Their length of service ranged from one to twenty years. Several of the men died within a year or two of their arrival in the province and a few returned to England.[6] Thirteen more ministers arrived in the colony between 1618 and the dissolution of the company in 1624. Their length of service varied: nearly half of the men served at least one year, two for about two years, and one each resided in the colony three, seven, 12, and 23 years. Two of the men were graduates of Cambridge and one of Oxford, while the colleges attended, if any, by ten of the men are unknown.[7] Their fate is uncertain, they may have been victims of the 1622 Good Friday Massacre at Henrico, or died of other causes.

At least two men appointed by the Virginia Company to serve congregations were not ordained. William Wickham arrived in the colony no later than 1616 and possibly as early as 1611.[8] He served as an assistant to Alexander Whitaker at the church in Henrico until the latter's death by drowning in June 1617 and continued to serve the congregation until his own death in 1622. Governor Sir Samuel Argall (1580?–1626) wrote to Sir Dudley Digges on 19 June 1617 requesting that Archbishop of Canterbury George Abbot grant Wickham permission to perform the sacrament of Holy Communion without ordination because there was no other person available to do it.[9] It is unclear whether the governor meant that there was no ordained clergymen in the colony to perform the rite or that there was no other minister in the parish, or a nearby parish, who could administer the sacrament.[10] On 10 March 1617/18 Governor Argall wrote again to Digges on behalf of Wickham, but to no avail.

Samuel Maycocke was the second unordained man to serve in the colony, presumably with the knowledge of company officials in London. A graduate of Gonville and Caius College, Cambridge University in 1614, he arrived in the colony in 1618 but was not associated with a parish.[11] At this point the record is silent; nothing came of the proposal for either man.

It is also unlikely that George Keith (1585–16xx), who arrived in Virginia from Bermuda in 1617, was ordained. In Bermuda, between 1612 and 1616, he conducted services on St George's Island and was in frequent conflict with another minister, the Reverend Leslie Hughes. Governor Mansfield of the colony wanted Keith to preach to the settlers in the place of Hughes but the people replied that 'he is no minister'. Mansfield answered, 'then we will make him a minister and then he will please you'.[12]

Although the clergymen were associated with a traditionally hierarchical church, their career paths in Virginia were narrow, single track, and virtually frozen. There was no opportunity for the usual advancement in the English church to, for example, serve as a prelate's archdeacon, administering a geographical district of clergy and churches in a diocese, or to be a dean or canon of a cathedral. The men's only option was to move laterally, from one parish to another, perhaps a move that offered the inducement of an increase in the value of their salary by payment in a more valuable grade of locally grown tobacco.

Discipline of Errant Parsons

Historians have briefly cast attention and generalized on the character and conduct of colonial Anglican ministers but usually without a systematic review of the individual circumstances, the discipline, if any, or the resolving of complaints.[13] In the seventeenth and eighteenth centuries, the key complaints filed against Virginia clergymen were usually related to immoral behaviour, drunkenness, and neglect of duties; serious matters, worthy of fair, prompt, and diligent attention. The conduct and discipline of eighteenth-century Virginia Anglican ministers has been examined by Joan R. Gunderson and John K. Nelson, leading to a revised understanding of the number and nature of the complaints against these men in the eighteenth century.[14] A few seventeenth-century ministers are noted on the pages of historical evidence as subjects of disciplinary action, or for contested disputes with their vestries and congregations over the payment of their salaries. But a judgment of the men's situations or the differences of the parties in disagreement is again limited. An analysis of the ministers' professional careers is constrined; we know nothing of the regularity of their services of worship, the style and refinement of their preaching, their readings, and the quality and range of their pastoral care.

Circumstances for appropriate disciplinary action in Virginia were rudimentary compared to those in England. Diocesan visitations reminded parish clergy in the homeland of their ordination vows and their canonical duties. Where there was scandal or neglect, the bishop would admonish, and, if that did not work, he might punish by the suspension and removal of the parson from his post. In Virginia such complaints were not so neatly resolved. In fact, several parties, including civil and ecclesiastical officials, exercised a power to hear and resolve such charges against ministers. There was no uniform process for reviewing such issues during the colonial era, and procedures differed from province to province.[15]

In the English Church, disciplinary authority for ministers ultimately rested in the hands of a bishop. The absence of such an official in Virginia, or America more generally, inevitably compromised efficient and effective oversight of complaints against clergymen. The need for adequate discipline of errant parsons was a common theme of the unsuccessful petitions for a colonial bishop.[16] In large measure, the two issues, the pleas for a prelate and the need to provide a process for clergy discipline, reflected the tension between civil and ecclesiastical officials in London and the provinces regarding the needs of the church. In several colonies the royal governor, sometimes with the assistance of the council, carried the primary responsibility for acting on charges against parsons, while in those provinces where commissaries of the Bishop of London were appointed and resided, those officials took action. By law, the Virginia vestries were entitled to initiate complaints against incumbents, but the basis of such actions seems suspect and may indicate sharply differing divisions within the congregation's membership. In any event, after drafting a complaint the vestry could refer the matter to the governor and colonial council for consideration, followed by suspension of a parson from his duties or some other punishment determined by the offence. Removal of a minister from office was the jurisdiction of the General Assembly, a procedure that departed from the practice in England.[17] Another channel for reviewing complaints was a convention of the clergy; these would usually be called by the commissary or a respected elder colleague in the province. It must be noted that none of these procedures for reviewing and resolving charges against a minister was predominant during the colonial period.

Table 6.1 shows that 42 ministers were charged with complaints of misconduct between 1607 and 1783. But only four of these incidents occurred during the seventeenth century.

Table 6.1   Disciplinary complaints, 1607–1739

1607–19	–
1620–39	2
1640–59	1
1660–79	–
1680–99	1
1700–19	2
1720–39	11
1740–59	15
1760–83	10
TOTAL	42

The earliest record of a complaint against a minister occurred in Virginia about January 1624/25, with a dispute between Greville Pooley and Robert Pawlett. Pooley is not noted in the pages of the published records, so was presumably sponsored by the Virginia Company. He arrived in Virginia in 1622 and served Martin's Brandon until 1629. The origin of the conflict is unclear; it may have simply been a clash between two exceptionally strong-willed individuals, a controversy that escalated when Pawlett sought to have the Sunday church services moved from the house of one member of the congregation to his house. Pooley immediately objected and vitriolic and vociferous exchanges occurred between the men. The dispute was heard by the court and both men were found guilty and required to acknowledge their offences, seek forgiveness before the congregation and pay a fine.[18]

Anthony Panton, minister of the congregation at York, Virginia, was publicly critical toward the policies of Governor Sir John Harvey in 1638, a conflict that prompted the ire and banishment of the parson from his post. A year later Harvey's replacement as governor, Francis Wyatt, revoked the charges against Panton and he returned to the church.

Arriving in Virginia in 1651, Thomas Higby, who may have been ejected from a living in England during the Puritan Revolution, served Hungar's Parish for three years. In his fourth year he was brought before the local court for 'scandalous speeches against Major Robbins', but the nature of the issue was not disclosed.[19]

Jeremiah Taylor succeeded Justinian Aylmer, a descendant of the controversial Elizabethan Bishop of London John Aylmer (1520/21–1594), as minister of the Elizabeth City Parish in 1667. William Meade notes that he served the congregation for a decade but at some point during his tenure he was charged with insolvency and misbehaviour in court. Taylor was committed to confinement at the court's pleasure. Sometime later, he reappeared to answer charges for drunkenness and slander.[20]

The long-time minister of the Petsworth church, Thomas Vicaris, served the congregation between 1666 and 1696 but we know little about him. What biographical detail has survived indicates that he was admonished for some unknown reason by the vestry, yet allowed to continue in his post 'and exercise his ministerial functions until the next shipping' in hopes of his reform. Vicaris agreed to leave the parish if he did not meet the approval of the precinct and vestry. Whatever the charge, or the process of adjudication and reform, he apparently met the test because he served the congregation until his death in 1696.[21]

A charge was levelled against John Waugh in the late 1680s. He arrived in the colony in 1667 and served Potomac Parish from 1667 to 1680 and Overwharton Parish from 1680 until his death in 1706. Waugh was censured for his politically seditious, anti-Catholic, and anti-James II sermons.[22]

Near the close of the seventeenth century, in 1698, Scottish born Samuel Gray was charged with whipping a slave to death. An incorporator of the College of William and Mary and a member of the board of visitors, he was forced to resign as minister of Christ Church Parish after eight years of service. The next year he and his colleague John Gordon of Wilmington Parish were embroiled in another controversy and hailed before the provincial council for having published a scandalous libel against King William III and the late Queen Mary and the government.[23] After being reprimanded by the governor and the Colonial Council, the work was ordered to be confiscated and destroyed.[24] Gray's legal circumstances, however, did not stop his appointment in 1698 as minister of Cople Parish, a post he held for the next decade.

Secondary occupations

In addition to performing their ministerial duties, a few of the clergymen in seventeenth-century Virginia pursued secondary occupations; three as schoolmasters, four as physicians, and one as a lawyer.[25] It is unclear whether the men practised these secondary occupations during a portion or their entire Virginia ministry. We do not know the number of students taught by the schoolmasters or the texts that were used for instruction. It is likely that the physicians and the lawyer practised their profession in a manner common for clergyman with such interests in England at the time. Perhaps several more of the 159 seventeenth-century parsons practised a subordinate occupation, but confirmation of such activity is absent from the historical records. In the eighteenth century a second occupation was more common, with at least 71 clergymen serving as schoolmasters, 26 as tutors to the children of nearby families, ten as physicians, 12 as college professors, and seven as members of the Provincial Council.

7
Divisions in the Virginia Pulpits: Anglicans, Puritans, and Nonconformists

Geographical distance did not isolate the Anglican church in Virginia from the divisions within the Church of England. Ministers and congregations were active and worshipped in the manner of traditional Anglicans, Puritans, or Nonconformists. The religious practices of a church may have reflected the preferences of the current minister or the sentiments of strong-willed members of the congregation. The question of how Anglican the seventeenth-century Virginia church was, evades a definitive answer. Was the practice of the church in the new colony an extension or variant of the Anglicanism represented by Henry VIII and Elizabeth I, or by such leaders as Archbishops of Canterbury Thomas Cranmer, George Abbot, or William Laud, or by such leaders as the codifier of the Ecclesiastical Laws of the English Church, Richard Hooker?

Virginia's history is without a chronicler after the English manner of a George Herbert (1593–1633), who offered in prose a description of a parson's personal and professional life, or a Ralph Josselin (1616–83) or James Woodforde (1740–1803), who routinely chronicled the daily rhythms and routines of a provincial village, church, and community.[1]

After the English Reformation the church was gripped with contentious divisions and controversy, clashes of opinions that were framed and sustained by differing views of theology, liturgical practice, the orders of the ministry, and clerical dress. The most prominent factions were the traditional or governmental State Anglicans, Anglican-Puritans who sought to reform the church from within, Puritan-Separatists, and Nonconformists. The institution did not speak with one voice or with uniform and common practices, and this exposed the church to many conflicting forces that buffeted and shaped its destiny. Understandably, the controversies and practices of the church at home were transferred to settlements overseas.

The fledgling Virginia institution was without the usual episcopal hierarchy and we do not know whether any of the ministers expressed their opinions on the controversies faced by the church in England. Any desire to discuss and print, either in support or in opposition to such sentiments, was restrained by the lack of a printing press in Virginia until about 1730. A helpful, though limited, source is the fragmentary biographical evidence available for 32 ministers who served congregations.

I have identified 159 men who were associated with the colonial Church between 1607 and 1700. Table 7.1 shows the number who arrived in the colony in each decade of the seventeenth century. I recounted in Chapter 5 that the period of service for the men varied greatly.

Details are sparse regarding their affiliation to the factions in the Church in England. The situation is particularly unclear for the men who arrived in the colony between 1607 and 1680, when Bishop of London Henry Compton was granted authority by the crown for jurisdiction and supervision of the overseas institution. He immediately implemented a requirement that any minister travelling to Virginia to accept a church post must be licensed by the London prelate to perform his professional duties. This was not a novel procedure – it was well established within the church in England. Presumably, the 64 ministers who arrived in Virginia between 1680 and 1699 had undergone a systematic evaluation that awarded them the licence and right to exercise their ministerial duties in the province. These 62 men comprised 39 per cent of the 159 ministers who served congregations in the colony during the seventeenth century. For the men who arrived in the colony

Table 7.1 The number of ministers who arrived in Virginia, by decade, 1607–1699

	Number of men	As a percentage
1607–29	25	15.72%
1630–49	18	11.32%
1650–59	21	13.20%
1660–79	31	19.49%
1680–89	33	20.75%
1690–99	31	19.49%
Totals	159	100.00%

before 1680 we have no information regarding their association with any of the religious factions active in the Anglican Church.

During the period that the Virginia Company of London was responsible for the recruitment of ministers (1607–24) it is probable that all 22 of the ordained men were allied with the Anglican-Puritan group within the church, if only because they were possibly recruited by Richard Hakluyt or Archbishop Abbot. The two men who were not ordained probably embraced the same opinions and practices. The 24 early clergymen represented 15 per cent of the total number of men serving congregations during the century.

The structure does not change for the period between 1630 and 1680, nor do we know how regularly or rigorously any of the men adhered to the offices and sacraments of the Book of Common Prayer, or how many of the ministers replaced the use of the Book of Common Prayer at services with the Directory of Worship in the 1640s and 1650s.

The Directory was a manual of directions for worship approved by parliament in 1645 to replace the Book of Common Prayer. It was linked to the submission of the 'Root and Branch' petition of 1640, which demanded 'that the said government [meaning the episcopal system], with all its dependencies, roots and branches be abolished'. Among the 'branches' was the Book of Common Prayer which was said to be a 'Liturgy for the most part framed out of the Romish Breviary, Rituals, [and] Mass Book'.

It was also something of a handbook of pastoral practice, containing a lengthy section on visiting the sick and a detailed section on preaching. Objections to the Directory were advanced by Dr Henry Hammond, later Chaplain to Charles I, in his *A View of the New Directory and a Vindication of the Ancient Liturgy of the Church of England*, published at Oxford in August 1645. He noted six basic characteristics purposely avoided in the Directory: (1) a prescribed form or liturgy; (2) outward or bodily worship; (3) uniformity in worship; (4) the people having a part through responses in prayers, hymns, and readings; (5) the division of prayers into several collects or portions; (6) ceremonies such as kneeling in communion, the cross in baptism, and the ring in marriage.

In this group were 68 ministers, or 43 per cent of the 159 men that served seventeenth-century congregations.

Table 7.2 shows the known affiliations of Virginia ministers during the seventeenth century, ranging across a spectrum from Anglican, Puritan-Anglican, Puritan-Congregational, Presbyterian, Congregational, or of an unknown religious group.[2] As the men were ministers of established

Table 7.2 The decades of service of ministers with identifiable churchmanship

1600–09	1610–19	1620–29	1630–39	1640–49	1650–59	1660–69	1670–79	1680–89	1690–1700
Robert Hunt[3]	Richard Bucke[4]		Nathaniel Eaton[5]		Samuel Cole[6]	Henry Parke[7]			John Alexander[8]
	Alexander Whitaker[9]	Patrick Copeland[10]		Thomas Harrison[11]					John Bolton[12]
				Thomas Bennett[13]	Philip Mallory[14]		Matthew Hill[15]	Josias Mackie[16]	
				William Tompson (I)[17]	Francis Doughty[18]		Daniel Richardson[19]	Andrew Jackson[20]	
					Matthew Hill[21]			Superior Davis[22]	James Bushnell[23]
					Alexander Cooke[24]	Morgan Godwyn[25]		Jonathan Davis[26]	
						William Tompson (II)		John Lawrence[27]	
						Richard Morris[28]		Robert Carr[29]	
								William Paris[30]	
								Charles Davies[31]	

Notes: Biographical details for each man are available at the 'Colonial American Clergy of the Church of England, 1607–1783 Database' at www.jameshell.com.

congregations it would be justifiable to conclude that in every church the offices of the Book of Common Prayer were regularly and uniformly observed.

The church's development during the seventeenth century was in the hands of civil, not ecclesiastical, leaders in London and Jamestown. Perhaps the distinguished geographer Reverend Richard Hakluyt suggested or approved the brief references to religion inserted in the Letters Patent issued to Sir Thomas Gates and others on 16 April 1606 for the settlement of Virginia and the propagation of the Christian religion among the 'infidels and savages'.[32] The Instructions and Orders issued to the Virginia Company officials seven months later, on 20 November 1606, state that:

> wee doe specially ordaine, charge, and require, the said presidents and councils of the said several [Virginia] colonies respectively, within their several limits and precincts, that they, with all diligence, care, and respect, doe provide, that the true word, and service of God and Christian faith be preached, planted, and used not only within every of the said several colonies and plantations, but alsoe as much as they may amongst the savage people which doe or shall adjoine unto them, or border upon them, according to the doctrines, rights, and religion now professed and established within our realme of England.[33]

Civil servants drafted the documents that referred to the extension of the church to Virginia, though it is possible that an ecclesiastical official, such as the Archbishop of Canterbury, was consulted regarding the conditions in the Virginia Charters of 1606 and 1609 that applied to the church. The laws promulgated by Sir Thomas Gates in 1610 and the statutes enacted by the House of Burgesses in 1619 neither amplified nor clarified the matter.

The establishment of the church in 1619 reaffirmed the laws and orders promulgated by the successive governors De La Warr, Argall, and Yeardley. The Virginia statute declared that 'All ministers shall duely read divine service, and exercise their ministerial function according to the Ecclesiastical Laws and orders of the Church of England.'[34] In addition, the clergymen and churchwardens were charged to 'seeke to prevent all ungodly disorders', and report the offenders, if they did not reform, to the governor for discipline and excommunication.[35] The law also noted that an effort should be undertaken in each 'town, borough, and plantation to convert the Indians to the Christian religion'.[36]

the brevity and perfunctory nature of references to the church in the colony suggest that the language may have been inserted into the law by a clerk. No mention was made of the Canons, constitution, the Book of Common Prayer, or the King as the Supreme Head of the Church. The question arises, what prompted the legislative action: was it a response to pleas by the governor, members of the assembly, officials of the Virginia Company of London, or even the Archbishop of Canterbury, George Abbot? He was knowledgeable in such overseas ventures through his protégé and younger brother Sir Maurice (1565–1642), a prominent merchant in London, founder and officer of the East India Company, and a Member of Parliament.[37] It is possible, though, that the archbishop may not have been in a position to play a strong role in the matter, as in 1619 his voice carried little influence.[38]

All references to the church in the Letters Patent, Charters, Instructions and Ordinances, and statutes between 1606 and 1642/43 were in general terms, 'to propagate the Christian religion... according to the doctrine, rights, and religion now professed within our realm of England'. Meeting on 5 March 1623/24, the General Assembly stated that every plantation should have a house of worship and 'that there be an uniformity in our church as neer as may be to the canons in England, both in substance and circumstance, and that all persons yield readie obedience unto them under paine of censure'.[39] In 1629/30 the legislature prescribed that all ministers were 'to conform to constitutions and canons of the Church of England' and stated that if 'there bee any that, after notice given, shall refuse for to conforme himselfe, he shall undergoe such censure, as by the said cannons, in such cases is provided for such delinquent. And that all acts formerly made concerning ministers shall stand in force, and bee duly observed and kept'.[40] In February 1631/32 the assembly reaffirmed that services of worship in the province were to 'conform to the constitution and canons' of the Church of England.[41]

It is puzzling why the details and specifications in the various legal documents relating to the church in Virginia were sparse, while in contrast arrangements and regulations for the organization and governance of the colony and the establishment of the courts were very thoroughly specified. It was not until soon after the arrival of the staunch Anglican, Governor Sir William Berkeley, that the assembly in 1642/43 mentioned the usage of the Book of Common Prayer in legislation. The delay in publicly acknowledging the use of the Prayer Book in services of worship may have been intended to tolerate alternative procedures to be practised in the colony.[42]

A critical review of the church occurred at the session of the General Assembly on 3 November 1647, when it was reported that several unidentified ministers neglected to read the Book of Common Prayer at Sunday services, contrary to the requirement of the Canons and Constitution of the Anglican Church. At the time there were only four ministers serving congregations in the colony, a low point during the decade.[43] Occupying posts at the time were Thomas Hampton (1640–81), Thomas Harrison (1640–48), Robert Powis (1640–52), and John Rosier (1640–60). The latter three served congregations of historically dissenting members, while Hampton, a son of a Church of England minister and a graduate of Corpus Christi College, Oxford, did not serve a parish between 1658 and 1680.[44] Immigration substantially increased the population of Virginia during the 1640s, from an estimated 10,442 persons in 1640 to about 18,731 inhabitants in 1650, an 80 per cent increase.[45] But the number of active clergymen in Virginia in 1640 stood at eight, and ten years later at six. That is, in 1640 there was one parson to serve 1,305 residents and in 1650 there was one for every 3,121.

Table 7.2 shows known affiliations among seventeenth-century Virginia ministers with the differing religious factions within the Church of England. The 32 men identified represent 20 per cent of the 159 ministers serving congregations between 1607 and 1700.[46] They served established Anglican congregations, but we are still entitled to speculate on questions that will not go away: How regular were the legally prescribed weekly or daily services of Morning or Evening Prayer, and the Sacrament of Holy Communion observed? How often and how many baptisms, marriages, and burials of parishioners were performed each year? What was the formula for pastoral care to the sick and bereaved? While we may be inclined to embrace the notion that the men appointed to serve a congregation rigorously adhered to performing the offices and sacraments of the Book of Common Prayer, the record is silent.

The influence of the Puritan party within the Church of England in the early seventeenth century was evident among a group of Virginia Company officials and the earlier stream of ministers arriving in the colony, including Robert Hunt (1568–1608), Alexander Whitaker (1585–1617), Richard Bucke (1584–1623), and several of their successors. Included also were John Lyford, Nathaniel Eaton, Thomas Bennett, Thomas Harrison, Francis Doughty, Mr. Moore, William Tompson, and John Lawrence. These men were all known for their Puritan or Nonconformist leanings, but how they came to serve Virginia congregations is unclear. Each of them had served at a church that had appointed a succession of Puritan ministers, but each of them stands out for a different reason: for conflicts over the payment of their salaries, for not using the Book of Common Prayer at worship, or liturgical practices that classified them as Nonconformists.[47]

In addition, several men who had been ordained in England migrated to New England in the 1620s and 1630s. Perhaps they had demonstrated Puritan leanings in the homeland but after residing in the new community embraced the Congregational Church. Among the clergymen, John Lyford (1576–1634) was the first to appear in Virginia. A native of Armagh, Ireland, he arrived on the *Anne* at Plymouth, Massachusetts in 1623. He immediately demonstrated a curious temperament and was welcomed to the colony as a preacher. He soon clashed with Governor William Bradford and other leaders over civil and church affairs.[48] Charged with mutinous conduct, an assembly of settlers reviewed the complaint and found him guilty and sentenced him to expulsion from the community. Lyford moved to Nantasket for about a year, before residing in Salem between 1625 and 1629.[49] Did he leave his post in Massachusetts in 1629 and move to Virginia because he learned that a congregation was seeking a Nonconformist minister? Or was he urged to move to the colony by a civil official? Despite the circumstances, Lyford served Martin's Hundred Parish without further incident from 1629 until his death five years later.

A decade later, in June 1637, Nathaniel Eaton travelled to New England with his wife Elizabeth (her maiden name unknown) and his brother Theophilus, who presumably shared his brother's enthusiasm for establishing a colony at New Haven. Nathaniel attended Westminster School in London and entered Trinity College, Cambridge, in 1629 but left the university three years later without taking a degree.[50] Nathaniel's religious experiences in England and Holland during the early 1630s suggest that he was wrestling with the ecclesiastical issues of the day. His father Richard was an Anglican minister at Great Budworth in Cheshire, but between 1632 and 1635 Nathaniel undertook religious studies at Franeker in Holland with the exiled Cambridge University Puritan scholar William Ames. Returning to Cheshire in 1635, he was presumably ordained and installed as curate at Sidington by Bishop of Chester John Bridgeman.[51] This prelate, influenced by his wife's leanings, tolerated Puritan ministers in his diocese.

Upon arrival in New England in 1638, Nathaniel became the first master of the school in Cambridge that became Harvard College.[52] His brief association with the school was marked with conflict and controversy and, disgraced, he was forced to leave the post under a dark cloud of suspicious conduct.[53] By 1639 he had settled on Virginia's Eastern Shore at Nansemond, and served as an assistant minister in Hungar's Parish in Northampton County until 1645.[54] After the loss of his first wife in about 1640, he married Anne Graves, a planter's daughter, but by 1646 he had deserted her and returned to England.[55]

Perhaps at the direction of the recently arrived Governor Berkeley, the General Assembly, at its session of 2 March 1642/43, addressed the issue and problem of Nonconformist ministers serving congregations in the colony. The legislature responded by enacting a statute that required all ministers to conform to the Church of England or to be compelled to leave the province.[56] Four years later the assembly revisited the matter, on 3 November 1647, and passed a law declaring that ministers refusing to read Common Prayer were not entitled to receive tithes or duties from their parishioners.[57] Soon afterwards, Thomas Bennett, a graduate of Trinity College, Cambridge and ordained by the Puritan Bishop of Peterborough Thomas Dove in 1628, settled at West Parish in Nansemond County in 1648, serving an independent congregation. On receiving the news of Bennett's appointment, Berkeley, an Oxford graduate and well connected to the royal court of Charles I, exercised the terms of his commission and royal instructions of office to foster and support worship according to the forms of the Anglican Church and immediately banished him from the colony. Bennett' was not heard from again.[58]

Another early Virginia parson, Thomas Harrison, was born in 1616 in Hull, Yorkshire, and was a graduate of the Puritan-leaning Sidney Sussex College in Cambridge. He arrived in Virginia in the late 1630s and travelled briefly to Boston, where he married a niece of Governor John Winthrop. After returning to Virginia he became the minister of the Elizabeth River Parish between 1640 and 1648.[59] But in 1648 he became a Nonconformist and was banished from the colony by Berkeley for not using the Book of Common Prayer. Harrison returned to Boston until 1650, and later returned to London, where he became the minister of St Dunstan-in-the-East in London (1651–53). Later he served as chaplain to Henry Cromwell in Dublin, Ireland (1654–58), and minister of St Oswald's Church in Chester (1658–62), until ejected from his post. A decade later he was licensed to preach in Chester in 1672, presumably conforming to the Church of England.

The dismissals of Bennett and Harrison from their posts in 1648 by Governor Berkeley remain puzzling: were the men discharged for replacing the Book of Common Prayer with The Directory for Public Worship of God authorized by parliament in August 1645?[60] Both men served churches with a long association with Puritan ministers and it may be that members of the congregation, on receiving news of political affairs in England, encouraged or required the ministers to substitute the Directory for Worship for the Book of Common Prayer. If so, how did the men receive their copies of the Directory for use in Virginia? By personal purchase or from interested Nonconformist leaders in London? Were copies of the book also available for use by members of the congregation?

If the Directory of Public Worship was used in certain colonial churches was it introduced at the sole discretion of the minister or with the support of the congregation? The number of congregations, if any, in the province that embraced the Directory is unclear, as is how often and how long it was used for. It is probable that the two Presbyterian ministers who occupied Anglican pulpits in the late seventeenth and early eighteenth centuries, Josiah Mackie (16xx–1716) and Andrew Jackson (1656–1710) used the Directory with the approval of the members of their congregations. It seems possible that if this were the case the Directory's usage ceased with Jackson's death in 1710, in step with stronger governance of the Virginia church under the aegis of successive royal governors and the Bishop of London's Commissary James Blair.[61]

Another Puritan parson, Francis Doughty, was born in 1616 in Bristol, England. He was the son of a merchant and alderman and was ordained by Bishop of Bath and Wells William Piers. Doughty was installed as a curate of the English parish of Chewton in 1635, and then at Boxwell, Leighterton, and Rangeworthy in Gloucestershire, before migrating to New England in 1639.[62] Arriving in Massachusetts, he served churches at Taunton (1638–39) and Cohasset (1639–42), but was expelled from Taunton for his Presbyterian views and Cohasset for preaching that Abraham's children should have been baptized.[63] He moved to Long Island and founded the town of Mespath in 1642 and from then, until at least 1647, he served the church in Flushing, New York, before migrating to Maryland.[64] By the mid-1650s he was in Virginia and served in turn at Elizabeth City (165x–56), Hungar's Parish (1655–59), and at Charles County in Maryland (1659–62). While serving the congregation in Maryland, and later in Northampton County (1662–65) and Sittingbourne Parish (1665–69) in Virginia, he was known for his troublesome but unsuccessful witch-hunting proclivities.[65] Doughty married twice, first to Bridget Stone at Oldbury in Gloucestershire, who died in Newtown (Flushing), New York about 1654, second, in 1657, to Ann Graves Cotton Eaton, the widow of two former Anglican clergymen in the colony, William Cotton and Nathaniel Eaton.

In a petition to Governor Berkeley in 1668, two men, John Catlett and Humphrey Booth, charged Doughty with 'nonconformity and scandalous living'. The substance of the complaint is not known but it may have been over his use of the Directory or the Book of Common Prayer at worship services.[66] Perhaps recognizing the seriousness of the complaint, Doughty petitioned the governor on 13 March 1669/70 that he wished to 'Transport myself out of the Colony of Virginia, into some other country and climate that may prove more favourable to my aged, infirm and decayed body'. He addressed certain legal matters and conveyed to Richard Boughton of Charles County, Maryland, 200 acres on the Rappahannock River for the use of his wife Anne, she being 'unwilling to depart the said countrey, she finding the same best agreeing with her health, besides her loathness and unwillingness to bid farewell to her deare and beloved children, and to her beloved kindred and relacons, all or most of them residing in the said colony of Virginia'. All trace of Doughty vanishes and all we know is that he died some time after 1669.

When the congregation in lower Norfolk County was searching for a clergyman in 1656, officials wrote to a 'Mr. Moore a minister in New England' inviting him to come to Virginia and serve their church'.[67] At this time there was no Anglican minister residing and officiating in New England and the only clergyman known as 'Mr Moore' living in the region was John Moore, a Congregational minister who had arrived in Southampton in Long Island, New York, in 1641.[68] At the time he was serving a congregation at Newtown (now Flushing), settled by persons from Ipswich, Massachusetts, which he served between 1651 and his death on 13 October 1657.

Because Long Island was claimed by Connecticut there was a steady stream of settlers from that colony as well as from Massachusetts' communities. Some of these residents established Congregational churches. It is likely that Moore's Virginia correspondent assumed that the Eastern section of Long Island was within the geographical region known as New England. The letter from the Virginia correspondent is significant for two reasons: first, it indicates that no civil or ecclesiastical official in London during the final years of Cromwell's government was charged with supervising the Virginia church. Second, it demonstrates that a group of laymen in the parish were assuming responsibility for initiating the search and arranging for the employment of a clergyman.

The number of former New Englanders in Virginia increased when a 1653 graduate of Harvard College, William Tompson, arrived in the colony in 1663 in search of relief from his ill-health.[69] He had previously served as a Congregational minister in Springfield, Massachusetts (1655–57) and as a missionary to the Indian tribes at Mystic and New London, Connecticut (1657–61). A year later he accepted the appointment to serve jointly the congregations at Southwark and Lawne's Creek, both churches had histories of employing Puritan ministers. But his service was brief because he died a year after his appointment.

Another probable Anglican-Puritan, John Lawrence, was a graduate, in 1654, of Emmanuel College, Cambridge, an institution that maintained strong Puritan intellectual sentiments and followed the Puritan liturgical practices during chapel services. The Book of Common Prayer was not used and no ecclesiastical vestments were worn.[70] Lawrence served as minister in Virginia at both Mulberry Island and Denbigh Parish between 1680 and 1684. In September or October, 1684 he died at Point Comfort, Virginia, and in his will he noted that he had lived in Maryland for three years before moving to Virginia but he found the presence of the Roman Catholics difficult.

In the spring of 1680, before Henry Compton, Bishop of London, was awarded ecclesiastical jurisdiction over the church in America by the Council of Trade and Plantations, an incident occurred regarding the professional qualifications of a practicing clergyman. It involved two men, John or Jonathan Wright and Jonathan Davis, both recently arrived in the colony, though probably Wright was the first to arrive. Both men resided in New Pocouson Parish and each began to exercise a ministry. Wright quickly lodged a complaint with Virginia's Council that Davis was not in fact a clergyman. We have no biographical details about Davis and for Wright we only know that he was a native of Suffolk in England, attended Puritan-leaning St Catharine's College in Cambridge, and that he received letters dismissory for priest orders from Archbishop of Canterbury Gilbert Sheldon on 23 January 1673/74.[71] Both men were ordered to appear before the Virginia Council on 28 June 1680 but what disposition was made of the case is unknown because there are no minutes of the council for that date.[72] Nothing further is known about either man.

However, it is known that two Presbyterian ministers occupied established church posts from at least the mid-1680s. The Elizabeth River church was served from 1684 to 1691 by Josias Mackie, a graduate of Edinburgh College in 1681, and Andrew Jackson, also a former student at Edinburgh in 1672, served the congregations at St Mary's Whitechapel (1683–1710) and Christ Church (1701–10), both in Lancaster County. Mackie left the Elizabeth River church under unknown circumstances.

It is unclear whether he had been ordained in the English church. He may have been removed from his post during the term of Governor Francis Nicholson, a professional imperial administrator and ardent advocate of the Anglican Church, during his two terms in office (1690–92, 1698–1705).[73] He explicitly followed the orders of the Council of Trade and Plantations that required all ministers holding livings in the province to be episcopally ordained, as in England. Mackie immediately became a minister of the Presbyterian Church and served congregations at Lynnhaven (1692–96?) on the Elizabeth River and at Great Neck in Princess Anne County (1696–1716).[74]

Events took a different turn for Jackson when the vestry of his church vigorously opposed the execution of the governor's order to remove him from his post and declared that because he had served the parish for twenty-five years, raised a large family, and developed a good glebe, the people were unwilling to dismiss him.[75] At his death in 1710 Jackson bequeathed his collection of books for the use of future incumbents of his church.

On the occasion of Bishop Compton's suspension from office in 1686 he directed Governor Francis Howard to correspond with Bishop of Durham Nathaniel Crewe on ecclesiastical matters in Virginia.[76] In a letter to Crewe sometime after 19 November 1686, Howard thanked the prelate for sending Thomas Finney to Virginia to serve a parish post.[77] But he requested that no minister come to Virginia without the bishop's knowledge:

> then I could be confident we should have none but men of ability and good manners, for I am jealous of those that come not so qualified, it hath all ill face that they refuse the advantage of your Lordships owning of them; and the regular way of making application as they ought but the many vacancy that are here force me to alow of them contrary to my judgment of respect to your Lordship.[78]

Governor Howard also informed the Durham prelate that in the spring of 1686, in accordance with his royal instructions, he had convened the clergy in the colony and 'inspected into their orders and qualifications'.[79] He continued:

> Som of them have no orders, and as little order in their lives whome I have prohibited from officiating in the holy function, others are of good lives, but not duely qualified, some only by their own direction of themselves to the ministry, those I have permitted still to officiate

till I have your Lordships direction, as to preaching and baptisme, but not to read the absolution nor administer the blessed Sacrament of the Lord's Supper, others have qualifications as to Deacons orders from Sir William Berkeley how that will qualify I beg Your Lordships directions.

Another group of ministers who served parishes in seventeenth-century Virginia may have been Presbyterians, because no records of their ordination have yet been found. Included in this group are John Bolton at Cople Parish (1693–98), James Bushnell at Martin's Hundred Parish (1696–1702), Robert Carr at Stratton-Major Parish (1680–86), Samuel Cole at Christ Church Parish and Planketant (1657–59), and Charles Davies, the minister at Wiconico and Old Farnham (1680–83). It remains difficult to determine the religious group with which these men were associated.

In addition, several other men arrived in the province who may not have been ordained. Their names do not appear in the records of the 'Clergy of the Church of England Database, 1540–1835', though I should note that names are regularly added to the project.[80] A Mr Richardson served Hungar's Parish in lower Northampton County for some-time before 1676, but we know nothing more about the man. Presumably he was a Puritan, as the congregation had a long history of service by Puritan ministers, including Francis Bolton (1621–30), Nathaniel Eaton (1639–46), and Francis Doughty (1655–59). Richardson may have been appointed to the post because of the difficulty encountered by the vestry in recruiting a clergyman. For some reason Governor Berkeley found him objectionable and dismissed Richardson from the post. He was replaced by Isaac Key; a graduate of St Catharine's College in Cambridge in 1662 who had served as vicar of Margaretting in Essex, England, from 1664 to 1672 and rector of Stanway Magna between 1671 and 1677, before travelling to Virginia. Governor Berkeley said that Key was well known to him and he served the congregation for two years.[81]

Occasionally civil means were applied for the appointment of a minister to serve a congregation. The residents of Middlesex County living on both sides of the James River were without a minister or vestry as early as the 1650s. To remedy the situation the local court reviewed the situation and appointed Samuel Cole (16xx–59) to serve as minister of a congregation located at Planketant. Cole's tenure in the post was brief, about two years, because he died sometime before 28 September 1659.[82] The court intervened again in church affairs in 1661 and appointed the churchwardens and a vestry for the congregation thereafter known as White Chapel Church.[83]

The profiles of occupants of Virginia pulpits between 1607 and about 1680 reflect in part the circumstances of the church in England. Many of the men had been educated at Cambridge or Oxford colleges and after ordination held minor posts in England.[84] Yet, at this time we have little evidence of the ordinations, dates, places, or officiating prelate of a majority of the men.[85] Governor Berkeley noted in 1671 that several ministers arrived in the colony after ejection from their English positions in the 1640s and 1650s.[86] But we know little about the men except their names, places, and possible years of service.

8
The Libraries of Two Seventeenth-Century Ministers

Ministers serving rural Virginia congregations were required to provide their own books for professional support and assistance. Access to printed volumes was essential for the continuing study of the biblical languages, literature, theology, history, and pastoral care. Each parson was responsible for acquiring his own books either before travelling to Virginia or while in residence. Two significant seventeenth-century library inventories survive that illuminate and provide a glimpse of the books owned by an Anglican and a Nonconformist minister serving in the province.

For early modern Church of England ministers living in the age of the recently invented printing press, books were a luxury but also were essential resources and companions for their professional development and performance. Among the 159 men who served established Virginia congregations during the seventeenth century 89 had attended a college or university. The ministers, as members of a learned profession, were in need of such printed references as works on theology, biblical criticism, liturgics, Greek and Hebrew languages, history, classical literature, and their distinctive personal interests of medicine, law, poetry, or literature. Among the Virginia clergymen the collections ranged in size from 'a few books', to a 'parcel of books'.

During the colonial era from 1607 to 1783 I have found evidence of book collections for 126 of the 1,289 men associated with the Church of England in America; 63 of the libraries were owned by Virginia parsons.[1] But among the 159 clergymen of 1607–1699 we know something of the collections of nine of them: John Banister (1650–92); Thomas Bargrave (1581–1621), who left his library to the proposed college at Henrico; Robert Bracewell (1611–68), whose books were valued at 500 pounds of tobacco; John Bromfield who left a 'parcel of books' valued at 800 pounds of tobacco when he died in 1681; Richard Bucke's (1584–1623) 18 books were valued at 3 shillings per pound of tobacco; Almeric Butler (1648–78) left his books to his brother and provincial minister William; Benjamin Doggett's (1636–82) extensive library was to be 'collected and packed in a great chest' and sent to England for sale; and Robert Dunster (16xx–56) left an unknown number of books.

It is the exceptional inventories of the books of John Goodbourne (1605–35) and Thomas Teackle (*c*.1624–95) that deserve attention. Both libraries represent significant collections in seventeenth-century Virginia and America. Yet the two men could not have been more different in backgrounds, education, intellectual interests, periods of service, and probably churchmanship. An analysis of the two collections offers a profile of the range of each man's intellectual and professional interests, and suggest possible sentiments of churchmanship, whether the parson could be classified in one of the factions of the English Church and nation of the day, such as Anglican, Anglican-Puritan, Puritan, Presbyterian, Nonconformist, or some other designation. An analysis of the two libraries indicates that the books acquired in England represented the uniquely personal scholarly interests of the men.

The two men

Both men were English natives, Goodbourne, of Dacre, in Cumberland was christened in 1605, but his personal background is a blank because we have no details about his parentage, nor do we know whether he was married, or had any children. We do know that he matriculated at Jesus College in Cambridge University in 1622 and received a B.A. degree in 1625/6. The historical record is silent about his career after graduation from the university and before sailing to Virginia in 1635. It is not known if he was ordained, or the name of the prelate and the place and date on which the ceremony took place.[2] Nor do we know if he served as a curate or minister at a country or urban parish in England before departing for America.

Circumstances surrounding Goodbourne's decision to travel to Virginia are also unclear. Perhaps he or his father was acquainted with or related to one of the merchant adventurers in London who had financial or commercial interests in the colony. Possibly Goodbourne had a conversation with Archbishop of Canterbury William Laud who, as the chief primate of the Church, was aware of the need for clergy in the colony and urged him to consider the prospect. Another connection may have been forged during his undergraduate years at Jesus College in Cambridge and discussions with his contemporary there, the Puritan-leaning John Eliot. Destined for a ministerial career as a student, Eliot followed in the train of the band of initial settlers migrating to New England, sailing on the *Lyon* in 1631 for the Massachusetts Bay Colony. Eliot, later known as the celebrated 'Apostle to the Indians' at Natick and translator of the Bible into the Algonquin language, possibly described in a letter to Goodbourne the engaging religious prospects of bringing the gospel to the Native Americans in the New World. If so the exchange of letters may have set Goodbourne on course to travel to Virginia where the Anglican Church was established in 1619. Regardless of the circumstances he sailed from England on the *Globe* in 1635 destined for the plantation 'Merchants Hope'.[3]

Teackle's, origins are obscure too, and only sketchily recounted in a family genealogical account that indicates he was born in Gloucestershire sometime in 1624.[4] Regretably, the chronicle is silent regarding the names of his parents or the place of his birth. The family surname was relatively common in the county in the late sixteenth and seventeenth century: there were Teackles residing in the villages of Bisley and Horsley.

We do not have details regarding Teackle's decision to travel to Virginia in the mid-1650s. He was about thirty years old when he arrived in the colony and may have been prompted to take the journey by the prospect of acquiring land. If he was born in Gloucestershire about 1624 or 1625 Teackle grew up in a nation and county that had experienced political and religious turmoil during the reigns of James I and Charles I. Christopher Hill reports that as early as '1622 Gloucestershire unemployed went in groups to houses of the rich demanding money and seizing provisions', a period, too, of riots of the weavers in the county.[5] There is no trace of evidence that Teackle matriculated and attended one of the colleges at either Oxford or Cambridge universities. His name does not appear in the usual published records of both institutions that note students admitted to a college, but that does not convincingly indicate that he did not attend either university, as the published accounts and archives of the colleges of the period are incomplete.

Soon after his arrival in America Teackle married Isabelle Douglas in 1658, the widow of Lieutenant Colonel Edward Douglas of Northampton County, on Virginia's Eastern Shore. She brought to the union 3,700 acres of land, wealth that may have supported and advanced his many later property investments and transactions.[6] The couple had four children, one son and three daughters. Isabelle died about 1674 and Teackle remained a widower for nearly twenty years until his second marriage in 1693 to Margaret Nelson of Accomack

County. She was the daughter of Robert and Mary (Temple) Nelson of Virginia, natives of Stantonbury, Buckinghamshire, in England. She gave birth to nine children but only four survived to maturity.[7]

Teackle began serving churches in Accomack and Northampton counties, Puritan and Nonconformist regions on the Eastern Shore of Virginia from about 1656 until his death in 1695. Despite his long service in the pulpit he remains an unfamiliar, shadowy, and enigmatic figure, He did not leave behind a cache of papers, diaries, journals, or correspondence that chronicled his family background, education, or professional experience. Today he is remembered not for his nearly four-decade-long career and influence as a clergyman, or as a participant in local civil affairs, but for the content, and number of titles in his substantial library.[8]

Limited details of Teackle's origins, family, and education are matched by the scanty information that has survived about his career as a minister. The Eastern Shore historically was inhabited by Quakers and Presbyterians rather by people embracing the tenets of the Church of England. Governor William Berkeley, a royalist and fervent supporter of the Church of England, expelled members of both religious groups from Virginia into Maryland in 1649.[9] Perhaps his strong-arm tactics represented an effort to publicly demonstrate his fulfilment of the religious duties described in his commission and instructions of office received from the crown. But the situation raises the question, how did Teackle come to be appointed the minister of a congregation in the region? From the years of Alexander Whitaker's service earlier in the century to Teackle's tenure it was not uncommon for nonconformist, Puritan, Independent, or Presbyterian ministers to occupy a pulpit of the established church and preside over a congregation, frequently for many years.[10] The congregation's records do not provide details of the procedures and terms for Teackle's selection and maintenance as minister of the parish.

The mystery of Teackle's religious affiliation is further deepened by a lack of traceable associations with Anglican clergymen in the province. We do not know if he attended the meeting of the colony's ministers summoned by Governor Francis Howard in the spring of 1686 and at which time he examined the credentials of the province's parsons.[11] Moreover, his name is not included in the collection of correspondence between Virginia clergymen and the successive bishops of London contained in the Fulham Palace Papers at the Lambeth Palace Library in London, nor is he mentioned in the minutes as attending the meetings of the Virginia ministers in July 1690 called by Commissary James Blair. Nor is Teackle mentioned in the correspondence of clergymen supporting the founding of what is today the College of William and Mary.

It seems likely that he kept his distance from the Anglican parsons because he was not a Church of England minister. If he were invited to the clergy meetings of the 1686 and 1690 it may have been on the basis that he was the minister of an established church congregation and not on whether he was an ordained Anglican clergyman. Teackle does not seem to have had any connection with such prominent clerical and intellectual leaders in the colony as Blair, John Clayton, or John Banister, or planters.[12]

We cannot escape raising the question of whether Teackle an ordained minister of the Church of England or associated with some other religious group. Was his ministry a reflection of the diverse religious character of the region? If he were an ordained Anglican minister do any records survive to confirm the date, place, and name of the official that performed the ceremony? Current historical resources available to identify men ordained during the period do not include any reference to him.[13] A single entry notes that a Thomas Tickle was ordained deacon and priest in 1633 but neither the name of the prelate who performed the ceremony or the place where it took place is noted. Further analysis of the slim biographical information available suggests that if the later Virginia resident was the man ordained in 1633, he would have had to have been born about 1610 and at least 23 years old, the minimum age required by canon law for admission to the priesthood. Therefore, if he arrived in Virginia about 1655, he would have been about 45 years old and at his death in 1695, nearly 85.

Regretably, the thirty-year-old Goodbourne did not live to see the Virginia shoreline or take up the post at 'Merchant Hope' plantation, he died at sea in 1635. Our personal knowledge of him is limited to his attendance and graduation from Jesus College in Cambridge and the surviving inventory of his books and possessions. The document was written in his own hand perhaps immediately before departing from England or during his voyage to Virginia. The inventory itemizes and values the titles of his books and identifies apparel and other objects that he was transporting to the colony. After Goodbourne's death the captain of the ship *Glove* placed the contents in a storehouse after arriving in the province and perhaps the books were later returned to England for probate with the inventory.[14]

The two libraries

The number and content of the two libraries is culled from the 1635 inventory of Goodbourne's books, and the 1697 inventory of Teackle's library.[15] The two collections have in common certain titles and categories of interest to a minister, such as theology, Biblical criticism, history, the classics of Greece and Rome, pastoral theology, and so forth. But we do not have any clues regarding the methods by which the men acquired their valuable collections of books. What was the source of funds for purchasing the collections, or were the books acquired by inheritance or gift?

Virginia clergymen arriving in Virginia in the seventeenth and eighteenth centuries had to bring their own books with them to the province. No church official or agency in London provided a collection of theological, liturgical, historical, biblical critical or other works for their use in parish duties. It was not until Thomas Bray's efforts to establish parish libraries in Maryland in the 1690s and provincial libraries in the Anglican churches of the key capital towns that a carefully selected core of books was available for the use of a clergyman.[16] His notable programme was later absorbed and continued by the Society for the Propagation of the Gospel (SPG) for the remainder of the colonial era for the congregations to which its missionaries were assigned, but because the SPG did not send its recruits to Virginia the churches there were not beneficiaries of the program.

Goodbourne, about twenty years older than Teackle and a graduate of Cambridge University, may have gathered his library while an undergraduate. The list of his books indicates that he had a tutored and scholarly turn of mind. He noted carefully in his document the acquisition costs of the printed materials and other items, including the value of his clothes. Many of the titles in Goodbourne's book collection ranged in value between one and five shillings but the value of two works are exceptional: Barnadi, *opera* at £11.0.0 sterling, and Dr. John Preston's (1587–1628) *Sermons* in 6 volumes, valued at £11.4.0. Preston's books stand out in Goodbourne's collection because he was an influential preacher and counsellor to such Puritans as John Cotton and Thomas Shepard, who settled in New England, and Richard Hooker, the author of the *Ecclesiastical Laws* of the Church of England. Goodbourne lists his cloth gown and two cassocks as new, with a value of £51.14.0, and two old cloth suits and a new cloth jacket at £21.0.0. The book collection of 162 titles was valued at the time at £321.16.6 sterling, representing in 2011 values about £717,000.00 or $1,124,000.00. His clothes and other personal items were valued at £271.13.8 (£605,000 or $960,000). On the basis of the value of his books and other belongings it is possible that Goodbourne was one of the wealthiest English clergyman to migrate to Virginia or any other American colony in the seventeenth century. What was the source of his wealth? It is likely that he drew on the family account for his acquisitions of books and clothes although we have no information about his father's finances, or commercial, political, or ecclesiastical connections. Perhaps his mother brought substantial financial resources from her family to the marriage that would have provided him with the necessary funds. Perhaps the wealthy London merchant and promoter of the plantation 'Merchant's Hope', William Barker, granted Goodbourne the money to acquire his possessions before travelling to Virginia to become the settlement's minister.

Historian Jon Butler estimates the value of Teackle's estate at probate in 1697 at about £550 but it is unclear if the sum represents the value in Virginia or English currency. He further suggests that perhaps the value of the collection of 333 books was about £50 or roughly an average of 3 shillings per title, a considerably more modest amount than the value of Goodbourne's books sixty years earlier. As a comparison, the £50 value of the books in 1697 would be worth about £98,000, or about $150,000, in 2011. The total estate value of about £550 corresponds to £1.1 million, or about $1.6 million, in 2011.[17]

The book collections of Goodbourne and Teackle are unique and represent the intellectual interests of each man. In number, Goodbourne's library was about half the size of Teackle's, with 166 against 333 titles respectively, and it is comprised only of books published before 1635. The two collections deserve an analysis at two levels. The libraries were acquired over different periods of the seventeenth century by men of varying ages, educational backgrounds, and career experience.

In the first instance an examination discloses that the libraries held in common the works of several prominent and influential scholars of the sixteenth and seventeenth centuries including copies of John Calvin's *Institutes of the Christian Religion* and critical study of the *Psalms*, and *Greek Grammar*, and Desiderius Erasmus, *Tomus primus, Paraphraseon Des. Erasmi Roterodami, in Novum Testamentum* (Basel, 1535), and William Perkin's protégé William Ames's publication, *Medualla S. S. theologiae: ex Sacris Literis, earumque, interpretibus, extracta & methodice disposita* (London, 1629).

Goodbourne's library seems to represent the interest of scholars at Cambridge at the time and held Calvin's critical study of the *First and Second Corinthians,* and *Catechism.* Teackle's collection included copies of Calvin's published sermons. Among Goodbourne's other books were Thomas Aquinas' *Summa Theologicae,* Peter Martyr's critical commentaries on *First and Second Kings, First and Second Samuel, Judges, First and Second Corinthians, Romans*, and his treatise on the *Eucharist*.

But the two libraries differed substantially in other ways. Goodbourne's collection included writings of St Augustine, his meditations on the fall of the Roman Empire, *The City of God*, and *Enchiridion*; Thomas á Kempis's *Opusculum*, Erasmus's *Militis Christiani Enchiridion, Adagia*, and Peter Lombard's *Sentences*. Also among the volumes were the works of the classical Roman and Greek historians and philosophers including Caesar, Seneca, Juvenal, Plutarch, Horace, and Eusebius, Homer, Thucydides, and Aristotle, as well as Bishop John Jewel's sixteenth-century *Apologia Ecclesiae Anglicanae*, and commentaries on *First and Second Thessalonians*, and the separatist minister and religious controversialist Henry Ainsworth's (1569–1622) writings on the *Pentateuch and Psalms*, and the Calvinist Thomas Beza's *De veris et visibilibus Ecclesiae Catholiciae Notis* (Geneva, 1579).

In contrast Teackle's library focused on theology, Biblical criticism, sermons, and medicine. His collection was well represented with the publications of the outstanding Puritan writers of the period, including the distinguished Cambridge Puritan scholar, William Perkins, *Armilla aurea, id est, Miranda series causarum et salutis & damnations iuxta verbum Dei* (Cambridge, 1590), and *A golden chaine: or, The description of theologie* (Cambridge, 1600). Also the works of the Cambridge academic and later leader of the New England theocracy John Cotton, *The way of life or God's way & course* (London, 1641), and Gerrard Winstanley's *The mysterie of God, concerning the whole creation, mankinde* (London, 1648).

Teackle maintained a strong interest in medicine, and his library included such works as Burton's *Anatomy of Melancholy*, Helkian Crooke, *A description of the body of man & etc.* (London, 1615), Edward Edwards, *The analysis of chyurgery, being the theorique and practique part thereof* (London, 1636), William Harvey, *The Anatomical exercises of Dr. William Harvey, professor of physick and physician to the Kings Majesty, concerning the motion of the heart and blood* (London, 1653), and Ambrose Paré, *The workes of that famous chirurgion Ambrose Paré* (London, 1649).

The second level for comparative purposes of the two libraries consists of an analysis with the probate inventories of book lists from the Vice-Chancellor's Court at Cambridge University during the Tudor and Stuart periods.[18] Goodbourne's library balances favourably with the 24 inventories of books.[19] His library reflects the influence of John Calvin and other Puritan writers on the Cambridge academic community during the sixteenth and early seventeenth centuries. Goodbourne's inventory indicates that he followed the collecting patterns of such Puritan bibliophiles and fellows of Cambridge colleges as Robert Some at Queen's, Robert Laudesdale at Jesus, William Gibson at Peterhouse, and Humphrey Tyndale at Pembroke.[20]

A comparative study of Teackle's collection differs from Goodbourne's perhaps in part because he did not attend a university. But an analysis of his book collection with the Cambridge probate records indicates that his library was not comparable with the books owned by Anglican parsons and university fellows.[21] In fact the authors, titles, and contents of Teackle's library suggest that he probably was not an ordained minister of the Church of England. Based on my examination of the 166 known collections of books of seventeenth- and eighteenth-century American Anglican ministers Teackle's library varies in an important manner from the books in nearly all other Anglican clergyman's libraries. First, his inventory does not include such basic works relating to the history, formularies, and organizational and administrative structure of the Church of England as Richard Hooker's *Ecclesiastical Polity*, the *Thirty-nine Articles of Faith*, or the *Constitutions and Canons of the Church*. Second the collection includes the writings of many Nonconformist ministers not usually found in the libraries of Anglican ministers. Among the authors represented are Thomas Adams (1583–1652), a Calvinist Episcopalian rather than a Puritan; William Ames (1576–1633), theologian and university teacher; Jeremiah Burroughs (bapt. 1601? –1646), an Independent minister; Joseph Caryl (1602–1673), an ejected minister and 1643 preacher in the House of Commons in favour of the Solemn League and Covenant; Thomas Case (bapt. 1598–1682), ejected minister; William Greenhill (1597/8–1671), an Independent minister; Edward Leigh (1603–71), a writer and fervent Puritan; Christopher Love (1618–51), a Puritan who refused episcopal ordination, evangelical preacher and author; Thomas Manton (baptized 1620–77), a nonconformist minister; William Perkins (1558–1602), theologian, Anglican clergyman, advocate of Calvinist doctrines among the group of moderate puritans in Cambridge; Robert Purnell (1606–66), a Baptist leader and author; and George Swinnock, an ejected minister.

A comparison of Teackle's library with the collection of the Massachusetts divine Increase Mather presents useful insights because both collections include works by prominent Puritan and Anglican authors. Mather's prized possession was his collection of books, more than seven hundred titles and nearly a thousand volumes. Assembled in part, perhaps, by his father, the library was supplemented by additions during Increase's lifetime and his visits to his brother in Oxford during his years as a student at Trinity College in Dublin. In the catalogue of the collection that he prepared in 1664 we find examples of his interest in the episcopacy issue in the Anglican Church. His library included such volumes as William Prynne's *Lord Bishops None of the Lord Bishops (London, 1640) and Sixteen Quaeres Proposed to our Lord Prelates*; David Calderwood's *The Pastor and Prelate*, of 1628; and *The Presbyterian Government is Divine*. These texts were side by side with the fundamental doctrines and laws of the Anglican Church, *Articles of the Church of England; and Canons Ecclesiastical of the English Church*. New England's most learned cleric had at his fingertips in his study the basic reference works on which he could launch his attack on the corrupted nature of the episcopacy, liturgical ceremonies, and the Prayer Book of the Anglican church.[22]

The paucity of information about Teackle's career does not allow a definitive classification of his religious preference as an Anglican, nonconformist, Puritan, Independent, or Presbyterian minister. In addition the social and religious character of Accomack and Northampton counties on Virginia's Eastern Shore suggest that a Nonconformist would have been much more compatible with the residents than an Anglican clergyman. The regions from early settlement in the 1620s were inhabited by numerous Quakers and Presbyterians.

Teackle did not leave a diary recording his reading habits, schedule, or the titles of the books he read in the course of a year. Nor did he leave behind after his death any sermons or manuscript to offer clues about the substance and style of his preaching. Yet the situation raises other significant questions. Why did the successive royal governors of the period and the Bishop of London's deputy allow Teackle's long tenure to continue as a Nonconformist minister on the Eastern Shore? He was serving as the clergyman of an established Church of England parish, and the civil and ecclesiastical leaders were entrusted with obligations to supervise religious affairs in the province as early as 1679 and 1685 respectively. Teackle seems to have avoided for nearly forty years the attention, discipline, and reprimands of governors William Berkeley and Francis, Lord Howard of Effingham. The royal instructions issued to the chief civil officers as early as 1679 provided that all clergymen officiating in Virginia parishes were required to be licensed by the Bishop of London.[23] Certainly Commissary Blair was familiar with the requirement but apparently he decided to overlook the matter with Teackle as well with two Presbyterian ministers who also occupied established church pulpits: Andrew Jackson (1656–1710) at St Mary's Whitechapel in Lancaster County between 1683 and 1710, and Josias Mackie (16xx–1716) at Elizabeth River Parish from 1684 to 1691. It was likely that the civil leaders were acknowledging the historically diverse religious sentiments of the residents of the Eastern Shore and were reluctant to impose the appointment of a Church of England parson. Replacing Teackle with a licensed Anglican parson would probably have prompted a public outcry of objection and heated controversy. The leaders may have decided to allow 'nature to run its course' and allow retirement or death to occur before making a change. Throughout the seventeenth century the settlers of the region had been allowed to recruit and maintain their ministers without the supervision or approval of civil and church leaders. Bishop of London Henry Compton may have known of the circumstances and if so urged Blair not to take action.

Succeeding Teackle at Accomack church about 1694 was the young Samuel Sandford (Sanford) a graduate of Pembroke College in Oxford University and ordained a deacon of the Church of England in 1691.[24] He served the congregation until 1702 and his return to Radnor in Wales.

Part III

9
An Age of New Imperial Policies: Church and State, 1660–1713

The tide of English interest in the imperial administration of Virginia and the other American colonies began to turn in the 1670s, an element in a wide-ranging effort by the Restoration government of Charles II to address critical matters at home and abroad. The chronicle of the Church in Virginia may be divided into two periods: from 1607 to 1680 and from 1680 to 1786. The new interest by the government in imperial polices and administration strongly influenced the subsequent course of affairs in Virginia and the other American provinces. But it is the period between 1680 and 1713 that we find a concentrated effort by the members of the Board of Trade and Plantations, the crown, and the Bishop of London to launch policies and governance that indelibly shaped Virginian and American affairs until the Declaration of Independence.

Led by the king's First Chancellor, Thomas Osborne (1632–1712), Lord Danby, civil officials came to believe that the Roman Catholic Church was growing to be a more serious influence in England as a result of Charles's flirtation with the king of France and the undisguised Romanism of James, Duke of York. To further his ends, Danby was particularly anxious to secure the cooperation of the Anglican Church, especially the bishops, who sat in the House of Lords, and to use them in support of a policy that it was equally in their interest to pursue.[1] In addition to the pressing religious issues the government addressed the need to increase revenues, and officials cast an eye on the opportunity to tap provincial sources in America.[2] Under Danby's charge the members of the Lords of the Council of Trade and Plantations, a committee of the Privy Council, reshaped and implemented stronger and more comprehensive policies for imperial administration.[3] The Council of Trade and Plantations launched policies that framed colonial administration for the next century, until the outbreak of the War of Independence.

In part the new era was shaped by political, diplomatic, and commercial forces in England. Parliament's passage of the Navigation Act of 1651 began a series of successively stronger acts of legislation for colonial affairs during the remainder of the century.[4] The statutes were an outgrowth of mercantilism, and followed principles laid down by Tudor and early Stuart trade regulations that intended to aid the expansion of English ships carrying trade. The governing precept was that the colonies would provide the commodities that England could not produce, and in turn would offer markets for English manufactures. Enumerated in the statute were such colonial articles as sugar, tobacco, cotton, and indigo that were to be supplied only to the homeland.

The rise of the Dutch carrying trade, which threatened to drive English shipping from the seas, prompted the 1651 Navigation Act, which was substantially re-enacted in the First Navigation Act of 1660 that was confirmed in 1661. This law underwent expansion and alteration with succeeding Navigation Acts of 1662, 1663, 1670, 1673, and by the Act to Prevent Frauds and Abuses of 1696. In the Act of 1663 the important principle required that all foreign goods be shipped to the American colonies through English ports. In return for restrictions on manufacturing and the regulation of trade, colonial commodities were often given a monopoly of the English market and preferential tariff treatment.

But English imperial interests were not limited to trade and commercial matters. For the purpose of this study my attention is focused on ecclesiastical affairs. After a half century the estimated population of Virginia in 1660 was at 27,020 white and 950 Negro persons.[5] In the wake of more than four decades of legal establishment and the increase of population, the church in the province in the 1660s was an institution stronger on paper than in fact. Although the county commissioners over the period had created between 45 and 48 parishes, there were only 8 churches built and 12 incumbent clergymen.[6] The isolated and rural congregations were sustained by a stream of successive clergymen performing their duties without a coherent sense of corporate identity or collegiality.

The new policies were shaped in part by several historical factors including the English government's failure to effectively and efficiently manage its first extra-territorial efforts in Ireland, the floundering administration of the Virginia Company of London, and the chequered experience of the American colony's first half century of development. At stake was the formula for an orderly extension and development of the civil and ecclesiastical institutions after the mid-1670s. But the anglicization policies intended to replicate in part the familiar structure of the English Church at home also carried seeds that gave rise to conflict and turmoil in Virginia. In retrospect, the affairs of the Church never reached the level of attention granted by London and provincial officials for civil administration, the judiciary, or defence and commercial affairs.

Following in the wake of news from New England of the outbreak of King Philip's War in 1675 reports of Bacon's Rebellion in Virginia reached London and stirred grave concern for North American affairs among Whitehall officials. At hand were the letters of Roger Green and John Yeo describing the dismal state of the Anglican Church in Virginia and Maryland. Leading the opening round of the discussion on colonial affairs was Bishop Compton. He may have been pressed to take the role by his patron and mentor, Thomas Osborne, the Earl of Danby. But it was an opportunity that the politically savvy prelate would have savoured. Personally he probably had two purposes in mind, first, to bring to the attention of the chief civil officers the dire situation of the church in England's first transatlantic settlement and second, to use the opportunity to establish the metropolitan bishop's jurisdiction and authority over ecclesiastical affairs in America. On both counts he was successful and implemented a template that governed his successors and the American church until the outbreak of the War for Independence.[7]

Compton presented to the Lords of Trade and Plantations in July 1677 a 'Memorial of Abuses which are crept into the Church of the Plantations', a document that was a synthesis and distillation of the critical reports offered by Green and Yeo.[8] He highlighted several basic shortcomings in the administration of the overseas church: including the denial of the crown's right of patronage and presentation of all clergymen to parishes, a procedure that was neither asserted nor acknowledged by the governors as the chief royal officials; that the salaries of the ministers were inadequate and precarious, and that some parishes were kept intentionally vacant to save the payment of a parson's salary; retaining lay readers rather that the appointment of ordained ministers to save the difference in salary; and the appropriation by the vestries of 'sole management of church affairs and exercising an arbitrary power over the Ministers'.[9]

Instructions on church affairs had been provided to Virginia governors as early as 1626 when Sir George Yeardley was charged to see that 'God be duly, and daily served', although there was no specific reference to the Church of England.[10] His successors, Sir Francis Wyatt in 1638 and Sir William Berkeley in 1650, received identical instructions that required them to see that God be 'duly, and daily served according to the Form of Religion as established in the Church of England'. They were also to oversee that every settled minister was provided with a parsonage and glebe. The governors were also granted authority to probate wills and issue letters of administrations.[11]

A committee of the Privy Council, a civil agency, the Lords of Trade included among its members the Bishop of London and Archbishop of Canterbury because they were great officers of state.[12] Policy for the overseas church was developed and implemented by the Bishop of London rather than an ecclesiastical body such as convocation of prelates under the supervision of the Archbishop of Canterbury.[13] In contrast to the Spanish and Portuguese ventures in the New World, England's effort in Virginia was launched without the entrenched sense of national mission for civil or ecclesiastical affairs. Policy for the overseas colonies was only gradually discussed and implemented between 1675 and 1690 by the Lords of Trade.[14]

Assisting with the introduction of a strategy for the extension of the Anglican Church to the New World was Danby's loyal protégé Henry Compton, Bishop of London (1632–1713). The sixth and youngest son of the second Earl of Northampton,[15] Compton was thrust to the centre of national ecclesiastical and political authority by his appointment to the Privy Council and the Committee on Trade and Plantations soon after his translation to London.[16] Mindful of Danby's strong support for the Church of England it was his policy to protect it from two enemies at home, Dissenters and Roman Catholics.[17] Compton took special interest in drafting the ecclesiastical responsibilities included in the instructions for royal governors in Virginia and the other American provinces.

Bishop Compton's sharply focused interest in American church affairs was partly driven by a 1662 letter from Roger Green (1614–73), a provincial parson who had written to then Bishop of London Gilbert Sheldon (1598–1677) reporting on the state of the church in Virginia.[18] Published in London a year later it was supplemented in 1676 by Reverend John Yeo's (1639–86) account to now Archbishop of Canterbury Sheldon on the situation in Maryland.[19] Sheldon turned to Compton and asked him to lay the matter of the church in America before Privy Council's Committee on Trade and Plantations for consideration.[20] In addition Compton appointed his first minister to Virginia, the 26-year-old John Banister (1650–92), a graduate of Oxford University. Undoubtedly aiding the young man's appointment was the strong interest in botany he shared with the prelate.[21] During the next decade Compton appointed a remarkable corps of accomplished men to serve Virginia congregations, including the naturalist, writer, and later member of the Royal Society, John Clayton (1657–1725); Deuel Pead (1647–1727), who after his return to London in 1691, as Chaplain to the Duke of Newcastle, was an acclaimed preacher; and James Blair as his commissary.[22]

He pressed for a detailed revision of the royal instructions affecting religion issued by the Privy Council to colonial governors in 1679 that charged the officials with several ecclesiastical duties. Central to their tasks was that The Book of Common Prayer should be read each Sunday, the Holy Communion celebrated according to the rites of the Church of England, and that no clergyman should be inducted into a benefice without a certificate from the Bishop of London.[23] A clause was added to the governors' instructions at Compton's prompting that directed them to see that suitable laws were enacted in their colonies for the punishment of blasphemy, profanity, adultery, polygamy, profanation of the Sabbath, and other crimes against common morality. The instructions also required that the laws be enforced by the civil courts upon testimony furnished by the churchwardens. Whenever new members of the provincial councils were to be appointed, their names were submitted to the bishop for any objections he might have to the religious principles of any of the men.[24] The Council of Trade referred all colonial laws touching on religion or religious questions to Compton for review as they may have encroached on his ecclesiastical jurisdiction, just as all statutes were sent to the crown's attorneys for any objection 'in point of law'.

On the one hand he was attempting to wrap his arms around the task of supervising the ecclesiastical affairs of an extra-territorial possession of England, while on the other hand he faced a range of questions and problems of procedures such as: how men were to be recruited to serve congregations in the provinces, how their transatlantic passages and annual salaries were to be paid. For the few congregations established in 1680, and then only in Virginia and Maryland, the looming question was how the necessary worship service books for each parish were to be supplied – Bibles, Books of Common Prayer, copies of the Thirty-Nine Articles and Canons of the Church of England, and so forth, and, importantly, at whose expense. Furthermore, there was the need to furnish plate and vessels for the celebration of the Lord's Supper on at least two or four occasions each year, but at whose bidding and cost? And finally, with a lack of books in the colonial parishes and no Anglican college established with a library for their use, how were ministers to be provided with the indispensable publications to enrich their professional performance? Searching for answers to these perplexing problems, Compton found the necessary resources at the Treasury.[25]

Bishop Compton corresponded regularly with the governors in Virginia on the state of ecclesiastical affairs in the province. His strong position among officials in London was unique because he enjoyed, for the first ten years of his episcopate, power in the church and at court. All of his successors in the eighteenth century cautiously imitated and did not exceed his innovative accomplishments on American affairs but did not enjoy his influential political capital, particularly during the critical decades of the 1760s and 1770s.[26]

But the assignment of ecclesiastical duties to their authority was at variance with historical procedure in England. The chief royal officials were vested with duties that were reserved to the jurisdiction of diocesan prelates in England. Colonial policy turned on the legal and bureaucratic notion that as the king was the titular head of state and the Supreme Head of the English Church, the monarch's chief royal appointee in the American provinces could be vested with the same authority. It became an arrangement that created tensions, confusion, and indifference between the governors, the church, vestries, and ministers in the decades before 1776.

In the aftermath of Bacon's Rebellion in 1675–76 and discussions in London with Lord Baltimore regarding Anglican Church affairs in Maryland, the Council of Trade and Plantations systematically revised the terms of the commissions and instructions issued to royal governors.[27] The instruments were intended to define and circumscribe the authority and duties of the chief royal official in a colony. Carefully crafted documents, the instruments were the product of several hands, including officials at the Admiralty, the Treasury, the Commissioners of the Customs, the Auditor General of the Plantation Revenues, and the Bishop of London.[28] The instructions were not public documents: they were meant for the eyes of the governor only. At the chief executive's discretion specific paragraphs might be shown to members of the colonial council, but only those items that related to their functions. But their influence upon provincial government was more significant because of their constant use and the variety of matters with which they dealt. The instructions included such details as the names of the members of his legislature, guidance on provincial financial affairs, justice, religion and morals, the militia, local defence, maritime affairs, land system, and trade and commerce.[29]

The governors were instructed to 'take especial care that God Almighty be devoutly and duly served' throughout his government, 'the Book of Common Prayer as by law established read each Sunday and Holy day, and the Blessed Sacrament administered according to the rites of the Church of England'.[30] He was required to see that the churches be well kept and that as population and prosperity increased in the province additional houses of worship were built. The colonial executive was charged to oversee that a 'competent maintenance' was to be assigned to each minister and that a parsonage and glebe were provided. After 1683 the royal officials were directed to ensure that colonial tobacco acts adopted for the support of ministers were observed.[31] But few leaders pursued that duty with zeal. When tobacco – the basis of the province's economy – returned a low yield, all incomes dependent on the crop were depressed and the condition of the minister's stipends received no special notice.

Before a governor could prefer a minister to a benefice of the Anglican Church the prospective appointee was requested to present a certificate from the Bishop of London of his conformity to the doctrine and discipline of the Church of England and of being of a 'good life and conversation'. If, somehow, a person of poor character in doctrine or manners occupied a living the governor was charged 'to use the best means for the removal of him', and to supply the vacancy temporarily with nearby clergy.[32]

Compton recommended that the governor's instructions should include a provision that each minister was allowed membership in the vestry of his parish, as was the procedure in England, and that no clergyman should be inducted into a benefice without a certificate from the Bishop of London.[33] A common practice in English dioceses, its application in the provinces was to be regulated by the governors, who were not to induct any parson into a parish without a valid licence to officiate. Governor Francis Lord Howard, Baron Howard of Effingham, issued a 'Proclamation concerning ministers and lay readers' on 8 July 1686 that recited the obligations of clergymen and vestries under the terms of his royal instructions.[34]

The vestry issue was the first topic to be addressed by the Committee for Trade.[35] Contrary to the traditional practices in England, the presence of delegated episcopal supervision restrained such developments, although the patron of a benefice – either a bishop, collegiate proprietor, or a local squire – could and did wield dominating influence. On the recommendation of the Committee for Trade, King Charles II issued an Order in Council on 14 January 1679/80, instructing the royal governors that every minister within their government was to be a member of the parish's vestry and in attendance at all meetings.[36]

The issue was complicated in Virginia where vestries since 24 February 1631/32 and 2 March 1642/43, and during the eighteenth century till the Revolution, reflected increasing lay-power in local church affairs.[37] Generally, the vestries were inclined not to present a minister for induction but rather retain him on a year-to-year basis without the full benefits of an instituted incumbent. Consequently, his status precluded a seat on the vestry. Throughout the colonial period the controversy was common between the ministers and the vestrymen. But successive governors were reluctant to intervene in these disputes since the laymen, usually politically influential persons in the neighbourhood, took the position that it was their sole right to supervise and maintain their parish's operation.[38]

A stipulation that was probably inserted by Compton in the governor's instructions required the official to accept and acknowledge the ecclesiastical jurisdiction of the Bishop of London in their provinces, except that the authority to collate ministers to benefices, grant licences for marriages, and probate wills was reserved for the governors.[39] The chief civil officers were granted authority to determine whether any man was exercising the priestly office in his province without episcopal orders and to report the situation to the London prelate. In addition they were required to oversee the placement of the table of marriages in every Anglican Church and urged to press the colonial Assembly for the necessary legislation to uphold the principles of the table.[40] In Virginia (1682–90) and New York (1668–88), the civil officials were required to observe that the Books of Homilies and Thirty-Nine Articles be placed, kept, and used within every Anglican Church in the province.[41]

The division of authority between governors and the Bishop of London over ecclesiastical affairs in Virginia and, later, elsewhere in America was a situation that at times flourished with relative ease while at other moments was gripped with confusion or conflict. Changing circumstances and the passage of time cast civil and church leaders in occasional conflict. Partly the situation may have been shaped by destructive temperaments and personalities and in part to novel politics and social demands in an increasing provincial population. There was no resident or visiting bishop present to oversee congregations, provide counsel to the clergy, adjudicate complaints against clergymen, and ordain native colonists seeking ordination. In addition, such episcopal duties were not fulfilled such as confirmation, ordination, and the consecration of church buildings. Furthermore, a colonial candidate for holy orders had to travel to England to receive ordination, a journey usually of four to seven weeks. The trip was expensive; it cost about

£100 round-trip, and was hazardous: not only on the high seas but in London, where the smallpox scourge was then present.

The Royal Commission and Instructions issued to Francis Lord Howard of Effingham by Charles II on his appointment at Lieutenant Governor General of Virginia were detailed instruments of a new age of imperial administration. Both documents were extensive in content and useful primers for provincial executive duty.[42] Under the Commission he was granted 'full power and authority to Collate any person or persons to any Church, Chappel, or other Ecclesiastical Benefice within Our said Colony, as often as they shall be void'.[43] His 77-paragraph Instructions carried the duty to 'take especial care that the Book of Common Prayer be read each Sunday and holy day and that the Blessed Sacrament administered according to the Rights of the Church of England'.[44] In addition he was to oversee that churches already built were kept orderly and more churches built as required. The ministers were to receive a competent salary, a house, and a glebe of 100 acres for their use.[45] And, of course, no minister 'is to be installed in a church without a certificate of the bishop of London stating that he is Conformable to the Doctrines and Discipline of the Church of England and of good life and conversation'. Any person that violated these standards was to be removed from office. The minister was to be a member of the vestry.[46] Finally, the governor was charged to take care that the Table of Marriages was installed in each church as required by Canon Law and that he carries with him to his provincial assignment 'a sufficient number of Books of Homilies and Books of the 39 Articles of the Church of England'.[47]

Armed with his Commission and Instructions, Governor Howard also received a list of 30 inquiries for answer from the Committee of Trade and Plantations on 27 September 1683. For our purposes only two questions are of concern to this study. He was asked how many parishes existed in the colony and what course of instruction offered 'the people in the Christian Religion'.[48] In addition the Committee wanted to know the number of churches and ministers in the colony, how many clergymen were without accommodation, and the religious groups active in Virginia with their relative proportion of the population.[49]

After nearly seven decades, the troubling and persistent issues facing the extension and development of the church in Virginia were harnessed. The Bishop of London was granted supervisory jurisdiction for the overseas church and through his efforts a procedure was instituted for the recruitment of clergymen for the colonies. Governors were issued Instructions for performing their civil and ecclesiastical duties and deputies of the London prelate were appointed in Virginia and other American provinces to provide a degree of supervision over the clergymen and congregations. Yet the church's historical ministry was incomplete, no bishop was appointed to perform ordinations and confirmations of members. No diocese had been created by parliament in Virginia or elsewhere along the Atlantic frontier. The English Church apparatus of cathedrals, bishops, deans and archdeacons remained unknown in England's first American colony, or any other province.

The London prelate exercised considerable influence at the court of Charles II, although his outspokenness against Roman Catholics created a strained relationship with James, Duke of York. As the reign of Charles II came to a close Compton identified himself with the hopes that the future rested in Protestant Mary and her Dutch husband, William of Orange. Compton was a relentless defender of the 'Ecclesia Anglicanae' and applied his extraordinary diplomatic skills to protecting the church and state from the prospect of Charles II's leanings toward the Roman Catholic faith and James's conversion. Doubtless this was a strong reason why he did not succeed Gilbert Sheldon as Archbishop of Canterbury in 1677.[50]

The accession of James II to the throne in 1685 and the rising constitutional controversy altered Compton's position at court. His anti-Catholic opinions and conflict with the king came to a head in November 1685, in a debate in the House of Lords on James II's claim to dispense with the Test Act and with the Bishop of London's refusal to silence a cleric critical of the policies of the monarch. Compton forthrightly declared that at issue was the English civil and ecclesiastical constitution and that his remarks reflected the opinion of the whole bench of bishops. Parliament was summarily prorogued the next day, and Compton was immediately dismissed from the Privy Council.

King James II as the Supreme Head of the Church appointed three loyal prelates to serve as the court of ecclesiastical commission to hear the charge against the London bishop that he failed to obey the royal command.[51] Denying the commission's competency, Compton, after a hearing, was suspended from office for three years. At the time John Evelyn noted in his diary that the proceedings were baseless and carried out on false pretences.[52]

Called before the court of ecclesiastical commission, the London prelate was charged with failing to obey the royal command. A committee of three prelates was delegated with the responsibility to supervise the affairs of the London diocese during Compton's suspension from office. Bishop of Durham Nathaniel Crewe was one of the panel to administer the diocese and American affairs.[53] After William III and

Mary assumed the throne in 1689 Compton was restored to his episcopal office, reinstated as a privy councillor, presided at the coronation of the king and resumed his administration of colonial church affairs.[54]

The London prelate's civil experience and discipline may have modified and sharpened his concern for the supervision of the American church. As the author of the provision in the governor's royal instructions that had split supervision over the Anglican Church between civil and ecclesiastical officials, Compton now boldly stepped forward to appoint his own deputies.[55] His decision testified to his active jurisdiction over matters that had not been delegated to the royal governors. It was a positive administrative step because the transplanted colonial church had many real disadvantages.

Under the Council of Trade's jurisdiction over the colonial church the bishop had the right to appoint commissaries for overseer duties.[56] Compton's appointments represented the strongest possible official substitute for a resident bishop. Their primary duty was to provide clerical supervision over the American church and to serve as the main link for communication between the London prelate and the ministers in each colony. Although the commissary's office was useful in England during the sixteenth, seventeenth, and eighteenth centuries it proved difficult to establish in the colonies.[57]

Building on the administrative experience of governors Sir William Berkeley and Francis, Lord Howard of Effingham the successive provincial chief civil officers were provided with detailed royal commissions and instructions to guide their duties and leadership in office.[58] Compton was charged with the supervision of church affairs and immediately addressed the need for policies to govern the duties of local vestries and recruit ministers to serve Virginia churches. After 1677 the pages of the official journals of the Board of Trade, the Privy Council, and the Treasury Office provide evidence of Compton's attention to overseas ecclesiastical matters. He recruited ministers and obtained funds from the Treasury to defray their transportation expenses to America.[59]

Compton appointed James Blair (1655–1743) to serve as his administrative deputy, commissary, in the province on 15 December 1689. For nearly sixty years he looms large on the horizon of Virginia ecclesiastical and civil affairs. Born in Banffshire, Scotland, he was the eldest of four sons and one daughter of Robert Blair and his wife, whose name remains unknown, a Church of Scotland cleric for 43 years or more of the parish of Alvah on the North Sea.[60] James Blair was baptized on

7 December 1655 at Banffshire and in time admitted to Marischal College, Aberdeen, in 1668 as a Crombie Scholar, aged twelve. The next year
he matriculated at the University of Edinburgh, proceeding to an M.A.
degree in 1673, and completing his theological studies in 1679.[61] He
was ordained a priest of the Church of Scotland by Bishop of Edinburgh
John Paterson (1632–1708) and served Cranston Parish in the Presbytery
of Dalkeith, ten miles southwest of Edinburgh, from 1679 until 1681.[62]

Political and religious turmoil in Scotland shaped a new path for
Blair's life and career. The Privy Council of Scotland on 22 December 1681 noted that Blair, like many Scottish Episcopalian clergymen,
had refused to swear and subscribe to the Test Oath that would have
placed the Catholic James II as the head of the Scottish church upon
his accession to the throne. Trapped in a moral and ethical quandary
he sought the assistance of his distinguished former Edinburgh University Professor of Divinity, Laurence Charteris (*c*.1625–1715), who
had resigned his academic appointment rather than sign the oath.[63]
Charteris promptly wrote to a fellow Scotsman in London, the well-
connected Gilbert Burnet (1643–1715), a former professor of divinity
at Marischal College, introducing and requesting his help on Blair's
behalf. Burnet, the distinguished preacher and writer of the Rolls Chapel
in London, was an anti-papist who had fled his homeland in discon-
tent over the extravagance of Scottish bishops and mismanagement of
ecclesiastical affairs.[64]

Aged 27, Blair travelled to London where through Burnet's efforts he
became an under clerk (1682–85) of the Master of the Rolls. Burnet
embraced Blair as his protégé and introduced him to such prominent
church leaders and personal friends as John Tillotson (1630–94), later
the Archbishop of Canterbury, and Henry Compton, Bishop of London.
In 1685 the London prelate was seeking men to fill posts in America and
recruited Blair to serve the Henrico Parish in Virginia.[65]

Blair's commissarial appointment granted 'all and every power of carrying out and performing... whatever pertains and belongs, or ought to
pertain and belong, to the office..., by law or custom according to the
laws, canons and constitutions followed and observed in the Church
of England'.[66] The traditional responsibilities of commissaries were delegated to summon the clergy, conduct visitations, administer oaths
customary in ecclesiastical courts, and administer discipline or judicial
proceedings to wayward clergy either by admonition, suspension, or
excommunication. Appeals from any judgments, decrees, or sentences
passed by the officer or an ecclesiastical court over which he presided in
the colonies, however, were to be allowed before the Privy Council. The

commissary was also allowed to appoint one or more of his ministerial colleagues as substitutes in his place whenever necessary.[67] An important exception to the traditional English episcopal privileges was the authority and powers for granting licences for marriages, proving wills, and conferring of benefices, reserved by the crown for the colonial governors and so stated in their royal instructions on ecclesiastical affairs.[68] Unlike the commissaries in England, however, the colonial officials were not appointed for life.

The commission granted to Blair was valid during the episcopal term of the grantor in the diocese of London. If a bishop died or was translated to another see, his successor decided whether or not to reappoint a commissary. The commission was terminated whenever the episcopal office became vacant.[69]

The transfer of the commissarial office from England to America was probably not as effective and successful as Bishops of London Henry Compton and Edmund Gibson (1723–48) had hoped. Although the position enjoyed a long history in the English church hierarchy, undertaking delegated episcopal administrative and political duties, it was neither a substitute for an American prelate nor adaptable to the provincial scene of the English church.

The turn of civil and ecclesiastical events and procedures in Virginia in the 1670s, 1680s, and 1690s set the Anglican Church on its course until the outbreak of the War for Independence. Nearly a century after the settlement of Jamestown the colonial institution was provided with administrative supervision in London and the province that did not duplicate the procedures in the homeland. Offered in its place was the barest of administrative structure possible without parliament's approval and creation of a diocese and bishopric. New civil issues and an increasing population supplemented by a steady flow of immigrants gradually gave a distinctive shape to eighteenth-century Virginia life, forces that presented new challenges and controversies for the established church.

10
The Peace Disturbed: Salaries and Controversies, 1696–1777

A topic that bridges the chronicle of the transfer and development of the Anglican Church in colonial Virginia is the payment of clergymen's salaries. The payment of clergy stipends was an issue of regular complaint and debate in provincial Virginia, especially in the 1750s. Unlike their colleagues in England the parsons were vulnerable and without a strong and respected official spokesman to represent their interests, such as the Archbishop of Canterbury or the Bishop of London. Williamsburg's printer published works that represented the conflicting positions and argued the positions of laymen and parsons. A stalemate occurred on the matter in a province increasingly exposed to popular rhetoric objecting to imperial policies. It represented a deep and open fissure in the colony's religious establishment.

The maintenance of ministers had been a common problem in England at least since the sixteenth century. In 1585 Archbishop of Canterbury John Whitgift (1530/31?–1604) complained that there were scarcely 600 livings (out of well over 9,000 in England) capable of supporting a minister. Livings generally were poorly endowed and many clergymen were forced to rely on additional sources of income either from a patron or impropriation, or by teaching, preaching, trading, or practicing a craft to survive.[1] The financial woes in England accompanied the clergymen to the New World in the seventeenth century. Newly established congregations were without the common English resources of endowments and patrons to address the financial insecurity felt by the men. In England the situation did not change until a major effort was undertaken to improve the salaries of ministers in the early years of the reign of Queen Anne.[2]

Before the era of Queen Anne the clergy were required to pay royal taxes known as First Fruits and Tenths to the crown on ecclesiastical dignities and benefices. The first fruits being the sum of money paid on entry into possession of any one of them, and tenths being a recurring annual charge of much smaller amounts. The taxes were recognized as a burdensome charge on underpaid clergymen.[3] Under the supervision of an agency known as 'The Governors of the Bounty of Queen Anne for the Augmentation of the Maintenance of the Poor Clergy' the Queen would release her revenues from First Fruits and Tenths and apply them to the augmentation of the poor clergy's income. Queen Anne's Bounty demonstrated the crown's generosity toward improving the financial circumstances of the poorer clergy of the Church.[4]

Financial circumstances for the clergy of the Church of Ireland were no less bleak than their English brethren in the early eighteenth century. Leading the charge to improve the men's salaries was the Dean of St Patrick's Cathedral in Dublin, Jonathan Swift (1667–1745), widely recognized as a satirist, essayist, political pamphleteer, and poet. Between 1707 and 1709 and again in 1710, he unsuccessfully urged upon the Whig administration of Sydney Lord Godolphin (1645–1712) for the claims of the Irish clergy to the First Fruits and Tenths which brought in about £2,500 a year, already granted to their brethren in England.[5]

Between 1607 and 1624 the Virginia Company was responsible for the payment of the salaries of parsons. On at least one occasion the company entered into an employment contract with one of the 18 clergymen it recruited to serve in the colony, and it may have been a common procedure for all of the men travelling from England to the province during the period.[6] The first known instance of such an arrangement occurred when Robert Pawlett (1590–1644) agreed on 15 September 1620 to travel to Virginia and serve as a chaplain, preacher, surgeon, and physician for one year at a salary of £20. He was free to return to England after one year's service under the terms of his employment contract.[7] In 1621 the population of the colony was about 4,000 residents and was served by six men, two of whom were not ordained.[8] Briefly serving as the minister at Martin's Hundred and Martin Brandon, Pawlett drops from sight after 1622 possibly dying in the Indians' Good Friday Massacre in 1622, or perhaps he returned to England with his wife and children.[9] Notwithstanding that the Company was responsible for the payment of a minister's salary the printed records do not disclose how many of the Company's clerical appointees encountered slow or no payment of their stipends. It remains unclear how many of the men encountered a similar financial experience.

A new page was written in the colony's history in 1619 when the Virginia Assembly, under the jurisdiction of the Virginia Company, enacted legislation to establish the church and set the salary for the six ministers residing in the colony and serving congregations.[10] The statute stipulated that the minister's salary was to be paid by tithes of the local residents in tobacco, the colony's most valuable commodity. Circumstances dimmed the need for the application of the law with the Good Friday Massacre of 1622 at Henrico, an event that undermined the validity of the province as a commercial venture. A devastated and diminished population was not supplemented with a stream of settlers and the company's charter was revoked by James I in 1624. Immediately Virginia became a royal colony and a new era of imperial administration began that continued until 1776.

In 1632, with only 1 clergyman in the province, the burgesses further defined the requirement of parishioners for the support of the minister and embraced the English precedent that granted ministers ten pounds of tobacco and one bushel of corn from each titheable in the parish.[11] Since the price of tobacco was depressed, a further allowance was made for the parsons to be paid in kind from the twentieth calves, goats, and pigs born on the plantations within the colony. In addition the clergy's professional fees were to be paid in tobacco, including a two-pound tobacco gratuity for the performance of a marriage, and one pound for either the churching of women after childbirth or for burying the dead. No fee was set for baptisms.[12] The statute remained on the law books for two years, when the section covering the tithes of the twentieth calf, pig, or goat was repealed.[13] Yet the precariousness of the annual support of the clergymen persisted, and the record of the General Court of 9 December 1640 declares that 'many controversie do daily arise between the parishioners and ministers throughout the colony concerning the payment of their duties owed to the minister'.[14]

Again, in 1643, the legislature addressed the issue of the tobacco stipend paid to the men and maintained the previous allowances but revised the scale of fees for their services. For performing a marriage ceremony without a licence the ministers were to receive forty pounds of tobacco, while the duty was considerably higher – one hundred pounds – for those who had a licence. Fees for burials and the churching of women were raised to ten pounds of tobacco.[15] Whenever a parish was too sparsely settled to support a parson on a tithe of ten pounds of tobacco per titheable, the assembly after 1646 gave the vestries the power to augment the rate as they thought appropriate.[16] With a population of about 30,000 persons in 1660 and 11 ministers serving congregations in the colony the legislature two years later set the salaries of ministers at 13,333 pounds of tobacco that were to be assessed and collected under the supervision of the vestries.[17]

By 1681 Governor Thomas Lord Culpeper (1635–89), successor to Sir William Berkeley (1605–77) on 13 July 1677, reported to the Board of Trade in London that the estimated population of Virginia was about 70,000 to 80,000 persons.[18] A year earlier the number of ministers serving congregations in the province stood at 29. Clergy incomes continued to be paid at the 1662 level until 1696 when after a three-year struggle the provincial clergy enlisted the aid of Governor Edmund Andros (1637–1714) and members of the colonial Council to increase by exactly one-fifth the value of their stipends.[19] The annual allowance for parsons was set at 16,000 pounds of tobacco.[20] We do not know how many of the payments were usually fully paid, partially remitted, negotiated, or disputed and settled by litigation.[21] Evidence exists that indicates that such disputes were not numerous but erupted occasionally in the province. Except for minor modifications enacted by the legislature in 1728 and 1748, the incomes of the ministers were those set by the 1696 statute.[22]

Without the apparatus of the hierarchical ecclesiastical organization of the church in England career opportunities for Virginia parsons were limited. Provincial ministers enjoyed no opportunity for advancement to a higher level of service with a commensurate increase in stipend, such as a prelate's archdeacon administering a geographical district of ministers and churches in a diocese, or as a dean or canon of a cathedral.

Disputes

Records indicate that the Virginia Company was tardy in paying the ministers their annual stipend. Richard Bucke (1584–1623), educated at Gonville and Caius College in Cambridge University, arrived in the colony in 1610, served as the minister at Jamestown. He explained his plight of not receiving a salary for several years in a 1621 letter to the former governor of the colony Sir Edwin Sandys (1561–1629), a substantial Company shareholder. Bucke sought his assistance for payment, declaring that his earlier written requests to the Company for payment remained unanswered.[23] The amount of his annual stipend is unknown but it was probably about £20, at the same level of Robert Pawlett's employment contract.[24] Married with four or five children, Bucke and the claim vanish from the historical record. We do not know if he or his survivors were ever reimbursed for his back salary.

After Bucke's complaint there is no evidence of the handful of ministers active in the colony for the next few years not receiving their stipend. The issue surfaces again when William Harwood, a leading resident of Martin's Hundred, took it upon himself to enter into a contract in late 1628 or early 1629 with Francis Doughty (1616–69) the recently appointed minister of the parish. Harwood agreed that the minister's salary would be 2,000 pounds of tobacco and a quantity of corn to be paid by the parishioners. But his authority to encumber the titheables of the parish was challenged in April 1629 when church members went to court, claiming that because the population of the plantation was very small Harwood had saddled them with an unfair and heavy burden. The court agreed with the plaintiffs and resolved the dispute by ordering that Harwood was personally responsible for paying Doughty a third of both the tobacco and the corn, and the parishioners to provide the rest.[25]

Arriving in the province in 1632 William Cotton (16xx–40) served as the first minister of Hungar's Parish in Northampton County. He is not remembered for his performance as a preacher or for attention to pastoral duties with his flock but for his sustained legal efforts to recover his salary. For the next six years, possibly with the assistance of his brother-in-law William Stone, the sheriff of the community, he regularly filed complaints in the county court against individual members of his congregation for non-payment of tithes due him.[26] In every instance his demands for redress and payment were successful and ordered.

Writing on behalf of the clergy on the south side of the James River in 1723 the Reverend Alexander Forbes (1685–1726) informed Governor Hugh Drysdale and members of the House of Burgesses that their tobacco allotments were often not collected in time for sale and shipment to England. Frequently, Forbes asserted, the tobacco was unfit for sale either to agents in England at a high price or to provincial dealers in Williamsburg who usually offered the men a lower cash allowance.[27] In response to Bishop of London Edmund Gibson's queries that were sent to the clergymen in his diocese in 1724, the returns indicated that the salaries in Virginia were similar to those in Maryland. Clergy stipends ranged from an annual maximum of £120 for one man, to £100–80 for ten men, to £70–50 for seven men, down to a minimum of £45–20 for four men. Legislation was enacted by the Virginia Assembly in March 1728 that required better and quicker methods of transporting the tobacco allotments of the parsons to market, thus offering them a chance to sell it at a more competitive price.[28] The fees of the attorneys and other public officials whose incomes were paid in tobacco were affected too. But the situation was not resolved and in 1732

Lieutenant-Governor Sir William Gooch (1681–1751), Hugh Drysdale's (d. 1726) successor, informed Bishop Gibson that although in the past the stipends of ministers were calculated at £80 sterling annually, the experience for many years indicated that the tobacco allotment brought no more than £40, £30, or even £20 income.[29] It was common for taxable residents in the parishes of Virginia and the adjacent colony of Maryland to discharge their rates for the support of the clergy with poor-quality tobacco. Awkwardly, and without a means of systematic recourse, the parsons on the one hand were trapped by the poor quality of tobacco that they received as payment and on the other hand by the low price the crop usually generated at market. It may be inferred that the financial circumstances probably prompted a number of the men to supplement their church incomes by serving as schoolmasters in their homes or at nearby plantations.[30]

The Parson's Cause

A heated dispute over clergy salaries in the 1750s surfaced again and became known popularly as the 'Parson's Cause'. It was hotly debated and shaped by a stream of essays from the pens of layman Richard Bland (1710–76) and the bishop of London's Commissary in the colony, John Camm (1718–79), also head of the College of William and Mary. While the disagreement touched the pocketbook of every clergyman in the province it was not drafted or vehemently argued by a resolution of the men in convention.

Candidly, Camm neither enjoyed nor entertained the political sagacity, authority, and influence of James Blair. Without demonstrating a need to enlist a coalition of support on behalf of the ministers' interest in the controversy his strategy rested on a foundation of simply 'we versus them'. The common political practice of seeking to find a compromise was not identified or pursued in the matter. It was a many-sided issue, partly a controversy over the payment of salaries when the market value of tobacco fluctuated, and partly an argument pressed in the absence of a bishop to supervise church affairs, providing an opportunity for lay members to demonstrate their will and authority over local parish affairs. The thorny debate was not attractive for intervention and resolution by successive royal governors or commissaries of the Bishop of London.

On the one hand the controversy may have been solely a recital of the disagreement over the fluctuating value of the tobacco paid to each minister heard first in the 1720s. While on the other hand the issue may have been more subtly about laymen's efforts to strengthen political control over parish and local affairs, a strategy to curtail the power vested in the parson. The 'Parson's Cause' took place at a time when the population of the colony had increased substantially from an estimated 18,731 persons in 1650 to about 168,000 white and 116,000 black persons in 1754.[31] There were pockets of differing religious groups in the colony from at least the 1620s but by the 1740s and 1750s there was an increased number of Presbyterians. Aiding popular familiarity with the heated issue was the establishment in the 1730s of a printer and printing press in Williamsburg that allowed for the regular publication of newspapers and the essays on the Parson's Cause debate.[32]

Historian Richard L. Morton has written that the Parson's Cause controversy over the Two-Penny Acts of 1755 and 1758 in Virginia was an economic issue of greater consequence beyond merely the payment of clergymen's salaries. A dispute moulded in part by the decline in the influence of the commissary of the Bishop of London after the death of James Blair (1655–1743); the increased secular control over the Church and the College of William and Mary; opposition to the royal veto in provincial legislative affairs; opposition to a Virginia bishopric; and an increasing dissatisfaction with the imperial policies of Great Britain.[33] For many observers the dispute over the Two-Penny Acts was an early sign of the escalating movement to Virginia's participation in the American Revolution.[34]

But what were the details of the controversy? In the summer of 1755 the colony suffered a severe drought foreshadowing a short crop of tobacco. By September the price of tobacco had increased three times and was selling at about four and a halfpence per pound Virginia currency. The provincial legislature, in an attempt to avoid hardships among debtors, passed a law authorizing the liquidation of tobacco debts during the next year at sixteen shillings and eight pence per hundred pounds, the equivalent of two pence per pound. Importantly, the payment could be commuted from tobacco to paper money. As tobacco sold for sixpence a pound the ministers considered themselves losers; as their entire incomes were dependent upon tobacco, they immediately criticized the law in Virginia and England. The parsons felt that the statute was directly aiding the well-to-do tobacco planters who were willing to pay debts with colonial currency, since it was constantly decreasing in value while tobacco could be sold in London or Amsterdam at a large profit.[35]

Their incomes, the ministers declared, seldom provided a sterling stipend of £80 per year, which, they countered, was not the equivalent of a curate's £40 stipend in England.[36] It must be noted that in addition to their salaries the clergymen received additional financial benefits, the use of a parsonage and glebe lands for the production of farm crops.[37] The value of these significant financial benefits at any time during Virginia's colonial history is not known. It is a matter worthy of further investigation.[38]

Yet the clergy's grievances antedated the first of the Two-Penny Acts in 1755. They were embittered by the provincial Assembly's 1748 act for the better support of the clergy that provided that the sole right of presentation of a minister to a parish shall be and remain in the hands of the vestries. The duty was recognized to be that of the lay-board rather than of the royal governors under the terms of his instructions or of the Bishop of London. The procedure was a departure from the practice in England. The eviction in 1753 of William Kay (1721–55), rector of Lunenberg Parish, from his post by a vestry guided by the mercurial Landon Carter led to a lengthy court case that was finally decided in Kay's favour. This was an incident with more than money at issue. It dramatically represented the power of the vestry over the appointment and tenure of the minister.[39] It was not an isolated episode; the ministers were also disturbed by the removal of the Reverend John Brunskill, Jr. (1729–1804), from Hamilton Parish in Prince William County by the Colonial Council, 'for monstrous immoralities, profane swearing drunkenness and very immodest actions'. The event, regardless of the merits of the case, further illustrated the vulnerability of the church and its parsons and undermined ecclesiastical responsibility and authority.[40]

After the passage of the first Two-Penny Act in November 1755, only a small group of the clergymen in Virginia opposed the measure and tried to secure Governor Robert Dinwiddie's (1692–1770) veto of it. When they failed in this they urged Commissary Thomas Dawson (1713–61), the recently elected president of the College of William and Mary, to call at once a convention of the clergy to formulate a 'public representation' on the issue to Bishop of London Thomas Sherlock, but the commissary preferred a less active and confrontational response of the matter by sending a 'private report'.[41] A handful of the parsons disagreed with the commissary's response, perhaps at the church's and college's expense during the remainder of the colonial period. Eight ministers immediately went over the head of the Governor and Assembly with a complaint to British authorities. Four of the parsons were professors in the College and clergymen trained in the English universities of Oxford and Cambridge and had little sympathy with the rising 'republican' spirit in Virginia. These men – John Camm, William

Preston (1720–81), Thomas Robinson (1715–17xx), and the lay Richard Graham – wrote the Bishop of London Thomas Sherlock (1677–1761) on 29 November 1755, accusing the Virginia Assembly, with the Governor's assent, of deliberately making a law 'too glaringly inconsistent with natural equity, the rights of the Clergy, the common liberty of the subject and his Royal Majesty's prerogative, to be spoken of without detestation'. This measure, which, they said would 'draw on the ruin of the Established Church', would not aid the poor people; it would benefit only the 'gentlemen of this Colony [who] have at present high notions of the advantage that will accrue to them by making indigo'. The act, they complained, was retroactive, since it regulated the amount of salary already due them. To the question why they opposed the act when others similarly affected were content, they answered that others had different means of support and while losing in one way by the act could gain in another; and they wrote spiritedly and convincingly of the high cost of living and the inadequate salaries of the Virginia clergymen.[42]

The first Two-Penny statute was only on the law books ten months. When a drought again curtailed tobacco production in 1758 a law similar to that adopted in 1755 was passed that immediately evoked strong opposition from the clergy. Again, had the law not been enacted, the high-priced tobacco would have meant a substantial addition to the income of clergymen. A number of ministers, particularly those situated in Williamsburg and serving as members of the faculty of the College of William and Mary, were determined to resist the Two-Penny legislation under the leadership of John Camm. It was Governor Dinwiddie's opinion that there would be 'constant animosities between the clergy and the laity in every scarce year of tobacco', should the clergy receive their full quota when the planters made small crops. As soon as the Assembly had adjourned, the disgruntled group of clergymen, led by Camm, urged Commissary Dawson to call a convention of the clergy to consider steps to oppose the act. When Dawson refused, they defiantly went over the head of the commissary and issued a call for a rump convention in their own names, as they had done in 1755. About thirty-five parsons out of a possible seventy in Virginia attended the rump session, and they were unanimous 'in sending Mr. Camm as their agent to England'.[43]

Camm left for England in late 1758 and took with him a 'Representation of the Clergy of the Church of England' in Virginia. This paper described the act of 1748 and others fixing salaries of the clergy and the Two-Penny Act; accused the Governor and Assembly of having caused the vestries to break their contracts with the ministers, who, ordinarily underpaid, could not take advantage now of the rise in the price of tobacco; and stated that the Virginia government had 'broken through' laws confirmed by royal authority and had disobeyed royal instructions 'to pass these pretended laws'. Finally, the clergy petitioned the Board of Trade to persuade the king to declare the acts null and void and to give 'explicit instructions and commands' to the Governor to pass no such 'pretended' acts changing in any way the act of 1748 regarding the salaries of the clergy. The Virginians did not underestimate the strength of the leader of the opposition. 'Mr. Camm', the Governor warned the Board of Trade, 'is a man of abilities but a turbulent man who delights to live in a flame'.[44]

Armed with the aid of Archbishop of Canterbury Thomas Seeker (1693–1768), Camm appeared before the Privy Council on 14 May 1759 and presented his case.[49] In turn the Bishop of London Thomas Sherlock sent a letter to the Board of Trade, 14 June 1759, that was read at the 19 June meeting of the Board and which included many of the details contained in the 'Representation'.[46] The letter later was included with the Board's report to the Privy Council on 3 July.[47] This letter is a remarkable document of misinformation, false interpretations, and misleading insinuations. It is apparent from this letter that the bishop was not familiar with the laws that he condemned, and the motives of the Virginia lawmakers and governors. In fact, a study of the legislation since the revision of the laws in 1696 shows that instead of trying to weaken the Church and oppress the clergymen, the provincial laws tended to strengthen the Church and make more secure the position of the clergy.

Camm's affairs now moved rapidly to a successful conclusion. On 3 July 1759, the Board of Trade recommended to the King and Privy Council the disallowance of acts of 1753, 1755, and 1758 relating to the ministers' salaries, as unjust in their principles and effects contrary to the King's instructions and the next day King George II signed the order.[48] After hearing the arguments in the case the King in Council, on 10 August 1759, disallowed: all the acts of the Virginia Assembly permitting salaries to be paid in tobacco; acts of December 1753 for paying ministers in the frontier counties of the counties of Princess Anne and Norfolk; the Two-Penny Acts of 1755 and 1758; and the two private acts not in the forms required.[49] To add a further blow to the Governor and Assembly in Virginia, the King appointed their chief adversary, John Camm, as his messenger to bring to them the official documents telling of their defeat.[50]

News of the disallowance of the Two-Penny Act greatly disturbed the Virginians and started a vigorous newspaper and pamphlet war chiefly between a pair of members of the House of Burgesses, Landon Carter (1710–78) and Richard Bland on one side, and Camm on the other. Carter, of Sabine Hall, fired the opening volley in the campaign in Richmond County. Familiar with the practice of contentious pamphlet warfare, he had published in London a decade earlier *A Letter from a Gentleman in Virginia, to the Merchants of Great Britain, Trading in that Colony* (London, 1754). Now, in his *A Letter to Right Reverend Father in God, the Lord B[isho]p of L[ondon]n* (Williamsburg, 1759), he wrote with resentment, an answer to the Bishop's charge that the General Assembly had been disloyal and had encouraged dissent.[51]

Bland, educated at the College of William and Mary and a member of the House of Burgesses since 1742, was author of the Two-Penny Acts. He joined the fray in 1760 with *A Letter to the Clergy of Virginia*.[52] This letter was also an answer to the Bishop of London's letter to the Board of Trade; but it was addressed directly against those memorialists who had led the bishop astray. The pamphlets of Carter and Bland were 'received with great applause' in Virginia.

Camm replied to Bland and Carter in similar tone and manner. He published a tough, direct, and lively pamphlet entitled *A Single and Distinct View of the Act Vulgarly Called the Two-Penny Act* (Annapolis, 1763). In this he condemned the 'justice and charity' ascribed to the act by Carter in his letter of 1759 and Bland's *salus populi* argument for it in his letter of 1760. Camm, the Professor of Divinity at the College of William and Mary, concluded with the observation that he was 'no less astonished at Col. Bland's casting the Conduct of Archbishop Laud in our Teeth;' and comparing the provincial clergymen 'to Romish Inquisitors', for their 'secret Machinations'.[53]

The debate continued when Carter rebutted with *The Rector Detected* (Williamsburg, 1764), a tract of persistent verbal sharpness, and Camm answered with *Review of the Rector Detected, or the Colonel Reconnoitered* (Williamsburg, 1764).[54] The final round of the controversy included Bland's trenchant contribution offered under the pseudonym, 'Common Sense', entitled the *Colonel Dismounted: or the Rector Vindicated* (Williamsburg, 1764), and Camm's *Critical Remarks on a Letter ascribed to Common Sense* (Williamsburg, 1765).[55]

At least five of the Church of England parsons, including Camm, took their grievances to court for the recovery of the full market value of their assigned quota of tobacco. In Hanover County the court ruled the 1758 act was invalid from passage, and the Reverend James Maury (1718–69), rector of a parish in Louisa County, brought suit to recover on his salary in 1762. Patrick Henry defended the parish in Louisa County, presenting no witnesses but assailing the ministers and the practice of vetoing laws necessary for the public good. The jury awarded Maury one-penny damages. In 1764 the General Court of the province held the law good until it was vetoed and left the ministers without any remedy. This was appealed to the Privy Council where the appeal was dismissed in 1767.[56]

The crucial decision in Camm's case, brought originally in the General Court on 10 October 1759, and deliberately delayed, it seems, was finally given on 10 April 1764. The Court, by a vote of five to four, rendered judgment against Camm. He appealed the decision to the Privy Council in London that heard the petition in 1767, and dismissed the suit on the ground that it was improperly drawn, doubtless a convenient excuse for avoiding a difficult and unpleasant decision.[57]

There are few traces of evidence relating to the opinions of Virginia ministers who opposed Camm's overtures and attacks on Carter, Bland, and the Two-Penny Acts. Commissary Dawson's unwillingness to call a convention of the clergy was a signal of the lack of support among the rank and file as well as with church leadership. A general Two-Penny Act was passed in 1769, and the ministers gave up the agitation.

The escalating popular resistance movement in Virginia and the other American colonies during the 1760s and 1770s marked and scarred the strongest provincial Anglican Church in America. Protests in New England and the Middle Colonies over such imperial policies as the Stamp Act, Townshend Act, Boston Massacre, Tea Party, the divisive but muted interest for the appointment of a colonial bishop, the Parson's Cause, the educational, financial, and disciplinary problems of the Anglican College of William and Mary were all argued publicly in the press.

Ironically, the talented and persistent essayist and protagonist of the Parson's Cause, the planter and civil leader Richard Bland, witnessed one of his sons, William (1742–1803), become a Virginia Anglican minister in 1767. Born on 26 December 1742 and educated at the College of William and Mary between 1758 and 1763, he was ordained deacon and priest by the Bishop of London in June 1767 and served as the minister at the James City Parish from 1767 to 1777. His views seem to mirror his father's political views because William signed the Virginia protest for the closing of the political port of Boston in 1774 and he served as Chaplain to the Virginia Regiment Militia in 1775 and 1776.[58]

The increased presence and activity in 1769 of the Presbyterians and Baptists in the province created a new situation for the Church.[59] The two religious groups began to pressure the members of the House of Burgesses to grant them religious toleration or liberty. The necessity for some revision of the statute relating to the Established Church had been recognized by the legislature as early as 8 May 1769, when the Committee for Religion was appointed and directed to prepare a bill for exempting dissenters from the penalties of the law.[60] Session after session the reform was put off until 1776.

The Declaration of Independence on 4 July 1776 and the outbreak of the War for Independence marked a dramatic reversal in the fortunes of the Anglican Church in Virginia and the American colonies. No other religious group encountered such a drastic change in its status and situation. With the collapse of imperial organization, the withdrawal of royal officials from colonial posts, and the outbreak of military campaigns the institution quickly became a casualty of fast-changing political events and its fate was in the hands of uncontrollable civil circumstances and persons.[61] For nearly two centuries the church's extension and survival in Virginia and the American colonies was dependent on the favourable and protective policies of the crown, the Board of Trade, the influence of provincial royal governors, and the supervision of the Bishop of London. All of these factors were either abruptly or steadily diminished or finally dismantled beginning in 1776.[62]

11

Virginia's Favoured Anglican Church Faces an Unknown Future, 1776

After 170 years the Anglican Church was not a fully-formed extension of the institution in Virginia nor was it an example of a distinctive American church. Its procedures and practices necessarily bridged the Atlantic; one foot was in England and one in the colony. The ministers were required to be ordained by a prelate of the English, Scottish, or Irish Episcopal Church and licensed by the Bishop of London to serve in the colony. It was placed in a difficult position. On the one hand it was an agent of a one-thousand-year-old legacy of the national church and state and on the other hand it faced an unknown, uncontrollable, and turbulent civil present and future.

Throughout the Church's long history after its first worship services at Jamestown in 1608 it was one of the three most prominent faces and symbols of the English imperial establishment in Virginia, in company with the royal government, and the College of William and Mary. Yet each of these institutions was exposed to the consequences of the Declaration of Independence and the War for Independence. Abruptly, imperial administration and the royal governor were swept away in 1776 and replaced by a new state government with Virginia leadership.

The Anglican Church and its ministers were absorbed in the vortex of emerging civil circumstances over which it had neither influence nor control. The institution was an extension of the English state church over which the demon King George III was the Supreme Head. On the provincial landscape its buildings and services publicly reinforced the notion that the church was a vital instrument of the English government and English ways, and not a novel, distinctive, and unfettered colonial religious group. The church established in the province by the House of Burgesses in 1619 popularly represented ties to the homeland and the bonds of objectionable imperial authority and civil policies.

We can only speculate and raise the question, would the English Church have flourished and survived in the province without the protection of official endorsement and support? We do not know. In the uncharted currents of the turbulent times following the Declaration of Independence the church was in a weak position, without leadership and without a unifying voice. A historically hierarchical institution, it was lacking a bishop to lead and speak on behalf of the band of Anglican parsons and congregations in Virginia. All ties with London ecclesiastical officials were severed in 1776 and the church's destiny was lodged in the hands of the members of the new state's General Assembly and not with the traditional custodians, the Bishop of London, the Archbishop of Canterbury, the crown, or parliament.

After about 1690 the Church was increasingly exposed to two contrasting cultural movements, the processes of anglicization and Americanization. On the one hand it enjoyed the favoured status and support of the stronger emerging imperial polices and administrative governance advocated by the Board of Trade in London; on the other, it was exposed to the gradually increasing anglicization movement that influenced American provincial culture. It was a transatlantic influence that was not limited to civil affairs but systematically extended to other aspects of the provincial experience including the architecture of houses, churches, and public buildings, and the dress of persons, and the topographical design of towns and cities. Richard L. Bushman has identified the era as the beginning of the 'age of refinement' in America that introduced 'the changes in America [that] were a variant of changes occurring in all of the British provinces at roughly the same time'.[1] It is difficult to measure the depth and breadth of the movement in terms of design and popular impact but there are markers to identify the cultural force of the process.

A thread of two colours is woven through the structural fabric of the colonial English Church in Virginia and subsequently in the other American provinces, representing a tension between the twin cultural forces. Generally the movement is recognized by historians as paralleling the introduction of stronger imperial policies and royal government in America about 1690. But the chronicle in Virginia is somewhat different because the movement is found in the earliest days of settlement at Jamestown in 1607. The settlers were familiar with only English ways and there was yet to emerge a cultural force that could be characterized as distinctively American. Most obviously, anglicization operated as a political force reshaping institutions of law and government to conform to English practice.[2]

The signposts for the anglicization movement in colonial Virginia are at once recognisable. Included among the most visible were the top-tier imperial officers serving in the provinces, the royal governors, customs officers, tax collectors, admiralty court judges, and military officers. The Anglican Church only partly fits into this civil and military structure. It was the English state church in America and its clergymen, under the supervision of the Bishop of London had taken an oath of allegiance to the crown and parliament when they were ordained. But the members of local congregations did not adhere to the structure of a local English parish church that was governed by either a local patron, a collegiate or corporate patron, or the bishop of the diocese in which the parish was located. In Virginia the members of the vestries were usually representing the local gentry and some were also members of the province's legislature. Only in a few instances, particularly during the seventeenth and eighteenth centuries, did governors intercede in the affairs of local congregations.[3] The anglicization and Americanization tension within the Church affected the English, Scottish, and Irish-born ministers as well as native-born colonists. It was a tension that was present in the affairs of individual congregations, most notably in the occasional conflicts between parsons, vestries, and congregations particularly over salary disputes.

The fledgling church was without the usual ecclesiastical structure familiar in England. Parliament had the authority to create archdioceses, dioceses, and bishoprics but had not done so for Virginia. From the settlement's earliest days the buildings, ministers, and services represented the introduction of the anglicizing religious process. The novelty of a new colony founded in a virgin land prompted new ways for the settlement to live, work, and govern. It was a development that was uniquely American and would gradually become stronger as one generation passed to another. Vestry members and other congregational leaders would exercise an interest in the recruitment, performance, and salaries of the ministers, the maintenance of church buildings, the glebe, and churchyards. The progressively increasing power of individuals in civic affairs also found reception in local parish matters.

The state of the Church during the post-war period and the decades afterwards invites the question, how effective were the royal anglicization policies that established the religious group in the seventeenth century? Was the church marked by the influence of imperial authorities, beleaguered by financial resources, and without strong popular support and loyalty? The momentum of the proceedings of the First Continental Congress in Philadelphia in September and October 1774, followed by the Declaration of Independence on 4 July 1776 and the outbreak of the War for Independence, signalled startlingly changed circumstances for the destiny of the Anglican Church.[4]

In the face of the civil movement during the 1770s and 1780s to disestablish the Church in Virginia attempts were vainly undertaken by Church leaders to preserve some of the privileges of the pre-Revolutionary War period. Their position was out of step with the popular temper of the times and of political leaders who were opposed to any state financial support for religion. No other religious group in the American colonies encountered such a drastic change in its status and situation.

While imperial officials and the royal government were swept away with the fast-paced civil events in the wake of the Declaration of Independence the Church remained. Yet the institution was severely scarred and reshaped by the radical course of action. Ironically, it was the Church's role as a national English institution that fostered its extension to Virginia and the other American colonies in the seventeenth century and that in the 1760s and 1770s exposed the church and its ministers to challenges of conspiratorial activity and questionable loyalties.

The ranks of ministers and church buildings were diminished by the upheaval of political and military events. Among the thirteen rebelling colonies the number of congregations and ministers of the Anglican Church in America was comparatively strongest in Virginia. In 1775 there were 95 primary and 154 secondary churches in the colony.[5] But it remains unclear how many of the churches conducted regular services during and after the war, and how many of the lay members drifted away from regular church attendance.[6] At least some buildings that closed did not reopen their doors again. In 1776 there were 120 active ministers in the colony but at the end of the war in 1783 the number had dwindled to 67 parsons. Death claimed 25 men, retirement another 15, while 12 parsons fled to England and 5 to another new state. In addition the clergymen demonstrated their support of the American cause in other ways: 25 became members of their county's Committee of Public Safety and 13 served as chaplains in either the Virginia militia or the Continental Army.[7]

Services of worship followed the Offices and Sacraments of the Book of Common Prayer, an English Church in an American colonial setting serving the residents of a local community. But there was an important difference, the ranks of the ministers were not entirely English or composed only of colonists. In 1775 the men had diverse origins including the following: Virginia, 42, Connecticut and Pennsylvania, 3 each,

New York and Maryland, 2 each, New Jersey, 1, Scotland, 28, England, 19, Ireland, 4, and 16 whose national origins are unknown. Many of the men had married into the gentry and were well established in the province.[8]

The pages of published vestry books covering the period between 1777 and 1783 rarely mention ministers holding worship services. Perhaps the clergymen were reluctant to do so because of the uncertainty that they would be paid. The legislature in 1777 terminated their annual payment in tobacco and shifted the responsibility to the vestries to raise voluntary contributions from members of the congregations to meet the parson's salaries. I have not found a vestry that was able to do so. Strained financial circumstances required vestries to rent glebe houses, church lands, and parish and vestry houses to generate funds to meet the obligations of serving the poor.[9]

Another turn of events that marked the Church followed political affairs and occurred at the annual meetings of the parish vestries in early 1777. Surviving records indicate that an initial round of resignations of members of the bodies occurred at that time and continued until 1784.[10] The pace of resignations held relatively steady until 1780 when the number increased coincidentally at the appearance of the larger British military presence on land and at sea. The first major British invasion of Virginia occurred in 1779 and was followed by Alexander Leslie's forces in October 1780, Benedict Arnold's in January 1781, and William Phillip's in March 1781.[11] General Charles Cornwallis arrived with the main British army in May 1781 for a campaign climaxing in his defeat by George Washington at Yorktown in October of that year.[12] The resignations of the vestrymen are of special notice because of the usual pattern of longevity of the members. Professor John K. Nelson has indicated that many members of the bodies frequently served for 20, 30, 35 or even 40 years and that certain planter and merchant families dominated the membership.[13] The evidence that survives does not provide us with a clue about the vestrymen's reasons for their resignations. Perhaps some of the men resigned their posts because of age, sickness, declining health, or simply for a release from the duty.

Before an elected vestryman or church warden could assume office he was required to swear six or seven oaths including the following: the Test Oath, of Conformity to the Doctrine and Discipline of the Church of England, of a Vestryman, of a Church Warden, of Allegiance to the King, of Abjuration of the Pope, and of Renunciation of the (Stuart) Pretender to the English throne.[14] Understandably in light of the changing provincial political situation and popular Patriot opinion the vestry members may have decided to disassociate themselves from the body and sever any connection with an English institution. Perhaps their decision was based on fear of personal political retribution over being allied with an English institution, or from a continuing membership with the body that would represent a loss of social prestige.

The condition came to the attention of the legislature on several occasions between 1775 and 1784 and the body attempted to resolve the matter. As early as December 1775 the General Assembly was concerned for the responsible and diligent governance of parish affairs by vestrymen. At that time the legislature instructed the vestrymen of Frederick Parish to abandon their negligent ways and resume their duties, and warned that if they refused to do so the body would be dissolved and a new vestry elected.[15] Beginning at the session in May 1775 and continuing until 1784 the legislative body of the new state from time to time enacted laws to dissolve individual parish vestries on the grounds that the bodies comprised self-perpetuating members not elected by the freeholders and housekeepers of the district.[16] However, the bodies were dissolved also by the legislature's reconfiguration of county and parish boundaries.[17] Professor Nelson has noted that it was a procedure that had been more commonly applied during the decades after 1740 to 1776 but in light of the war now took on a new complexion.[18]

Cascading radical civil and military events cast eroding shadows over the provincial Church. No longer embraced by the state the institution was unleashed from its political and financial moorings after more than 160 years and required to subsist on voluntary contributions. New legislation in 1777 required that all financial obligations for each congregation, including the payment of the parson's salary and the construction and maintenance of church buildings, were terminated and transferred from the state to the local congregation's vestry. It faced a change of name too from the English Church or the Anglican Church to the Episcopal Church. New circumstances required the need to create a diocese, elect a bishop, and recruit clergymen to reinforce the diminished corps to serve the languishing pre-Revolutionary War congregations.

In 1786 the church was disestablished by the legislature with relative ease, and a political heritage dating from 1607 and 1619 was dissolved. The new age required the colonial church to reconstitute and reconstruct itself and subsist on the contributions of members. The Episcopal Church in Virginia, as it became known in the 1780s, was marked and scarred for decades and would not recover its eighteenth-century position until after the Civil War and during the 'Gilded Age'.

Writing from the vicarage in Epsom, County Surrey, in England in the mid-1790s, the exiled Loyalist and former Virginia and Maryland schoolmaster and parson Jonathan Boucher offered his observations on the state of the American church. He arrived in Virginia in 1759 as a schoolmaster and returned to London for ordination. After serving parishes in Virginia for a decade Boucher moved to Annapolis in 1771 as rector of St Anne's Church. But writing more than twenty years after he had fled his church in Maryland, Boucher unhesitatingly complained that the American situation was plagued by British officials who had little information of provincial commercial affairs, and worse, took no initiative to inform themselves on such matters. He pungently observed that those colonial officials entrusted with providing such details were 'either too ignorant, or too knavish to give any to be depended upon'.[19]

As early as 1769 the parson supported colonial opposition to the Townshend Acts, 'I do think the American opposition the most warrantable, generous, and manly that history can produce'.[20] He pointed his finger at the weakness of imperial government in America that reflected a general feebleness of social institutions, of which the precarious English Church was a primary example. Where there was no loyalty to the church, he wrote, there could not be loyalty to the state. He lamented the absence of bishops in the colonies, and the poverty and indifferent discipline of the church. Americans, he remarked, were 'not sufficiently aware of the importance of externals in religion'.[21]

Boucher declared that in the south [Virginia], the discipline of the Church of England was more nearly Presbyterian than Episcopal, and the ministers had to cater to the tastes of their congregations to an undignified degree: '*Voice and action*...almost constantly carried it'.[22] With so little attention by the state to the church, 'it was small wonder', Boucher thought, that nothing was 'so wholly without form or comeliness, as government in America'.[23]

Turning his attention to the state of the parsons Boucher declared that they were 'so established as in no small degree to be still dependent on the People, and on them alone. In Virginia, they were elected to their benefices by the People; and though, by examination of the Virginia acts of establishment as those acts appear on paper, the Clergy, after their election, might have been thought to have been placed beyond the reach of popular control, yet every man who had a practical acquaintance with the country before the revolution must know that this was not the case'.[24]

His trenchant recollection of the state of the Church in Virginia and Maryland in 1775 declared that 'excepting the provision made for the maintenance of ministers (which merely through a change of circumstances during a long course of years has in some instances become considerable and handsome) everything relating to religion is formed on a narrow and contracted scale. Our churches, in general, are ordinary and mean buildings, composed of wood, without spires or towers, or steeples, or bells, and placed for the most part, (like those of our remotest ancestors in Great Britain), no longer perhaps the depth of forests, yet still in retired and solitary spots, and contiguous to springs or wells'.[25] The interior of the churches were bleak and simple where 'there is rarely even an attempt to introduce any ornaments; it is almost uncommon to find a church in Maryland that has any communion plate, as it is in England to find one that has not; in both Virginia and Maryland there are not six organs'.[26]

A visiting French layman and officer to Virginia during 1780, 1781, and 1782, the Marquis Francois-Jean de Chastellaux a talented gentleman and member of the French Academy, observed the state of the Virginia Church.[27] He wrote in his *Travels in North America* that 'The predominant [religion] before the Revolution was the Anglican religion, which, as is well known, requires episcopacy and that every priest must be ordained by a bishop. Before the war people went to England to study and be ordained. It is therefore impossible under present circumstances to fill the pastorates that have become vacant. What has been the consequence of this? The churches have remained shut, people have done without a minister, and have not even thought of any future arrangements for establishing an Anglican church independent of England. The most complete tolerance has been established; nor have other communions made any gains from the losses of the former; each sect has remained as it was, and this sort of religious interregnum had caused no disorder. The clergy, furthermore, have received a further setback in the new constitution, which forbids them any share in the government, even the right of voting at elections'.[28]

Following the Revolutionary War and the severance of ties to the English Church, to the Bishop of London and the Archbishop of Canterbury, the remnant of the colonial Church of England in the United States had to be reorganized and reconstituted in each state and nationally.[29] The celebrated jurist John Marshall thought the Church was 'too far gone ever to be revived'. After a decade of service Bishop James Madison, a nephew of the future president, in 1800 found his Virginia diocese so diminished by the loss of clergy and communicants that following years of attempting to revive interest in the church he abandoned the struggle. He limited his efforts to serving as president of the College of William and Mary.[30]

Dublin native Isaac Weld noted in his travels through Virginia in the spring of 1796 that in Norfolk there 'are two churches, one for the episcopalians the other for Methodists. In the former, service is not performed more than once in two or three weeks, and very little regard is paid by the people in general to Sunday. Indeed throughout the lower parts of Virginia that is between the mountains and the sea the people have scarcely any sense of religion and in the country parts the churches are falling into decay. As I rode along, I scarcely observed any one that was not in a ruinous condition, with the windows broken, and doors dropping off the hinges, and lying open to the pigs and cattle wondering about the woods; yet many of these were not past repair. The churches in Virginia, excepting such as are in towns, stand for the most part in the woods, retired from among houses, and it does not appear that any persons are appointed to pay the smallest attention to them'.[31]

Throughout the new thirteen United States the experience of the church was similar; it had been dislocated, disrupted, and weakened by the war. Everywhere the congregations were smaller, the church buildings in disrepair, and the ranks of the parsons significantly reduced. The General Convention of the national church held in New York City in 1792 included only 19 clerical and 14 lay delegates and five recently consecrated bishops. In the 1811 Journal of the General Convention it was noted that 'the Church in Virginia is from various causes, so depressed, that there is danger of her ruin, unless great exertions ... are employed to raise her'.[32] Three years later at the triennial convention of the Church Virginia did not report the number of ministers either residing or ministering but it is estimated that about 50 parsons were serving churches in the state. The saga of the church was unchanged, with one observer noting that the institution had 'fallen into a deplorable condition' in many places her ministers have thrown off their sacred profession; her liturgy is either contemned or unknown, and her sanctuaries are desolate. It would rend any feeling to heart, to see spacious temples venerable even in their dilapidation and ruins, now the habitations of the wild beast of the forest'.[33]

Uncontrollable circumstances dictated the Church's tenuous and uncertain position shaped by the unravelling of the old order and partly trapped by the vortex of noisy and escalating radical political rhetoric. After more than 170 years in the colony the Church was vulnerable to the ideas and whims of popular opinion. Its status as an extension of the English state church and an association with a succession of impe-rial governors in league with the statutes enacted by the members of the provincial legislature fashioned its position. On the east wall of the most prominent Anglican churches in Newport, New York City, and else-where was displayed the coat-of-arms of the English monarchy, a visible reminder that the reigning monarch, George III, was the Supreme Head of the Anglican Church.

The Church in Virginia in 1776 was represented by a chain of indi-vidual congregations. Events closed churches, services were suspended, and the political opinions of the parsons frequently challenged by neighbours. Like the former provincial imperial government the church represented the old order linked to the authority and power of the crown and parliament. It was not at worship or in polity a distinctively American church as were the Congregational, Presbyterian, Baptist, and other religious groups.[34] Yet the church was not a fully formed Anglican institution with the traditional English and Irish episcopal appara-tus of bishops, deaneries, archdeaconries, dioceses, archdioceses, and cathedrals. Such an ecclesiastical structure was unfamiliar and probably unwanted by non-Anglican observers and critics and Anglican lay per-sons. Republican ideas of civil government replaced the former regime and spilled over to influence the procedures for reconstructing and reconstituting the colonial Anglican Church in a framework embracing democratic and republican political thought. There were no 'patrons of livings' such as bishops, colleges, or landed gentry overseeing local parish affairs. Instead there was an elected vestry of local community residents providing oversight of congregational matters.

Virginia became the first state to adopt a declaration of rights, on 12 June 1776, and, on 29 June, the first republican constitution. Fol-lowing the Continental Congress's Declaration of Independence on 4 July in Philadelphia the Virginia Convention later in the month addressed a political agenda and introduced and approved changes in the Prayer Book of the Church of England in the province. The leg-islative body eliminated from the Daily Offices all references to the king and royal family and inserted prayers for the magistrates of the Commonwealth.[35]

Notwithstanding the large ranks of English ministers in Virginia the strongest printed contributions in support of or in opposition to the colonial radical resistance movement to the English imperial policies in the 1760s and 1770s came from the pens of colleagues in the New England and Middle Colonies. We do not find in Williamsburg or the major towns of any other American colony a prominent public official or layman who stood up in the heat of the times and declaimed or published an essay in defence of the tenets and presence of the Anglican Church. We are left to question, why were the lay members of the Church silent? What did the church mean to them? Was the institution of so little importance in their personal lives that it could not nudge a few lines and offer sentiments on its behalf?

Anecdotal evidence suggests that a number of persons left the church after 1776. Was the movement a modest or larger migration of persons, or a mass exodus? Because it was the English Church, and anti-English sentiments loomed large in wartime Virginia, members could easily register their disaffection by walking away from the institution and not supporting the new independent church. We learn from the pages of the post-war and nineteenth-century proceedings of the triennial General Convention of the reconstituted Protestant Episcopal Church in the United States of America that the ranks of Virginia ministers and members were significantly reduced for several decades after the War for Independence.[36]

Virginia, the strongest church in the thirteen colonies and now the new states, played a modest role in the reorganization and reconstitution of the colonial Church as the Protestant Episcopal Church in the United States of America. For the establishment of an American episcopate and an American edition of the Book of Common Prayer the key leadership was exercised by clergymen from the former New England and Middle Colonies including William White of Pennsylvania, Samuel Provost of New York, Samuel Parker of Massachusetts, and Samuel Seabury of Connecticut.[37]

Between 1790 and 1876 four men served in succession as bishop of the Virginia Church including James Madison (1790–1812), Richard C. Moore (1814–41), William Meade (1842–62), and John Johns (1862–76). Each prelate struggled with common and unique problems. Madison attempted to revitalize the church but became disillusioned about the prospects and largely confined his efforts to serving as president of the struggling College of William and Mary for 35 years. Moore followed and focused his attention on the beleaguered congregations. At the time of his death in 1841 the Church was served by 95 clergymen, a number below the 120 members of the corps in 1775 but 28 more ministers than were available in 1783.[38] Following Moore in the episcopal office was the historian and antiquarian William Meade (1842–62), who led the church to the early years of the Civil War and withdrew it from the national church. He became the presiding bishop of the recently formed church in the Confederate states. Johns succeeded Meade in

1862 and after the war brought the church back into the fold of the national church.

In retrospect, the Anglican Church enjoyed the immense advantage of imperial favour yet was not the beneficiary of entrenched and loyal popular support nor free of financial concerns. Shielded on the one hand as an erastian institution, the church was challenged on the other hand by critics of the Book of Common Prayer, the legitimacy of the episcopal office, and other factors including the social and religious consequences of the Great Awakening, the appearance of new religious groups, an increased population, and the flow of immigration from non-English nations. It was exposed to strident criticisms to its historical traditions and practices by non-Anglican ministers in New England and the Middle Colonies, the essays being occasionally reprinted in the Williamsburg newspapers during the 1760s and 1770s. It was forceful commentary that deserved and required a reply. The issues could not be ignored and turned an esoteric ecclesiastical debate into a civil and constitutional issue.

Historically the strongest link to the early Virginia Church is the group of surviving late seventeenth- and eighteenth-century church buildings. Their notable and attractive exterior and interior architectural features reflect in part the tensions that gripped the church over the long colonial era. Apparent are the traces of English ecclesiastical form and the uniquely American style of the meeting house. But our eyes are framed by the memorable design of such colonial church building as Bruton Parish in Williamsburg and two Christ Churches, one in Philadelphia and the other in Boston, all reminders of a connection with the London churches designed by Christopher Wren in the early eighteenth century.

In step with political events in Virginia and the other twelve colonies, the War for Independence closed the colonial period for the Anglican Church. It was launched on a new and uncertain period for the institution without the burdensome ties to the state or English religious leaders. The task at hand was to reshape and reorganize the colonial Church as an American religious body.

12
The College of William and Mary Faces an Unknown Future, 1776

The College of William and Mary, the Anglican Church, and the royal governors were the most prominent figureheads of crown authority in the colony, but the college was the weakest of the three. The institution was continuously financially fragile and in need of funds to build and maintain its facilities, recruit faculty members and meet operating expenses. Its urgent need for funds was not resolved after the War for Independence and the institution faced decades of difficult circumstances and financial uncertainty.

The college encountered the same forces of anglicization and Americanization that were faced by the English Church. It also confronted an unknown future in the wake of the disruptive civil and military events of the 1770s and 1780s. The institution had been plagued with annual shortfalls of operating funds and a constant need to recruit students from among local residents. It was not a regional or national institution of the status of Harvard or Yale in New England. Ingrained in its history was an account of an institution constantly teetering on the brink of insolvency from its beginning. The college was affiliated with the church and lingered until the 1880s when it was finally rescued from financial collapse and became a state institution.

Commissary James Blair, the Bishop of London's chief deputy in Virginia since 1689, was the leader in seeking the establishment of a college.[1] His efforts in London beginning 1 September 1691 included gaining the support for the charter by such influential ecclesiastical and state leaders as Bishop of Salisbury Gilbert Burnet, Bishop of London Henry Compton, and Archbishop of Canterbury John Tillotson (1630–94).[2] Blair's efforts culminated in King William and Queen Mary granting a Royal Charter for the College of William and Mary on 14 February, 1692/93.[3]

Under the terms for granting the charter King William requested that Blair provide Bishop of London Compton with details for funding the institution. If agreeable to the prelate and the Archbishop of Canterbury John Tillotson the matter would be further considered by the Lords of Trade, a committee of the Privy Council. The Privy Council on 28 July 1692 authorized the charter providing that the attorney general confirmed the legitimacy of the financial support offered by the crown.[4] The document designated Henry Compton Bishop of London as chancellor and Blair as president of the College for life.[5]

The idea and effort to establish a college had flourished irregularly since 1617 and seems to have been intimately linked to the founding of Trinity College in Dublin in 1592.[6] Trinity represented one element of the anglicization policies of the English government to aid the consolidation of English rule in Ireland in the last decade of Elizabeth I's reign.[7] It has been regarded by historians as the first of the colonial colleges founded by thrifty Puritans, preceding Harvard by forty-five years and Yale by more than a century.[8] During the first two centuries Trinity was a College exclusively for those known as the 'Protestant Ascendancy' in Ireland, and Cambridge influence was strong. Trinity's first five Provosts were educated at Cambridge, at the time the seedbed of Puritan writings and thought.[9]

As early as 18 November 1618 the Virginia Company of London included the need to establish a college in the colony in the Instructions granted to the new Governor George Yeardley.[10] In lockstep the House of Burgesses at the first session of the delegates on 31 July 1619 petitioned the Treasurer of the Council of the Virginia Company of London seeking 'workmen of all sorts fit for the purpose of constructing the buildings of a University and College'.[11] Presumably the applicants were requesting the recruitment and services of such craftsmen as woodworkers, joiners, brick-makers, masons and so forth.[12] The same year the Company moved to grant 1,000 acres of land in the colony to support the founding of the University of Henrico with special attention for an Indian College, and English prelates raised about £1,500 to aid and launch the proposal.[13] Over the next few years a handful of persons in Virginia and England contributed books and funds for the benefit of the proposed institution.[14]

But any substantial efforts on behalf of the college were terminated by the Good Friday Massacre at Henrico on 22 March 1622 waged by the Algonquin warriors, at which men, women, and children were slain in a raid that provoked a series of retaliatory actions. The event shook to the foundation the commercial viability of the colony, terminated discussions about the college, and called into question the prospect of the province's survival.

The next round of interest for a college did not occur until October 1660, when the General Assembly of the sparsely settled province of about 27,020 persons renewed efforts to found an institution with three purposes: 'that the Church of England in Virginia may be furnished with a seminary of ministers of the gospel, and that the youth may be piously educated in good letters and manners, and that the Christian faith may be propagated amongst the Western Indians, to the glory of Almighty God'.[15] Five months later, at the March 1660/61 Assembly the delegates stated that a college was necessary 'for the education of ministers that are in short supply' and that the distance from Virginia to Oxford or Cambridge universities was a handicap for native colonists as prospective students. The legislators agreed that land should be set aside and allotted for a free school and college as soon as possible and the construction of a building undertaken.[16] But rather than the legislature leading and offering an appropriation or urging contributions from the public, the Assembly members enacted a statute that declared efforts should be undertaken to raise funds in England for a college and provincial schools and requested that Oxford and Cambridge Colleges should be enlisted to recruit ministers for Virginia congregations.[17] The governor, council members, and burgesses led the way by contributing 'considerable sums of money and quantities of tobacco to be paid to the General Assembly or Treasurer'.[18]

Public efforts on behalf of the college were probably delayed by the cross-currents of political unrest in Virginia and England during the 1670s and 1680s. Civil events cast a conflicting shadow over provincial affairs in the 1670s, particularly in 1675 and 1676 with actions that led to Bacon's Rebellion, while in the 1680s constitutional issues in England following the death of Charles II in 1685 and the flight from the throne of James II in 1688 created political instability and a constitutional revolution.

Blair, on his journey to London to obtain a charter for the college, carried an additional task: the lawmakers urged him to solicit financial support to aid the construction of buildings for the institution and to meet the operating expenses.[19] After his return to Virginia, Blair seems to have moved quickly to establish the college: the Grammar School opened in 1694 with a few students in a temporary building in Middle Plantation before the cornerstone for the college building was laid on 8 August 1695.[20] But two years later the building remained unfinished and some subscribers had not paid their contributions.[21] The trustees of the college reported to Governor Edmund Andros in early 1697 that 'the building and furnishing of the College was almost at a stop for want of money' and stated that 'we have desired Mr. President Blair to go to England [again] to procure what he can towards finishing it'.[22] Contributors failed to complete pledges, the legislature substituted land grants for cash appropriations, there was little support from local well-to-do planters and merchants, and there were no benefactors in the colony or England of the stature and substance of John Harvard and Elihu Yale, whose philanthropy was honoured in the naming of two early New England institutions.

On the occasion of the granting of a charter in 1693 King William and Queen Mary provided the College with 'near two thousand pounds in ready cash out of the Bank of Quit Rents' to apply upon the erection of the building. In addition, 'Towards the Endowment the king gave the neat (i.e. net) produce of the Penny per pound in Virginia and Maryland, worth £200 per annum; and the Surveyor-General's tax of one pence on each hundred weight of tobacco shipped from Virginia to any other American colony worth about £50 per annum.[23] It was not a steady and stable stream of income until the Surveyor General's death in 1695, after which it became possible for the college to collect fees for surveyor's licenses.[24] To provide financial assistance for Trinity College in Dublin, Elizabeth I in 1597 granted 20,000 acres of land to the institution and James I gave additional properties in 1610 and 1613.[25] The Virginia the General Assembly followed suit nearly a century later and offered the institution the choice of 10,000 acres in Pamunkey Neck and 10,000 more on the south side of Blackwater Swamp. In addition the legislature gave the College a duty on 'Skins and Furrs worth better than £100 a year'.[26] The total amount pledged by people in the colony for the college when subscriptions were first received was more than £2,500. But Blair said that on account of the attitude of Governor Andros, no further pledges were made and not more than £500 of the amounts pledged could be collected.[27]

One observer, Mungo Inglis, a recently arrived Scottish clergyman and faculty member commented in 1697, that 'the people of Virginia are at present in a kind of lethargy in regard to so noble a building as well as pious design as no doubt it was originally. And by I know not what mismanagement of those that have it in their hands they think it either as cheap as their children's education as capable of improving elsewhere as now in the college, which argues no great dependence on the President'.[28]

The institution's first years of instruction and fund raising were cut short when a fire in 1705 destroyed the College building and forced the College to suspend admission of students. It was not until Queen Anne contributed £1,000 in 1709 that it became possible to begin to rebuild the facility but it was not until 1716 that it was reconstructed and classes resumed.[29] The financial situation was so desperate that Blair's salary was suspended between 1705 and 1721. He travelled again to England and spent much of 1726–27 raising funds for the institution with the assistance of Bishop of London, Edmund Gibson.[30] In 1729, nearly three and a half decades after the College opened, Blair entered formally on the duties of the office as president.

Blair linked the College's continuing financial crisis directly to the lack of leadership and support of several successive royal governors in the province. He claimed that the governors were not fulfilling the terms of their royal commissions and instructions to serve the interests of the college and the Anglican Church.[31] He complained to Bishop of London Henry Compton, a member of the Board of Trade, in a 1697 'Memorial' that Governor Andros neglected to serve the needs of the provincial church and college.[32] He argued that 27 of the 50 congregations in Virginia were without ministers; that parson's salaries were deficient; and that the recently founded college was in need of urgent provincial financial assistance.[33] Countering the commissary's complaints Andros criticized Blair's supervision of the church: declaring that too many Scotsmen were appointed as instructors at the college; that Blair exercised little discipline over erring ministers; and that the deputy drew more than enough salary from college funds (£150 colonial currency annually). The heat of the controversy favoured Blair and forced Governor Andros to resign his post.

Six years later Blair attacked Francis Nicholson, Andros's successor, when he complained to Bishop Compton that the governor demonstrated a personal streak of "hypocrisy and profaneness'.[34] Joined by five members of the Virginia Council, Blair presented to Queen Anne in 1703 a 'Memorial' disparaging the arbitrariness and maladministration of Nicholson's regime.[35] The governor counter-attacked by summoning the Virginia clergy to a convention at Williamsburg on 25 August 1703 for a discussion of the dispute.[36] Twenty of the 38 ministers active in the colony at the time were in attendance at the meeting and, after hearing a presentation of the two adversaries, supported Nicholson's position and his administration.[37] The men concluded that Blair's action had stirred-up public contempt for the clergy. They recommended to the

Bishop of London that Blair should be required to confine himself to furthering his ecclesiastical duties with the aid of the colony's well-to-do planters rather than indulge in such divisive political affairs. Yet Blair's unrelenting criticism carried the day and forced the Board of Trade to recall Nicholson in 1705.[38]

Nearly twenty years later, Blair's dispute with Governor Alexander Spotswood in 1719 and 1720 brewed for several years: although it was not primarily about college affairs the debate probably impeded and impaired its development and status.[39] Blair objected outspokenly to Spotswood's efforts to impose additional imperial authority over such local institutions as the judiciary, the Colonial Council, and the right of vestrymen to induct into parishes ministers of their choosing. He revisited a key complaint against Andros two decades earlier that claimed Andros had withheld granting the use of glebes to several ministers because the vestries had not presented the men to the livings, a situation that led Andros not to intercede and induct the clergymen.[40] Following Nicholson's example, Spotswood called the clergy to a convention in 1719 with the specific purpose of bluntly challenging Blair's charges. Again the clergy were divided in their support of the commissary and the governor. Yet Spotswood emerged from the controversy a blighted official and in 1722 was recalled by the Board of Trade.

Following Spotswood as governor on 25 September 1722 was the Irish-born Hugh Drysdale (d. 1726). He was a son of an archdeacon, an experienced army officer, and a classmate at Queen's College, Oxford, of Bishop of London Gibson.[41] In rapidly failing health he nonetheless delivered a message to the members of the House of Burgesses on 12 May 1726 strongly recommending financial assistance for the institution because 'It lies in a languishing state and wants help to found their full number of Masters, which when once perfected will make a Nobel Seminary not only for the Education of your young Gentleman in the Liberal Arts and Sciences but for furnishing your churches with a sett of sober divines born of yourselves and bred among you, advantages of greater importance than at present you may be aware of'.[42] The governor's urgent plea went unanswered.

Financial matters did not improve over the next few years, and in mid-January 1734/35 Blair informed the Chancellor of the College, Bishop Gibson, that 'we have had a fatal blow of late in our Revenues, the penny per pound [of tobacco] which King William and Queen Mary gave for the support of the President and Masters being now so sunk, that (through the fraud of the Exporters to the West Indies) it doth not yield above £100 per annum instead of £400 it yielded formerly'.[43] He stated that the recent session of the General Assembly have provided some funds but that it would be about eighteen months before any benefit was derived from the appropriation. Blair anticipated that the institution would accumulate a deficit of about £1,000 for the academic year. Continuing he indicated that the governor and council could easily assist the college and he believed they would do so 'if they had a line of encouragement from our Superiors out of a fund here raised for the support of this Government'.[44] President Blair asked Gibson if he 'could think it proper to sound Sir R[obert] Walpole or his brother our Auditor [of the Plantations, Horatio Walpole] on this subject, perhaps a favourable letter might be obtained, for it is a fund solely appropriated to this Country'.[45]

Later in the year Blair renewed his plea on behalf of the College and detailed the provincial fund that could be tapped for assistance.[46] 'The Revenue of this country is either what we call the quitrents or the Two shillings per hogshead of tobacco exported'. He informed the bishop: 'The first of these is a small duty paid annually to the King, and excepting some Grants his Majesty or his predecessors have made out of this, there is no Authority here pretends to meddle with it, but it is from time to time transmitted to England. I know it would be difficult to obtain a grant of any part of this, and therefore took care to acquaint your Lordship that it was not this revenue of quitrents, out of which any relief to the college should be proposed'. 'The other Revenue of two shillings per hogshead', ... is an account 'appropriated by law to defray all the charges of the government here, such as the Governor's and Council's salaries, repairs of the Governor's house, messages &c and all other both ordinary and extraordinary charges of the government and applied only to this use, and the accounts are yearly transmitted to the auditor of the plantations, this fund is never transmitted to England, but has been applied by the Governor and Council to those services of the Country, to which they are appropriated by law'. Blair declared that there was a surplus balance in the fund and it could be tapped to aid the college's financial needs.[47]

The London prelate informed Blair that he presented the matter to government officials but a response had not been received.[48] Blair's pleas to Gibson coincided with the bishop's decline in influence with the Walpole government in parliament over the Quaker Relief Bill in 1736. The eclipse marked his episcopacy until his death in 1748.[49] Neither Blair nor Gibson discussed the matter of the Walpole government's financial assistance for the college again before Blair's passing in 1743.

President Blair never retreated in his efforts to raise funds to build or rebuild college facilities and did not abandon the need to recruit students and faculty.[50] In 1699, 29 students were enrolled at the institution, about 21 in 1705, and 60 in 1737.[51] In 1712 the faculty consisted of Blair and Mungo Inglis, who served as an usher, writing master, and Professor of the Grammar School.[52] A Professor of Mathematics was appointed later in the year and a Professor of Philosophy in 1717.[53] During the next 20 years the foundation for Brafferton House to serve as a place for instruction and residence for Indian students was laid (1723), the Chapel opened (1732), and the residence for the President begun (1739).[54]

The College's origins differed significantly from the two Anglican-related institutions established in the Middle Colonies in the 1750s. In Pennsylvania, the College of Philadelphia, now the University of Pennsylvania, was established in 1753 under the leadership of the Scotsman William Smith in concert with a coalition of local Anglican, Presbyterian, and Quaker leaders.[55] While in New York City, King's College, now Columbia University was founded in 1754 by an alliance of Dutch Reformed and Anglican community leaders who recruited as its first president Samuel Johnson, a Yale graduate. A former tutor at Yale College and a convert from the Congregational Church, he served as minister of the Church in Stratford, Connecticut.[56] Both institutions were from their beginnings stronger collegiate institutions than William and Mary in financial support, faculty, and curriculum.

Blair faced the continuing task of recruiting faculty members and protecting the charter from falling under the control of political leaders and other lay persons. In the first instance the charter of 1693 was in urgent need of revision and compliance with the original terms of the document. The governance of the institution was required to be transferred from the authority of the founding trustees as soon as a president and six masters were in office.[57] At the time Blair and the Reverend Stephen Fouace were the last two surviving men of the original founders of the college and they initiated the efforts to transfer the governing authority of the institution to the President and Masters.[58] Blair and Fouace's position was to expand the responsibilities of the 1693 charter for the governance, faculty structure, curriculum, and student discipline for the college. But they also introduced an unclear division of authority between the faculty and the Board of Visitors for the governance of the College.[59] Blair energetically recruited and appointed new faculty members during 1728 and 1729 to meet the obligation and fulfil his mission.[60] It was a politically complicated process and Blair was fixed on transferring the charter into the hands of the institution's faculty. The original charter noted that the faculty, on the occasion of the transfer of responsibilities, would supervise day-to-day matters at the college and manage the institution's financial affairs. Given the lack of financial support for the college after more than 35 years Blair probably felt strongly that the duty should be reserved to the faculty. While the Board of Visitors gained new power including the right to amend the statutes and to appoint faculty, the authority to dismiss faculty members remained unclear and would be a key issue in dispute between the two parties later.[61] On 15 August 1729 the transfer of the charter occurred from the hands of the original trustees to President Blair and the faculty members and was fulfilled at their next meeting when they were required to subscribe to the Thirty-nine Articles and swear allegiance to George II.[62] For the next forty years the statutes were a source of contention between the faculty and the Visitors in persistent efforts to intrude and influence collegiate affairs including the recruitment and dismissal of faculty.

Blair's death in 1743 concluded the first phase of the college's story, one that was firmly anchored in the last days of the seventeenth century and the strong designs of imperial anglicization policies of the Council of Trade and Plantations. His passing also marks the beginning of a new 40-year era in London's civil and ecclesiastical leadership. New faces and names guided imperial policies and administration from London through the years before the outbreak of the War for Independence, including kings George II and George III (1727–60, 1760–1820), Prime Ministers Robert Walpole (1730–42), the Earl of Wilmington (1742), Henry Pelham (1743–46), and twelve additional leaders until 1783. Between 1737 and 1783 five men served as Archbishop of Canterbury: John Potter (1737–47), Thomas Herring (1747–57), Matthew Hutton (1757–58), Thomas Secker (1758–68), and Frederick Cornwallis (1768–83). Only Secker among the corps of civil and ecclesiastical leaders took a keen interest in advancing American church affairs.[63] It remained the duty of the Bishop of London to play a central role in American church affairs and between 1723 and 1787 six men served: the politically neutralized Edmund Gibson (1723–48), Thomas Sherlock (1748–61), Thomas Hayter (1761–62), Richard Osbaldeston (1762–4),Richard Terrick (1764–77), and Robert Lowth (1778–87). Among the group Sherlock stands out as the lone prelate exercising an informed and active effort to support and assist the church in the colonies but, for various reasons, he received no support from the five successive governments serving in England during his episcopate.[64]

Following Blair's passing, seven men successively served as head of the college during the next forty years.[65] In contrast to Blair's long leadership at the institution his immediate heirs served a range of between three and nine years, with an average of five-and-a-half years in office. They held the position under changing and increasingly thorny political circumstances. But none of the men were able to follow in Blair's footsteps and achieve his level of influence in provincial affairs as a member of the Colonial Council or with civil and ecclesiastical leaders in London. He was familiar with the details of the colonial government's imperial policies and financial affairs and his wily headship and association with high-level London ecclesiastical leaders and provincial civil officials were not duplicated again. It was a tumultuous period for the institution.

During the two decades before the Declaration of Independence two major external issues involved members of the College faculty: the debate over the Parson's Cause of 1755 and the Two-Penny Acts of 1755 and 1758, and the dispute over the prospective appointment of an American Anglican bishop in 1769, 1770, and 1771. The Parson's Cause argument pitted the faculty against the college's president and Thomas Dawson, the commissary of the Bishop of London, and continued through his successors in the post, William Yates (1761–64), and James Horrocks (1764–71). The short-lived controversy surrounding the prospect of the appointment of an American bishop divided the faculty members along the line of either supporting or opposing the proposal.[66]

After the transfer of the Charter in 1729 to the President and Masters of the College the members of the Board of Visitors, or trustees, differed regularly over the administration of the institution, the quality and performance of faculty members, the statutes of governance, the effectiveness of the president, and the efficiency of student discipline. The disputes were at heart a clash of authority over issues that customarily belonged to the faculty and those that were reserved for the Visitors. But the faculty's resolve and opposition had been shaped by four decades of attempts by the Board of Visitors to impose lay authority over the affairs of the college. The faculty faced, too, during the 1760s and 1770s relentless criticisms by the members of the Board of Visitors regarding the college's instruction.[67]

Seeking total control over the affairs of the college and faculty the Visitors in the 1760s were intent on a revision of the college statutes.[68] The institution was in a vulnerable position, three persons served in quick succession as president and several faculty members were discharged for failings in personal conduct and behaviour.[69] Unlike Harvard and Yale, whose faculties were by now largely drawn from their own graduates, the College of William and Mary throughout the colonial period was dependent on the recruitment of a majority of its faculty from England.[70] Perhaps it is coincidence that conflict between the Visitors and faculty raged so vigorously between 1764 and 1768 in tandem with the popular objections over such imperial policies as the Stamp Act (1765) and the Townshend Act (1767). The controversy ground to an inconclusive halt about 1768, with the Visitors maintaining some control over finances and claiming authority over the college while the faculty continued to hold their professorships along with parish posts.

Students

The student enrolment of the College of William and Mary remained small in the 1760s and 1770s, serving primarily the local community in the same manner as Harvard drew on students from eastern Massachusetts and New Hampshire, Yale from Connecticut, and the College of New Jersey (now Princeton University) from New Jersey, New York, and Pennsylvania residents (see Table 12.1).

Among the colleges of the period Harvard and Yale were in a class by themselves, enrolling 180 and 170 students respectively, with the

Table 12.1 Enrolment at colonial colleges

College and year of founding	Number of students enrolled annually
Harvard (1636)	180
William and Mary (1693)	80
Yale (1701)	170
New Jersey (Princeton, 1745)	100
King's (Columbia, 1754)	50
Rhode Island(Brown, 1764)	41
Queen's (Rutger's, 1766)	25
Dartmouth (1769)	60
Newark (Delaware, 1769)	25
Total	731

Source: Beverly McAnear, 'College founding in the American Colonies,1745–1775', *Mississippi Valley Historical Review*. 42 (1955): 33.

College of New Jersey (Princeton) and William and Mary following with 100 and 80 students each. The recently founded institutions, Philadelphia (1753) and King's (1754) enrolled 30 and 50 students respectively. According to Professor McAnear the median age of students at entrance for the years between 1750 and 1775 at Yale was 16 or 17, at Philadelphia, 16, and at King's, 15 years.[71] Professor Samuel Eliot Morison has written that at Harvard the median age of an entering freshman rose from a low of a little over fifteen years in 1741 to seventeen years in 1769.[72] I have not found any details to aid in the establishment of the median age of students at entrance to the College of William and Mary.

It must be noted that, perhaps as a consequence of the turmoil at the college, a stream of Virginia residents began to seek their education at the College of New Jersey. By the mid-1750s native-born residents were drawn in gradually increasing numbers to register and attend the college in Princeton. Between 1755 and 1783 at least 35 Virginians matriculated at the institution, including a future President of the United States, James Madison.[73]

It is difficult to provide a comprehensive profile of the College of William and Mary students in the manner of Conrad Edick Wright's admirable analysis of Harvard College's student body in the years before the American Revolutionary War.[74] We have at hand only limited anecdotal evidence to indicate that the college's administration and instruction was challenged by a core of outspoken students and parents. One Virginia resident, George Washington, wrote in 1773 to the Reverend Jonathan Boucher, the sometime schoolmaster of stepson Jack Custis, that he felt that the College of William and Mary was not a desirable place to send Custis. Washington remarked that 'the In attention of the masters, added to the number of Hollidays, is the Subject of general complaint, and affords no pleasing prospect to a youth who has a good deal to attain, and but a short while to do it in'.[75] Washington remarked that he had decided to enrol Custis at the College of Philadelphia and asked Boucher to write a letter of introduction on his behalf.[76] Boucher responded to Washington and urged him not to send his stepson to the College of New Jersey but to consider King's College in New York, at which he matriculated.[77] Despite his election as Chancellor of the College of William and Mary in 1788, a post he held until his death in 1799, Washington's views of the institution did not change. In early 1798 he wrote to David Stuart, who had married the widow of Jack Custis, regarding the education of his step-grandson George Washington

Parke Custis and recommended that Stuart consider Harvard for his enrolment.[78]

The fate of the college was disrupted by events of the War for Independence, just as were the Anglican-related colleges in Philadelphia and New York. In New York, King's College closed, the college buildings were commandeered by a Committee of Safety in 1775 and soon afterwards by the British troops as a hospital. Instruction continued for the remainder of the war in a private house, because New York remained in British hands until November 1783. The College of Philadelphia met a similar experience with a local Committee of Safety and suspended instruction in the spring of 1777. Its buildings were used first as a Continental army barracks and then as a British hospital, but reopened in September 1778 after British troops evacuated the city.[79]

A 1771 graduate of the college, the Reverend James Madison, was a teacher at William and Mary as the hostilities of the American Revolution broke out. News of parliament's passage of the Tea Act in 1773, the Tea Party in Boston Harbor, and the Coercive Acts of the next year divided the political loyalties of the students, Visitors, and faculty. The students and members of the Board of Visitors were aligned with the Patriots' cause while the faculty, other than Madison, was Loyalist.[80] Madison expressed his sentiments by organizing the students into a local militia. During 1777, he served as chaplain of the Virginia House of Delegates and succeeded John Camm as the institution's eighth president in October, 1777.

Madison's first task was to work with the new leaders of Virginia, most notably Thomas Jefferson, on a reorganization of the college, which included the abolition of the Divinity School and the Indian School. The latter, intended to 'civilize' Indian youth, was begun in 1700 but Native American parents resisted enrolling and boarding their children. It was never very successful in achieving any quantity of conversions to Christianity, but did help educate several generations of interpreters.

In June 1781, as British troops moved down the Peninsula, Lord Charles Cornwallis, twin brother of Archbishop of Canterbury Frederick Cornwallis, made the president's house his headquarters, and the institution was closed for a few months of that year, which saw the surrender at Yorktown on October 19. After the war the prospects for the college remained uncertain, despite the persistent efforts of President Madison. During the late eighteenth century and first half of the nineteenth century the institution remained a local college with generally ineffective leadership, constant annual financial pressures and problems of student discipline.[81]

During the 1830s and 1840s officials of the institution sought, without success, public funding to aid its desperate financial position.[82] Between 1846 and 1862 a succession of presidents and disputes over their selection paralysed college affairs.[83] In 1859 only 47 students were enrolled at the institution and a fire destroyed the main building and the college library of 8,000 volumes.[84]

At the outset of the American Civil War (1861–1865), enlistments in the Confederate Army depleted the student body. On 10 May 1861 the faculty voted to close the college for the duration of the conflict. The college building was used as a Confederate barracks and later as a hospital, first by Confederate, and later Union, forces. The Battle of Williamsburg was fought nearby during the Peninsula Campaign on 5 May 1862, and the city fell to the Union the next day. The Brafferton School building was used for a time as quarters for the commanding officer of the Union garrison occupying the town. On 9 September 1862, drunken soldiers of the 5th Pennsylvania Cavalry set fire to the college building, purportedly in an attempt to prevent Confederate snipers from using it for cover. Much damage was done to the community during the Union occupation, which lasted until September 1865.

Following the end of the Civil War and the restoration of the Union in 1865 Virginia was devastated. On the campus the classroom building needed to be rebuilt, and this shortcoming forced a suspension of classes in 1868–69.[85] The college's 16th president, Benjamin Stoddert Ewell finally reopened the school in 1869 using his personal funds. College officials faced a daunting task in attempting to ensure the institution's survival: students needed to be recruited and funds to operate solicited. The college did not receive any financial assistance from the Episcopal Church in Virginia or from the state. Finally, after some years of struggle, the college closed in 1882 due to lack of students and funds.[86] Ewell sought war reparations from the U.S. Congress, but he was repeatedly put off, Federal funds were finally appropriated in 1893.

In 1888, William and Mary resumed operations under a substitute charter when the Commonwealth of Virginia passed an act appropriating $10,000 to support it as a state teacher-training institution. Lyon Gardiner Tyler (son of U.S. President and alumnus John Tyler) became the college's seventeenth president following President Ewell's retirement. Tyler, along with eighteenth president Julian Alvin Carroll Chandler, expanded it into a modern institution. Then, in March 1906, the General Assembly passed an act taking over the grounds of the colonial institution, and ever since it has remained publicly-supported.[87]

The world of James Blair died with him in 1743. His astute political instincts, sense of purpose, and accomplished diligent leadership on behalf of the college was unequalled by his successors for more than a century-and-a-half, until Lyon Gardiner Tyler became president in 1888 and inaugurated a new era of professional purpose for the colonial Anglican institution.

13

Epilogue: A New Age: Breaks with the Past

In 1606 the centre of power for the formation of England's effort to expand its imperial interest to the Western Hemisphere was lodged in London and in the hands of James I, a stalwart advocate of the divine right of kings.[1] At the close of the colonial era in 1776 the balance of power had shifted to America and to the cities of Boston, Philadelphia, and Williamsburg and into the hands of such radical political leaders as Samuel Adams, John Adams, Benjamin Franklin, Thomas Jefferson and James Madison. On 4 July 1776, after 167 years in the thirteen American colonies, royal authority was swept away with the Continental Congress's proclamation of the Declaration of Independence from England. The ultimate authority for the present and future of the American Church was no longer in the hands of English civil and ecclesiastical officials but passed into the hands of the emerging legislative leadership in each new state. At bottom the destiny of the church rested with political leaders and not with the prominent members of each state's local congregations.

The civil and ecclesiastical roles of empire and religion varied significantly between the two early seventeenth-century American colonies. Virginia and Massachusetts Bay represented different faces of the Reformation of the English Church: Anglican and Puritan in theological doctrine, ecclesial polity, and liturgical practices respectively. Social, civil, and ecclesiastical divisions in England were extended to both the New England and Chesapeake colonies. In Virginia the Church of England, and in Massachusetts the Congregational Church, were established by the provincial legislatures and in both instances the church was the dominant religious group throughout the colonial era. Yet in both provinces the churches' harmonious sentiments encountered dissident religious voices.

The Virginia colony began as an unsuccessful commercial venture 3,700 miles across the Atlantic Ocean from London. During its first 60 years as a royal province it received little attention from London-based imperial officials. The office of governor was a commodity, usually filled by persons who had purchased the position, and the transaction was granted some level of endorsement by royal representatives. Imperial administration and religion in the American colonies were little affected by civil and ecclesiastical conflict and change in England between 1607 and the 1680s. Circumstances changed abruptly in the late 1670s, 1680s, and 1690s with the initiation of new policies and procedures for governance and administration of the colonies by the Board of Trade with the approval of the Privy Council. For nearly a century, until the Declaration of Independence, the civil and ecclesiastical affairs of Virginia and the other provinces were monitored by London officials at Whitehall.

The heritage of the seventeenth and eighteenth century provincial Anglican Church contrasts sharply with the experience and legacy of the Congregational Church in the Massachusetts Bay Colony. The twenty-first-century memory of the Church in Virginia during the colonial period is largely shaped by the attractive exterior and interior architecture of the surviving church buildings. Ironically, no copy has survived of the two key manuals required for worship use by Canon Law: the Book of Common Prayer and the Great Bible. In contrast eleven copies are extant of the *Bay Psalm Book* published in Cambridge, Massachusetts, in 1640. Historians have long recounted the incompleteness of the Church in Virginia and America during the colonial period without the supervision and ceremonial role of a bishop or the territorial organization of the institution into a diocese or dioceses. Absent too from Virginia and the history of the church in the twelve other American colonies is a sense of the cultural and intellectual character of the institution. The account is in sharp contrast to the New England story. Perhaps the situation is anchored in the different patterns of settlement of the two regions: a township pattern in New England and a rural model in Virginia. Another difference was the availability of printing presses in Massachusetts from as early as 1638 while the first such equipment in Virginia did not appear for another century. Schools established in Massachusetts towns appeared early and were more common than in Virginia.

Massachusetts civil and church leaders contributed during the early and later years of settlement to the formation of a rich literary tradition. It was led by such authors of the history of the colony and theories of the state as John Winthrop, John Cotton, Roger Williams, Nathaniel

Ward, Jonathan Mitchell, William Stoughton, Samuel Willard, John Wise, Increase and Cotton Mather, and Samuel Sewall. Anne Bradstreet, Michael Wigglesworth, and Edward Taylor established a New England poetic tradition. While Henry Dunster, an early president of Harvard College published in London in 1643 a 26-page tract on *New England's First Fruits* with a section 'In Respect on the Colledge, and the Proceedings of Learning Therein'.

The first Anglican Church minister in the Western Hemisphere, Robert Hunt, arrived with the first ship carrying settlers to England's first colony at Jamestown, Virginia, in 1607. Over more than the next seventeen decades the ranks of parsons associated with the church in the thirteen mainland American colonies gradually increased to a total of 1,289 men and 492 churches. The distribution of men and churches was not equal or uniform through the years in the eventual thirteen colonies. Differing political character, composition of the population, gave rise to different religious circumstances in the provinces. Table 13.1 enumerates the number of Anglican ministers that served churches in each of the provinces. The largest concentration of the men was in the Chesapeake Colonies of Maryland and Virginia with 749 ministers or 58 per cent of the total number of 1,289 clergymen. Virginia was home to 534 ministers or 41 per cent of the American corps of clergymen associated with the Church, the largest representation in the provinces during the colonial period. Regionally the Middle Colonies claimed 234 men or 18 per cent of the total number of clergymen, the Southern Colonies, 218 ministers or 16.91 per cent, and the New England colonies 145 clergymen or 11.24 per cent of the men. In the Massachusetts and Connecticut provinces the number of men serving numbered 63 and 52 respectively or 72.4 percent of the 145 clergymen in the region. The New York men numbered 92 or 39.3 percent of the ministers serving in the Middle Colonies. South Carolina accounts for 139 or 63.76 percent of the 218 men serving churches in the Southern colonies. In contrast the New England colonies numbered 2,064 ministers among which were 1,586 Congregational Church clergymen (77 percent) and 217 Baptist (11.5 percent) ministers.

Captain John Smith recorded that the first Anglican Church service was conducted under an awning spread between trees at Jamestown on 14 May 1607. Soon afterwards a building was constructed within the fort at the new English settlement. We do not know the actual or an estimated number of churches in the province that were built, repaired, replaced, or abandoned during the long colonial era. Several monuments survive, most notably churches that were erected in

Table 13.1 The distribution of the men associated with the Church of England in early America

Colony	Number	Percentage of Region	Percentage of Total
New England			
Massachusetts	63	43.44	4.88
New Hampshire	5	3.44	38
Rhode Island	25	17.24	1.93
Connecticut	52	35.86	4.03
Total	145	100.00	11.24
Middle Colonies			
New York	92	39.31	7.13
New Jersey	49	20.94	3.80
Pennsylvania	57	24.35	4.42
Delaware	36	15.38	2.79
Total	234	100.00	18.15
Chesapeake Colonies			
Maryland	215	28.74	16.67
Virginia	534	71.25	41.34
Total	749	100.00	58.02
Southern Colonies			
North Carolina	54	24.77	4.18
South Carolina	139	63.76	10.78
Georgia	16	7.33	1.24
East Florida	4	1.83	31
West Florida	5	2.29	.387
Total	**218**	**100.00**	**16.91**

Source: James B. Bell, Colonial American Clergy of the Church of England Database, www.jamesbbell.com.

the late seventeenth and early eighteenth centuries in key provincial capitals including Bruton Parish in Williamsburg, Christ Church in Philadelphia and Boston, and Trinity Church in Newport; buildings that were architecturally linked to the visionary designs of Christopher Wren in London but represented in detail the handiwork of talented and skilled colonial craftsmen. Table 13.2 enumerates the 492 churches that were serving congregations in 1775. By regions there were 66 Anglican churches in New England or 13.43 percent of the total of 492; the Middle colonies included 63 church buildings or 12.80 percent of the inter-colonial total; the Chesapeake provinces included 332 churches or 67.47 percent of the total with Virginia accounting for 249 or 50.6 percent of the buildings; and the Southern colonies numbered 31

Table 13.2   Primary and secondary churches in use by colony in 1775

	Primary	Secondary	Total	Percent of Region	Percent of Total
New England Colonies					
New Hampshire	2	1	3	4.5	.603
Massachusetts	10	5	15	22.7	3.04
District of Maine	2	2	4	6.0	.8
Rhode Island	3	1	4	6.0	.8
Connecticut	17	23	40	60.60	8.13
Total	34	32	66	100.00	13.41
Middle Colonies					
New York	16	7	23	36.5	4.67
New Jersey	8	9	17	26.98	3.45
Pennsylvania	6	2	8	1.26	1.62
Delaware	4	11	15	2.38	3.04
Total	34	29	63	100.00	12.80
Chesapeake					
Maryland	55	28	83	25.0	16.86
Virginia	95	154	249	75.0	50.60
Total	150	182	332	100.0	67.47
Southern Colonies					
North Carolina	2	8	10	32.2	2.0
South Carolina	11	5	16	51.61	3.25
Georgia	3	2	5	16.12	1.0
Total	16	15	31	100.00	6.30
Grand Total	**234**	**258**	**492**		**52.43**

Source: James B. Bell, Colonial American Clergy of the Church of England Database, www.jamesbbell.com.

churches or 6.30 percent of the 492 English churches. Comparatively, the total number of Congregational Churches in Massachusetts numbered 344 and in Connecticut 200 or 47.77 percent and 27.77 percent respectively of the total of 720 churches in the New England provinces.

The Anglican Church began in America as a frontier institution in 1607 on the westernmost edge of England's first empire. It remained in essence a frontier Church throughout the long colonial period and individually was merely a shadow of a metropolitan London congregation and more akin to an English country parish or, in the provincial capitals, to a church in one of England's market towns. Yet admittedly it was led by a number of able persons through the decades by men of uncommon talent including James Blair in Virginia, William Smith in Pennsylvania, and Samuel Johnson in Connecticut and New York. But among the ranks there were not preachers of the oratorical skills, inspiration, and eloquence of John Donne or Lancelot Andrewes, or theologians of the rank of Thomas Cranmer or William Laud, or a philosopher of the calibre of George Berkeley.

Crown officials seldom interfered in the internal governance and supervision of Virginia or the Massachusetts Bay Colony until the 1680s. London officials did not seem to take notice or intrude on the New England disputes of Thomas Hooker and Roger Williams who hived off to found Connecticut and Rhode Island respectively, or of Quakers Mary Dyer and Anne Hutchinson. The problem of church membership among the Massachusetts clergy remained a controversy confined to the leaders of the provincial church. In Virginia little attention was given to the bands of Quakers, Puritans, and nonconformists who were settled among the larger population of colonists.

American affairs changed dramatically beginning with the reign of Charles II and the government's new interests in the overseas colonies. The Board of Trade and Plantations considered and recommended to the Privy Council new policies and procedures for governing and administering the provinces. Charters were revoked in the Massachusetts, New York, Maryland, and Pennsylvania provinces and were placed under royal jurisdiction until the Declaration of Independence in 1776. Royal governors were appointed as the chief administrative officers to the colonies and granted detailed Commissions and Instructions for the execution of their duties. The governors and the successive bishops of London were delegated specific responsibilities for the oversight and supervision of the church in the colonies.[2] On the recommendations of the Boston-based Commissioner of Customs Edward Randolph and governors Francis Nicholson of Maryland and Benjamin Fletcher of New York, the Anglican Church was introduced in Maryland in 1692, in Massachusetts in 1686, in New York in 1693, in Philadelphia in 1695, in Newport about 1700, and in Charleston in 1680, the largest capital towns of their respective provinces.[3]

The extension of the Anglican Church into the religiously diverse colonies of New York, Pennsylvania, and Rhode Island during the 1690s may have been a strategy largely defined and undertaken by royal civil officials. But the effort may have been partly encouraged too by the terms of the Act of Toleration approved by parliament in 1689. The events leading up to the Glorious Revolution and the subsequent Toleration Act of 1689 had religion and religious beliefs at their core. To be sure, much of the impetus behind the Toleration Act came from a desire to avoid Catholic religious freedom while also uniting Protestants. Prior to the Glorious Revolution of 1688 and the Act, Protestants were divided and there were legal penalties for not adhering to the strict tenets of the Church of England. Nonconformists were persecuted and parliament could not agree on a way to keep the Anglican Church happy while also allowing religious freedom only to Protestant Dissenters and not Catholics. In 1689 passage of the freedom of worship law came with ease, and the less favoured sects of Protestantism gained an improvement in religious, legal, and social status. The Act was a culmination of religious and political manoeuvring that began after the restoration of the Stuart monarchy of Charles II. The statute granted freedom of worship to Nonconformists of the Church of England, to Protestant dissenters like Quakers, Presbyterians, and Baptists. But Catholics and Unitarians were deliberately excluded from this grant of religious freedom.

The importance of the Toleration Act at the time of its inception can be summed up in the words of A.V. Dicey in that, it 'gave from the moment it was enacted substantial religious freedom to the vast majority of English people'. The Act left the Church of England virtually unchanged. All of its rights and endowments and privileges remained intact, but its jurisdiction became somewhat limited so that the church was no longer coextensive with the nation. The statute gave Protestant Dissenters a legally recognized existence, under certain terms and conditions. As far as parliament was concerned, before 1689 Nonconformists could not legally hold any sort of prayer meetings. During the Restoration period, the heyday of the Church of England's ascendancy, mob-harassment of Nonconformists' places of worship was commonplace. However, during the reign of William III, the rights of public worship and self-government were among the new rights afforded to the previously restrained groups. These benefits extended to Independents, Baptists, Presbyterians, and Quakers exclusively. These parties were all free to build their own chapels, take out licenses, regularize their positions in the eyes of the law, and even publicly appeal for new members. Practically speaking, the impact of the new freedoms provided by the law was seen in the vast proliferation of places of Dissenting worship.

Coincidentally, the long-championed and finally enacted statute of Toleration became the law of England at about the same time as the first signs of the anglicization movement appeared in the American colonies. Perhaps the timing of the appearance of the contrasting legal and cultural forces was mere coincidence and that there was no significant link or association. Yet the circumstance may be argued that the tenets of the Act of Toleration granting religious freedom to individuals and groups inspired and gave rise to the movement to assert English style and taste in early America. If so, it may have become in part a template under differing circumstances of various 'nativist' movements that have appeared in the course of American history since the 1840s.[4]

The transfer of the English Church to colonial Virginia was incomplete and without the familiar hierarchical structure of the homeland. It was at worship a traditional episcopal church without a prelate to ordain candidates for the ministry, provide the sacrament of confirmation to members, or consecrate churches, churchyards, and cemeteries. The launch of new interest in imperial administration by the English government's Board of Trade and Plantations in the 1670s, 1680s, and 1690s embraced but did not significantly alter colonial ecclesiastical affairs before the War for Independence. Successive commissaries of the bishop of London served as resident overseers of the provincial ministers and the Church in certain colonies.

A new and active era of English imperial administration in America occurred after the Treaty of Paris in 1763 and the close of the French and Indian War that launched a sustained round of colonial rhetoric in opposition to English governance. Civil provincial leaders decried the terms and consequences of a chain of legislation enacted by parliament including the Sugar Act (1764), the Townshend Act (1767), the Tea Act (1773), and the Coercive Acts (1774). Colonial legislatures were set on an inevitable track of conflict and rebellion. The Anglican Church did not escape notice from the critical voices of English imperial administration. After the first session of the legislatures the Continental Congress in the fall of 1774 adopted a policy for the establishment of Committees of Safety in each colony. The Church and its ministers came under popular suspicion for possibly holding pro-English rather than Patriot sentiments and were exposed to criticism and harassment. The urgent public question was simply, is the parson favourable to the revolutionary cause and a Patriot, or does he maintain an allegiance to the crown and parliament of England as a Loyalist?

Rising popular criticism and rhetoric by colonial leaders of English trade and tax policies following parliament's passage of the Stamp Act in 1765 began the gradual erosion of the status of the provincial church. Because of its English heritage the church was in a weak position. Loyalties to and members of the church could easily be terminated and transferred to another religious group, perhaps more aligned with Patriot sentiments including the Presbyterian and Congregational.

Edmund Burke, a Member of Parliament, in his analysis of Britain's imperial policies in the run-up to the American controversies identified the effort in a 1775 speech in the House of Commons as an era of 'Salutary Neglect'. It was an historical course of action that was partly masked but not changed by the policies of the Council and later the Board of Trade and Plantations in the 1670s, 1680s, and 1690s to revitalize and reshape the procedures for imperial governance. It reflected a longstanding and undocumented policy of non-interference by the government in colonial trade affairs that became a key element of the administration of Sir Robert Walpole in the eighteenth century. The policy intended to keep the overseas colonies obedient to the mother country. From the first settlement of Virginia in 1607 the province's civil and ecclesiastical affairs were shaped by 'Salutary Neglect' and were not altered until the Treaty of Paris of 1783.

England's colony, Virginia, came to an end with the Declaration of Independence in 1776. The distillation of contemporary civil rhetoric was presented by Thomas Paine in his pamphlet, *Common Sense* published in January 1776. Paine had arrived in America two years earlier at the suggestion of Benjamin Franklin. Paine was a genius with his pen and is recognized as the leading propagandist of the Revolution. He spoke of independence in words that every American could understand. In a sense Paine's tract was a popular, republican work that was published and read with urgency and popular authority.[5]

After a series of battles in the New England and Middle Colonies the War came to an end in October 1781. England's colony founded 170 years earlier at Jamestown came to an end in the fields surrounding Yorktown, merely twenty-one miles across Virginia land.

Despite the Patriot leanings of a majority of the 120 active clergymen in 1776, the destiny of the Church was in jeopardy in Virginia and elsewhere in America. Not one layman, in Virginia or in any other place in America, raised his voice or gripped his pen to declare or defend the interests of the Anglican Church. Without the company of an articulate prelate or a band of prominent and respected members the institution's interests were unheard in the colonial cities, towns, and countryside. At the Declaration of Independence and the outbreak of war in 1776 the Virginia church was severely affected and disarrayed: its clergy ranks were diminished by retirements and death, services of worship suspended and churches closed temporarily and permanently. It was not an American church or an American republican ecclesiastical symbol. It was identified as an English Church and a symbol linked to the government and policies that the colonists objected to and were rebelling against.

Members migrated to other religious groups such as the Presbyterian, and the legislature terminated state support of clergymen.

The colonial civil and ecclesiastical structure of the empire cobbled together was suddenly and completely dismantled. Civil affairs were drastically altered and the Anglican Church, because it was the state Church of England in six colonies, lost its power, influence, and status. Its position, status, and state was unalterably diminished and transformed, a victim of the revolutionary circumstances. A century of transforming changes to the civil and religious fabric by the Board of Trade and Plantations with the approval of the Privy Council, by parliament's approval of the Toleration Act of 1689, the Declaration of Independence, and the influential intellectual currency of the ideas of the Enlightenment, new circumstances prevailed. Ironically, in Virginia, the new design and situation of the church was shaped in part by Thomas Jefferson and James Madison, two prominent Virginian Anglicans. Jefferson was the author of the Virginia Act for Religious Freedom of 1786 that granted to all religious groups the right to meet and worship. Disestablishment of the church in the same year led to years of litigation over the status of glebes and parsonages and gave way to a post-Revolutionary War church that was financially independent and required the voluntary support of its members to maintain it. The Anglican Church in Virginia and elsewhere in the new United States faced the additional task of undertaking a reconstitution and reconstruction. The tumultuous military and political events launched with the two sessions of the Continental Congress, the battles at Lexington Green and Concord Bridge, and the Declaration of Independence at Philadelphia had dispossessed it of all support. Swept away were the imperial and ecclesiastical ties to London officials fashioned over 169 years, the financial support of colonial legislatures in the six states in which the church had been established, and the salaries of the missionaries of the London-based Society for the Propagation of the Gospel. English law prohibited the Bishop of London from exercising supervision over the church in the recently independent nation in the unlikely event it should be requested. As a consequence of political circumstances and the War for Independence the church was a legatee of the English Reformation and the imperial origins of the religious group in early America. The institution wore, uncomfortably, two hats, one shaped in the past and the other fashioned in an emerging new nation. It sought to embrace and continue the hierarchical ministerial authority of the Church of England and an American version of Thomas Cranmer's Book of Common Prayer.

The place of the English Church in Virginia was in question, in peril, and exposed for structural modification. The Virginia legislature terminated the payment of ministers' salaries and transferred the responsibility, along with the maintenance of church buildings, to the local congregation's vestry. Churches were closed, the ranks of parsons diminished, many members migrated to other religious groups such as the Presbyterian Church and many vestry members resigned their posts.[6] The church faced the arduous task of reorganizing and reconstituting itself locally and nationally, and eventually re-naming itself. It did not recover a semblance of its colonial status and strength until after the Civil War and the years of the Gilded Age of the 1870s and after.

During the formative years of the new republic each state and the nation grappled with the tasks of drafting and approving constitutions and organizing the elements of civil government. As Frederick V. Mills, Jr., has systematically chronicled, the church, too, faced a similar assignment but did not speak with one voice on matters of institutional structure.[7] After the formal cessation of hostilities between England and the United States in 1783 a prelate of the Church of England could not ordain American candidates for the ministry under English law. At ordination to the episcopate it was necessary for a candidate to take an oath of allegiance to the crown and parliament, a requirement that no citizen of the new United States could undertake. No longer could the church be known as the Church of England; a change of name was necessary and in 1785 it became the Protestant Episcopal Church in the United States of America.[8] Throughout the new states the experience of the church was similar; it had been disrupted and weakened by the war. The experience of the Virginia church was repeated everywhere: congregations were smaller, church buildings in disrepair, and the ranks of the parsons significantly reduced by exile, retirements, and death.[9] Clergy and lay leaders in each of the states met in conventions to reorganize the church but were rent in factions between 1784 and 1850.[10] At the Triennial General Conventions of the national church during the period reports repeatedly recounted the divided and impoverished situations in each state.[11]

Efforts to establish church-related colleges were slowly rekindled by local leaders in the 1820s. Hobart and William Smith College in Geneva, New York, was founded in 1822, Trinity College in Hartford, Connecticut, the next year, and Kenyon College in Gambier, Ohio, in 1824. The professional education of candidates for the ministry engendered a debate within the national church lasting more than two decades which was not settled until the founding of the General Theological Seminary in New York City in 1817.[12]

The Old Dominion Church was established and closely associated with English imperial policies and administration throughout the colonial period. We can only speculate and raise the question, would the English church have flourished and survived in the province without the umbrella protection of official favour? We do not know. The clarity of distant hindsight suggests that the subsequent fortunes of the church were tied to a link that was finally forcefully shattered and swept away and not placed on the shoulders of the residents who remained.

The religious culture of Virginia was not a seamlessly uniform Anglican practice after the Church's establishment by the legislature in 1619. Nonconformist ministers served several congregations occasionally on the Eastern Shore and in the region south of the James River during the seventeenth century. It was a situation that reflected that reflected the religious situation in England at the time. For nearly half-a-century before the Declaration of Independence controversies irregularly erupted and rocked the College and the Church. Beginning in the late 1720s and the need to legally transfer the charter of the College of William and Mary from the control of the last surviving founders to the members of the faculty clashed with the lay members of the Board of Visitors. It was a pattern of conflict between the two parties that persisted until the outbreak of the War for Independence. During the 1750s the extensive legal manoeuvrings of the Parson's Cause in Williamsburg and London affected the financial affairs of every congregation and clergyman. A polemical presentation of the issues in dispute published in several essays gave a popular cast to the controversy. It was followed in the 1760s and 1770s by rising critical rhetoric over a succession of imperial policies including the Stamp Act, the Townshend Act, the closing of the port of Boston, and the long-feared appointment of an American prelate; all stirred continuing popular debate and conflict. The Virginia English Church, of which King George III was the supreme head, was a reminder to civil leaders and the public that the church was tied officially to the crown, parliament, and civil and ecclesiastical leaders in London.

Between the 1720s and 1770s Virginia was transformed by an increasing population of diverse national origins and religious allegiance, Scots-Irish Presbyterians and Baptists settled in the backcountry of the province and were increasingly served by initially itinerant, and later settled, like-minded preachers. The Declaration of Independence was not the first signal that concluded the state and status of the church in Virginia but it was the decisive civil act. The rising influence and acceptance of a population of non-Anglicans was linked to the half-a-century decline of the fortunes for the Anglican Church and college. Nearly a century after parliament's passage of the Toleration Act of 1689 it remained for the legislature of the new state to enact a political accommodation that would grant and tolerate the presence and practice of all religious groups and remove the former Anglican Church from sole favour.

Unlike the circumstances in England between the sixteenth and nineteenth centuries, motivating the quest by dissenting religious group for toleration, there was no inter-colonial American established church.[13] In British North America churches were established in nine of the thirteen provinces at the beginning of the War for Independence including the Congregational Church in Massachusetts, the District of Maine, Connecticut, and New Hampshire. The Anglican Church was established in Virginia, Maryland, and the four lower counties of New York, South Carolina, North Carolina, and Georgia.[14] In America the agenda for religious liberty was set by the legislatures of the several states in which the Congregational and Anglican churches were established. Anti-English sentiments over civil and commercial policies supported by accounts of the heroic exploits of continental and colonial militias at Lexington and Concord, Valley Forge, and Yorktown contributed to relatively easy and quick disestablishment of the English Church in the former colonies. The drive for religious liberty in the New England states survived for about two generations when disestablishment occurred first in Connecticut in 1818, followed by New Hampshire in 1819, Maine in 1820, and Massachusetts in 1833. The first amendment of the Bill of Rights of the Federal Constitution adopted in 1791 declared that 'Congress shall make no law respecting an establishment of religion, or prohibiting the free exercise thereof'.

Appendix I. Clergymen who arrived in Virginia between 1607 and 1699

Name	Birth and Death	Place of Birth	College	Year Ordained	Parishes Served	Years	Comments
Alexander, John	1665–17xx	Scot.	Scot.?	Unk.	Sittingbourne	1696–1704	
Alford, George	1611–16xx	Eng.	Oxf.	1619	Lynnhaven	1658	Exeter
Allardes, Thomas	1676–1701	Scot.	Aber.	1699	Unk.	1699–1701	King's
Anderson, Charles	1669–1718	Scot.	Glas.	Scot.?	Westover	1693–1718	
Armourier, John	15xx–16xx	Eng.	M.A.	Yes	Hungar's	1651–54	
					Wicomico		
					Christ Church		
Aylmer, Justinian	1638–1671	Eng.	Camb.	Unk.	James City	1671	
					Elizabeth City		
Ball, John	1665–17xx	Eng.	Oxf.	Unk.	Henrico, St Peter's	1679–89	
Banister, John	1650–92	Eng.	Oxf.	1674	Charles City	1678–92	
Bargrave, Thomas	1581–1621	Eng.	Camb.	Unk.	Henrico City	1619–21	
Bennett, Thomas	1605–16xx	Eng.	Camb.	1628	Nansemond	1648	
Bennett, William	15xx–16xx	Eng.	Camb	1616	Warwisqueake	1623	Jesus
Blair, James	1653–1743	Scot.	Edin.	Unk.	Henrico	1685–1743	
					James City		
					Bruton		
Bolton, John	1635–16xx	Eng.	Camb.	Unk.	Cople	1693–98	Christ's

(Continued)

Name	Birth and Death	Place of Birth	College	Year Ordained	Parishes Served	Years	Comments
Bolton, Francis	1595–16xx	Eng.	Camb.	Unk.	Elizabeth City	1621–30	
					Accomac?	1623–26	
					Warwisqueake		
Bowker, James	1665–1703	Eng.	Camb.	Unk.	Kempton	1690–1703	
					St Peter's		
Bracewell, Robert	1611–68	Eng.	Oxf.	Unk.	Isle of Wight	1653–68d.	
Bucke, Richard	1584–1623	Eng.	Camb.	Unk.	James City	1610–23	
Bushnell, James	16xx–17xx	Unk.	Unk.	Unk.	Martin's Hundred	1696–1702	
Butler, William	1647–17xx	Eng.	Camb.	Unk.	Washington	1677–81	
Butler, Almeric	1648–78	Eng.	Camb.	Unk.	Sittingbourne	1671–78d.	
Calvert, Sampson	1603–16xx	Eng.	Oxf.	1626	Elizabeth River	1649	
Cant, Andrew	16xx–17xx	Scot.	Edin.	1691	Lawne's Creek	1696	
Carr, John	1643–85	Eng.	Camb.	1684	St Peter's	1684–85d.	
Carr, Robert	16xx–17xx	Eng.	Oxf.	Unk.	Stratton-Major	1680–86	
Clack, James	1673–1723	Eng.	Unk.	1695	Ware	1695–1723d.	
Clayton, John	1657–1725	Eng.	Unk.	Unk.	James City	1684–86	
Clough, James	16xx–84	Eng.	Unk.	Unk.	James City	1676–84d.	
					Southwork		
Cole, Samuel	16xx–59	Eng.	Unk.	Unk.	Pianketant	1657–59	
					Christ Church		
Cooke, Alexander	16xx–16xx	Eng.	Unk.	Unk.	Christ Church	1652–57	
Cotton, William	16xx–16xx	Eng.	Unk.	Unk.	Hungar's	1632–45	
Culverius, Mr.	15xx–16xx	Eng.	Un?	Unk.	Hampton	1644	
Davies, Charles	16xx–16xx	Unk.	Unk.	Unk.	Wicomico	1680–83	
					Farnham		

Name							
Davis, William	16xx–97	Eng.	Oxf.	1697	Unk.	1697d.	
Davis, Jonathan	16xx–16xx	Eng.	Unk.	Unk.	New Poquoson	1680–81	
Davis, Superior	16xx–16xx	Eng.	Unk.	Unk.	Christ Church	1682–83	
Doggett, Benjamin	1636–82	Eng.	Camb.	Unk.	Christ Church	1669–82	
Doughty, Francis	1616–69	Eng.	Unk.	Unk.	Hungar's	1655–5	
					Elizabeth City	1659–62	
					Northampton County	1662–65	
					Sittingbourne	1665–69	
D'Oyley, Cope	1658–1702	Eng.	Oxf.	1682	Elizabeth City, Denbigh, Bruton	1687–1702	
Dudley, Samuel	1654–85	Eng.	Oxf.	Unk.	Sittingbourne	1680–85	
					South Farnham		
Dunster, Robert	16xx–56	Eng.	Camb.	Unk.	Isle of Wight	1651–56d.	
Eaton, Nathaniel	1609–74	Eng.	Camb.	1635	Hungar's	1639–46	
Eburne, Samuel	1645–17xx	Eng.	Camb.	1667	Bruton	1688–95	
Farnifold, John	1635–1702	Eng.	Oxf.	Unk.	Old Fairfield	1670–1702	New
					Boutracey	1690–1702	
Fenton, Mr.	15xx–16xx	Unk.	Unk.	Unk.	Elizabeth City	1624	
Finney, Thomas	1659–87	Eng.	Oxf.	Unk.	Charles	1686–87d.	
Flowers, Ralph	16xx–16xx	Unk.	Unk.	Unk.	York	1690–91	
Folliott, Edward	1610–90	Eng.	Oxf.	Unk.	York	1652–90d.	
Fordyce, Francis	1651–16xx	Scot.	Aber.	Scot.?	Southwark	1696–99	
Fouace, Stephen	16xx–17xx	Unk.	Leyden	1684	York Hampton	1690–1702	
					Martin's Hundred	1702	
Glover, Nicholas	1567–1611	Eng.	Camb.	Unk.	Jamestown	1611	
Godwin, Morgan	1640–85	Eng.	Oxf.	1665	Marston, York	1665–66	
Gordon, Thomas	16xx–16xx	Eng.	Unk.	Unk.	Farnham	1671	

(Continued)

Name	Birth and Death	Place of Birth	College	Year Ordained	Parishes Served	Years	Comments
Gordon, John	1674?–17xx	Eng	Unk.	Unk.	Washington, St Peter's	1695–1702	
Gorsuch, John	1600–56	Eng.	Camb.	Yes	Lancaster	1654–57	Pembroke
Graeme, Rowland	16xx–16xx	Unk.	Unk.	Unk.	Unk.	1628–29	
Gray, Samuel	16xx–1709	Scot.	Edin.	1689	Christ Church, Cople St Peter's	1690–1709d.	
Green, Roger	1614–73	Eng.	Camb.	1639.	West, Jamestown	1653–71	
Gregg, Stephen	16xx–16xx	Unk.	Unk.	Unk.	Abington	1691–95	
Gwynn, John	1642–16xx	Eng.	Oxf.	Unk.	Abington	1672–88	
Hampton, Thomas	1609–16xx	Eng.	Oxf.	Unk.	James City, [No church1658–80] Hampton Wilmington Wallingford	1640–81	
Harrison, Thomas	1616–82	Eng.	Camb.	Unk.	Elizabeth River	1640–48	
Heyley, Willis	1591–16xx	Eng.	Unk.	Unk.	Mulberry Island	1634–35	
Highby, Thomas	1600–54	Eng.	Unk.	Unk.	Hungar's	1651–54	
Holt, Joseph	1668–17xx	Eng.	Camb.	Unk.	Stratton-Major Petworth	1696–1700	
Hopkins, George	1581–1645	Eng.	Unk.	Unk.	Hampton	1643–45	
Housden, William	1657–90	Eng.	Camb.	1677	West Newport	1680d.	
Hudson, George	1642–96	Eng.	Camb.	1677	Williamsburg	1694–96d.	

Name	Dates	Origin	University	Ordination	Location	Tenure
Hunt, Robert	1568–1608	Eng.	Camb.	Yes	Jamestown	1607–08d.
Jackson, Andrew	1656–1710	Unk.	Unk.	Presb.	St Mary's Whitechapel Christ Church	1683–1710d.
James, Richard	1592–1638	Eng.	Oxf.	1617	Unk.	1628–29 [to Maryland, 1629–38]
Johnson, Edward	16xx–65	Unk.	Unk.	Unk.	York	1664–65d.
Jones, Richard	16xx–16xx	Unk.	Unk.	Unk.	Martin's Brandon	1650–55
Jones, Rowland	1643–88	Eng.	Oxf.	1666	Bruton Martin's Hundred	1674–88d.
Jones, Samuel	1637–16xx	Unk.	Unk.	Unk.	James City	1671
Keith, George	1585–16xx	Scot.	Aber.	Scot.?	Kecoughtan, Elizabeth City	1624–26
Kenyon, Abraham	16xx–1704	Unk.	B.A.	Unk.	Cople	1684–85
Key, Isaac	1644–16xx	Eng.	Camb.	Unk	Hungar's	1676–78.
Lake, Thomas	1633–16xx	Eng.	Camb.	Unk.	Southwark	1655
Lansdale, Peter	1603–16xx	Eng.	Camb.	Unk.	Jamestown	1658–60
Lawrence, John	1633–84	Eng.	Camb.	Unk.	Mulberry Island, Denbigh	1680–84
Lette, William	1587–16xx	Eng.	Camb.	Unk.	Unk.	1622
Lidford, Matthew	1663–93	Eng.	Oxf.	1688	Christ Church	1693
Lindsay, David	1603–77	Scot.	Unk.	Unk.	Wicomico	1655–77d.
Lyford, John	1576–1634	Ire.	Oxf.	Unk.	Martin's Hundred	1628–29
Mackie, Josias	16xx–1716	Ire.	Edin.	Presb.	Elizabeth River	1684–91
Mallory, Philip	1617–61	Eng.	Oxf.	Unk.	Lynnhaven York County, James City	1657–61d.
Martin, Lazarus	16xx–16xx	Unk.	Unk.	Unk.	Henrico City	1629

(Continued)

Name	Birth and Death	Place of Birth	College	Year Ordained	Parishes Served	Years	Comments
Maycocke, Samuel	1594–1622	Eng.	Camb.	No	Unk.	1618–22	
Mease, William	1574–16xx	Eng.	Unk.	Unk.	Kecooughtan, Elizabeth City	1610–20	
Mitton, Roger	1663–1740	Eng.	Camb.	1689	Unk.	ca. 1698	
Monroe, John	1662–1723	Scot.	Unk.	Scot.?	Hungar's	1692–1723	
Moray, Alexander	1646–17xx	Scot.	Aber.	Scot.?	Ware	1653–72	
Moreau, Nicholas	16xx–17xx	Unk.	Unk.	Unk.	St Peter's All Faith's	1696–9x	
Morris, Richard	16xx–16xx	Unk.	Oxf.	Unk.	Pianketant, Lancaster Christ Church	1663–66	
Mullett, William	16xx–16xx	Eng.	D.D.	Unk.	Christ Church	1683–93	
Munro, John	16xx–16xx	Scot.	Unk.	Scot.?	Stratton-Major	1650–55	
Mynnarad, Mr.	15xx–16xx	Unk.	Unk.	Unk	Martin's Hundred	1628	
Owens, John	16xx–16xx	Unk.	Unk.	Unk.	Wicomico	1673–75	
Page, John	16xx–88	Unk.	Unk.	Unk.	Elizabeth City St Peter's	1677–88	
Palmer, Samuel	16xx–17xx	Unk.	Unk.	Unk.	Hungar's	1695–1702	
Palmer, Thomas	16xx–16xx	Unk.	Unk.	Unk.	Hungar's	1647–48	
Panton, Anthony	16xx–16xx	Unk.	Unk.	Unk.	York, Chiskiack	1637–40	
Paris, William	16xx–16xx	Unk.	Unk.	Unk.	Washington	1682–86	
Parke, Henry	1638–87	Unk.	Unk.	Unk.	St George's Accomac	1666	

Name	Dates	Nationality	University	Ordained	Parish	Tenure	College
Parke, Robert	16xx–16xx	Unk.	Unk.	Unk.	Warwisqueake	1680	
Paulett, Robert	1590–16xx	Unk.	Unk.	Unk.	Martin's Hundred, Martin's Brandon, Weynoke	1619–22	
Pead, Deuel	1646–1727	Eng.	Camb.	1668	Christ Church	1683–90	
Pendleton, Nathaniel	1650–74	Eng.	Camb.	1673	Unk.	1674	Corpus Christi
Perkins, Thomas	16xx–16xx	Unk.	Unk.	Unk.	Sittingbourne	1684	
Poole, John	1584–16xx	Unk.	Oxf.	Unk.	Jamestown	1611	
Pooley, Greville	15xx–1629	Unk.	Unk.	Unk.	Weyanoke, Martin's Brandon	1622–29	
Porter, James	16xx–83	Ire.	Unk.	Unk.	Lynnhaven	1678–83	
Powis, Robert	16xx–52	Wales?	Unk.	Unk.	Southern Shore Lynnhaven	1640–52	
Pretty, Henry	1656–17xx	Eng.	Camb.	1680	Unk.	1696	
Richardson, Daniel	16xx–16xx				Hungar's	1676	
Robertson, George	1662–1739	Scot.	St And.	1691	Bristol	1693–1739	
Rodgers, John	16xx–16xx	Eng.	Oxf.	Yes	Hungar's	1664	Christ Church
Rosier, John	1604–60	Eng.	Camb.	Unk.	York, Hampton, Cople	1640–60	
Sandford, Samuel	1669–1710	Eng.	Oxf.	Unk.	Accomac	1694–1702	
Sandys, David	1573–1625	Eng.	Oxf.	1619	Hog Island	1624–25	
Saunders, Jonathan	1670–1701	Eng.	Oxf.	Unk.	Lynnhaven	1695–1701	
Sax, Thomas	16xx–16xx	Unk.	Unk.	Unk.	Lancaster	1650–54	
Sclater, James	1657–1723	Eng.	Oxf.	Unk.	Charles	1686–1724	
Sellake, William	1617–16xx	Eng.	Oxf.	Unk.	St Peter's	1680–82	
Semple, William	16xx–16xx	Unk.	Unk.	Unk.	Unk.	1689	
Shepard, John	1646–82	Eng.	Oxf.	Unk.	Christ Church	1668–82	
Smith, Patrick	16xx–16xx	Scot.?	Unk.	Scot.?	Southwark	1690–91	

(Continued)

Name	Birth and Death	Place of Birth	College	Year Ordained	Parishes Served	Years	Comments
Stockton, Jonas	1588–1628	Eng.	Oxf.	1610	Henrico Kecoughton	1621–28	
Taylor, Jeremiah	16xx–16xx	Unk.	Unk.	Unk.	Elizabeth City	1667–68	
Taylor, John	16xx–16xx	Unk.	Unk.	Unk.	Fairfield Chicacone	1668–70	
Taylor, Thomas	16xx–16xx	Unk.	Unk.	Unk.	Blissland	1680–81	
Teackle, Thomas	1625–95	Eng.	Unk.	Unk.	Accomac	1658–95	
Tompson, William	1633–65	Eng.	Harvard	Cong.	Southwark Lawne's Creek	1664–65	
Tompson, William	1598–1660	Eng.	Oxf.	Unk.	Nansemond	1642–43	Brasenose
Towers, William	16xx–16xx	Eng.	Camb.	Unk.	Wicomico	1672	
Vary, Isaac	16xx–16xx	Eng	Unk	Yes	Wallingford	1682–85	
Vicaris, Thomas	16xx–96	Unk.	Unk.	Unk.	Petsworth	1666–96d.	
Wadding, James	16xx–16xx	Eng.	Oxf.	Unk.	Petsworth James City	1672	
Wallace, James	1667–1712	Scot.	Glas.	Scot.?	Elizabeth City St Peter's	1691–1712d.	
Ware, Jacob	16xx–1709	Unk.	Unk.	Unk.	Henrico	1690–1709d.	

Name	Dates	Country	University		Location	Years
Watson, Ralph	1602–45	Eng.	Oxf.	1625	York County	1645
Waugh, John	16xx–1706	Eng.	Unk.	Unk.	Stafford	1667–1706
					Overwharton	
Wayre, John	16xx–16xx	Eng.	Unk.	Unk.	Lawne's Creek	1680
Wern, William	16xx–16xx	Unk.	Unk.	Unk.	Elizabeth River	1680
Whitaker, Alexander	1585–1617	Eng.	Camb.	1609	Henrico	1611–17d.
White, Thomas	1595–1624	Eng.	Oxf.	Unk.	Elizabeth City	1622–24d.
White, George	1601–16xx	Eng.	Oxf.	Unk.	Denbigh	1635
White, William	16xx–58	Eng.	Unk.	Unk.	York	1658
Wickham, William	15xx–16xx	Eng.	Oxf.	No	Henrico	1616–22
Wilkerson, William	16xx–16xx	Eng.	Oxf.	Unk.	Lynnhaven	1635–37
Williams, Paul	16xx–16xx	Unk.	Unk.	Unk.	Weyanoke	1680
					Martin's Brandon	
Williams, William	1657–17xx	Wales	Oxf.	Prob.	St Stephen's	1680–1700
Wilson, John	16xx–1640	Unk.	Unk.	Unk.	Elizabeth River	1637–40
Wood, John	1641–16xx	Eng.	Oxf.	Unk.	Upper Parish	1684–85
Wright, John	1643–16xx	Eng.	Camb.	Unk.	Towson	1680
Wyatt, Hawte	1594–1638	Eng.	Oxf.	Unk.	James City	1621–25
Yates, Robert, Sr	1673–17xx	Eng.	Oxf.	1696	Christ Church	1699–1703
Young, George	16xx–17xx	Scot.	Edin.	Scot.?	Petsworth	1699–1700
Zyperius, Michael	16xx–16xx	Unk.	Unk.	Dutch Reform	Kingston	1680–87

Appendix II. Clergymen who arrived in Virginia by decade between 1607 and 1699

Name	Birth and Death	Year Ordained	Parishes	Served Years
1600–09				
Hunt, Robert	1568–1608	Yes	Jamestown	1607–08d.
1610–19				
Bargrave, Thomas	1581–1621	Unk.	Henrico City	1619–21
Bucke, Richard	1584–1623	Unk.	James City	1610–23
Glover, Nicholas	1567–1611	Unk.	Jamestown	1611
Maycocke, Samuel	1594–1622	Unk.	Unk.	1618–22
Mease, William	1574–16xx	Unk.	Kecoughtan Elizabeth City	1610–20
Paulett, Robert	1590–16xx	Unk.	Martin's Hundred Martin's Brandon Weynoke	1619–22
Poole, John	1584–16xx	Unk.	Jamestown	1611
Whitaker, Alexander	1585–1617	Yes	Henrico	1611–17d.
Wickham, William	15xx–16xx	Unk.	Henrico	1616–22
1620–29				
Bennett, William	15xx–16xx	1616	Warwisqueake	–1623
Bolton, Francis	1595–16xx	Unk.	Elizabeth City Accomac	1621–30
Fenton, Mr.	15xx–16xx	Unk.	Elizabeth City	1624
Graeme, Rowland	16xx–16xx	Unk.	Unk.	1628–29

185

Name	Dates	Ordained	Parish	Tenure
James, Richard	1592–1638	1617	Unk.	1628–29 [to Maryland, 1629–38]
Keith, George	1585–16xx	Unk.	Kecoughtan; Elizabeth City	1624–26
Lette, William	1587–16xx	Unk.	Unk.	1622
Lyford, John	1576–1634	Unk.	Martin's Hundred	1628–29
Martin, Lazarus	16xx–16xx	Unk.	Henrico City	1629
Mynnarad, Mr.	15xx–16xx	Unk.	Martin's Hundred	1628
Pooley, Greville	15xx–1629	Unk.	Weyanoke; Martin's Brandon	1622–29
Sandys, David	1573–1625	Unk.	Hog Island	1624–25
Stockton, Jonas	1588–1628	1610	Henrico; Kecoughton	1621–28
White, Thomas	1595–1624	Unk.	Elizabeth City	1622–24d.
Wyatt, Hawte	1594–1638	Unk.	James City	1621–25
1630–39				
Bennett, Thomas	1605–16xx	Unk.	Nansemond	1648
Cotton, William	16xx–16xx	1605	Hungar's	1632–45
Calvert, Sampson	1603–16xx	1626	Elizabeth River	1649
Eaton, Nathaniel	1609–74	Yes	Hungar's	1639–46
Heyley, Willis	1591–16xx	Unk.	Mulberry Island	1634–35
Panton, Anthony	16xx–16xx	Unk.	York; Chiskiack	1637–40
White, George	1601–16xx	Unk.	Denbigh	1635
Wilkerson, William	16xx–16xx	Unk.	Lynnhaven	1635–37
Wilson, John	16xx–1640	Unk	Elizabeth River	1637–40
1640–49				
Culverius, Mr.	15xx–16xx	Unk.	Hampton	1644

186

(Continued)

Name	Birth and Death	Year Ordained	Parishes	Served Years
Hampton, Thomas	1609–16xx	Unk.	James City [No church, 1658–80] Hampton Wilmington Wallingford	1640–81
Harrison, Thomas	1616–82	Unk.	Elizabeth River	1640–48
Hopkins, George	1581–1645	Unk.	Hampton	1643–45
Palmer, Thomas	16xx–16xx	Unk.	Hungar's	1647–48
Powis, Robert	16xx–52	Unk.	Southern Shore Lynnhaven	1640–52
Rosier, John	1604–60	Unk.	York Hampton Cople	1640–60
Tompson, William	1598–1660	Unk.	Nansemond	1642–43
Watson, Ralph 1650–59	1602–45	1625	York County	1645
Alford, George	1611–16xx	1619	Lynnhaven	1658
Armourier, John	15xx–16xx	Unk.	Hungar's. Wicomico Christ Church	1651–54
Bracewell, Robert	1611–68	Unk.	Isle of Wight	1653–68
Cole, Samuel	16xx–59	Unk.	Pianketant Christ Church	1657–59
Cooke, Alexander	16xx–16xx	Unk.	Christ Church	1652–57

Name	Dates	Status	Location	Years
Doughty, Francis	1616–69	Unk.	Hungar's	1655
			Elizabeth City	165x–56
			Northampton	1662–65
			Sittingbourne	1665–69
Dunster, Robert	16xx–56	Unk.	Isle of Wight	1651–56d.
Folliott, Edward	1610–90	Unk.	York	1652–90d.
			Cople	
Green, Roger	1614–73	Unk.	West, Jamestown	1653–71
Gorsuch, John	1600–56	Unk.	Lancaster	1654–57
Higby, Thomas	1600–54	Unk.	Hungar's	1651–54
Jones, Richard	16xx–16xx	Unk.	Martin's Brandon	1650–55
Lake, Thomas	1633–16xx	Unk.	Southwark	1655
Lansdale, Peter	1603–16xx	Unk.	Jamestown	1658–60
Lindsay, David	1603–77	Unk.	Wicomico	1655–77d.
Mallory, Philip	1617–61	Unk.	Lymnhaven	1657–61d.
			York County	
			James City	
Moray, Alexander	1646–17xx	Unk.	Ware	1653–72
Munro, John	16xx–16xx	Unk.	Stratton-Major	1650–55
Sax, Thomas	16xx–16xx	Unk.	Lancaster	1650–54
Teackle, Thomas	1625–95	Unk.	Accomac	1658–95
White, William	16xx–58	Unk.	York	1658
1660–69				
Doggett, Benjamin	1636–82	Unk.	Christ Church	1669–82
Godwyn, Morgan	1640–85	Yes	Marston	1665–66
			York	
Johnson, Edward	16xx–65	Unk.	York	1664–65d.
Morris, Richard	16xx–16xx	Unk.	Pianketant	1663–66
			Lancaster	
			Christ Church	

(Continued)

Name	Birth and Death	Year Ordained	Parishes	Served Years
Parke, Henry	1638–87	Unk.	St George's Accomac	1666
Rodgers, John	16xx–16xx	Unk.	Hungar's	1664
Shepard, John	1646–82	Unk.	Christ Church	1668–82
Taylor, Jeremiah	16xx–16xx	Unk.	Elizabeth City	1667–68
Taylor, John	16xx–16xx	Unk.	Fairfield	1668–70
Tompson, William	1633–65	Cong.	Chicacone Southwark	1664–65
Vicaris, Thomas	16xx–96	Unk.	Lawne's Creek Petsworth	1666–96d.
Waugh, John	16xx–1706	Unk.	Stafford Overwharton	1667–1706
1670–79				
Aylmer, Justinian	1616–69	Unk.	James City Elizabeth City	1671
Ball, John	1665–17xx	Unk.	Henrico, St Peter's	16xx–71 1679–89
Banister, John	1650–92	1674	Charles City	1678–92
Butler, William	1647–17xx	Unk.	Washington	1677–81
Butler, Almeric	1648–78	Unk.	Sittingbourne	1671–78d.
Clough, James	16xx–84	Unk.	James City Southwork	1676–84d.
Farnifold, John	1635–1702	Unk.	Old Fairfield, Boutracey	1670–1702
Gordon, Thomas	16xx–16xx	Unk.	Farnham	1671
Gwynn, John	1642–16xx	Unk.	Abington	1672–88

Name		1666		
Jones, Rowland	1643–88	1666	Bruton; Martin's Hundred	1674–88d.
Jones, Samuel	1637–16xx	Unk.	James City	1671
Key, Isaac	1644–16xx	Unk.	Hungar's	1676–78
Owens, John	16xx–16xx	Unk.	Wicomico	1673–75
Page, John	16xx–88	Unk.	Elizabeth City; St Peter's	1677–88
Pendleton, Nathaniel	1650–74d.	1673	Unk.	1674d.
Porter, James	16xx–83	Unk.	Lynnhaven	1678–83
Richardson, Daniel	Unk.	Unk.	Hungar's	1676
Towers, William	16xx–16xx	Unk.	Wicomico	1672
Wadding, James	16xx–16xx	Unk.	Petsworth; James City	1672
1680–89				
Blair, James	1653–1743	Unk.	Henrico; James City; Bruton	1685–1743
Carr, John	1643–85	Unk.	St Peter's	1684–85d.
Carr, Robert	16xx–17xx	Unk.	Stratton-Major	1680–86
Clayton, John	1657–1725	Unk.	James City	1684–86
Davies, Charles	16xx–16xx	Unk.	Wicomico	1680–83
Davies, Jonathan	16xx–16xx	Unk.	New Poquoson	1680–81
Davis, Superior	16xx–16xx	Unk.	Christ Church	1682–83
Dudley, Samuel	1654–85	Unk.	Sittingbourne; South Farnham	1680–85
D'Oyley, Cope	1658–1702	1682	Elizabeth City; Denbigh; Bruton	1687–1702

(Continued)

Name	Birth and Death	Year Ordained	Parishes	Served Years
Eburne, Samuel	1645–17xx	Yes	Bruton	1688–95
Finney, Thomas	1659–87	Unk.	Charles	1686–87d.
Housden, William	1657–90	Unk.	West Newport	1680d.
Jackson, Andrew	1656–1710	No	St Mary's Whitechapel, Christ Church	1683–1710d.
Kenyon, Abraham	16xx–16xx	Unk.	Cople	1684–85
Lawrence, John	1633–84	Unk.	Mulberry Island Denbigh	1680–84
Mackie, Josias	16xx–1716	Unk.	Elizabeth River	1684–91
Mullett, William	16xx–16xx	Unk.	Christ Church	1683–93
Pead, Deuel	1646–1727	Yes	Christ Church	1683–90
Paris, William	16xx–16xx	1638	Washington	1682–86
Parke, Robert	16xx–16xx	Unk.	Warwisqueake	1680
Perkins, Thomas	16xx–16xx	Unk.	Sittingbourne	1684
Sclater, James	1657–1723	Unk.	Charles	1686–1724
Sellake, William	1617–16xx	Unk.	St Peter's	1680–82
Semple, William	16xx–16xx	Unk.	Unk.	1689
Taylor, Thomas	16xx–16xx	Unk.	Blissland	1680–81
Vary, Isaac	16xx–16xx	Yes	Wallingford	1682–85
Wayre, John	16xx–16xx	Unk.	Lawne's Creek	1680
Wern, William	16xx–16xx	Unk.	Elizabeth River	1680
Williams, William	1657–17xx	Unk.	St Stephen's	1680–1700
Wood, John	1641–16xx	Unk.	Upper Parish	1684–85

Name				
Wright, John	1643–16xx	Unk.	Towson	1680
Williams, Paul	16xx–16xx	Unk.	Weyanoke; Martin's Brandon	1680; 1680–87
Zyperius, Michael 1690–99	16xx–16xx	Dutch Reformed	Kingston	
Alexander, John	1665–17xx	Unk.	Sittingbourne	1696–1704
Allardes, Thomas	1676–1701	Unk.	Unk.	1699–1701
Anderson, Charles	1669–1718	Unk.	Westover	1693–1718
Bolton, John	1635–16xx	Unk.	Cople	1693–98
Bowker, James	1665–1703	Unk.	Kempton, St Peter's	1690–1703
Bushnell, James	16xx–17xx	Unk.	Martin's Hundred	1696–1702
Cant, Andrew	16xx–17xx	Unk.	Lawne's Creek	1696
Clack, James	1673–1723d.	1695	Ware	1695–1723d.
Davis, William	16xx–97	1697	Unk.	1697d.
Flowers, Ralph	16xx–16xx	Unk.	York	1690–91
Fordyce, Francis	1651–16xx	Unk.	Southwark	1696–99
Fouace, Stephen	16xx–17xx	1684	Yorkhampton; Martin's Hundred	1690–1702; 1702
Gordon, John	1674?–17xx	Unk.	Washington; St Peter's	1695–1702
Gray, Samuel	16xx–1709	1689	Christ Church; Cople; St Peter's	1690–1709d.
Gregg, Stephen	16xx–16xx	Unk.	Abington	1691–95
Holt, Joseph	1668–17xx	Unk.	Stratton-Major; Petworth	1696–1700
Hudson, George	1642–96	Unk.	Williamsburg	1694–96d.
Lidford, Matthew	1663–93	1688	Christ Church	1693

192

(Continued)

Name	Birth and Death	Year Ordained	Parishes	Served Years
Mitton, Roger	1663–1740	Unk.	Unk.	ca. 1698
Monroe, John	1662–1723	Unk.	Hungar's	1692–1723
Moreau, Nicholas	16xx–17xx	Unk.	St Peter's, All Faith's	1696–9x
Palmer, Samuel	16xx–17xx	Unk.	Hungar's	1695–1702
Pretty, Henry	1656–17xx	Unk.	Unk.	1696
Robertson, George	1662–1739	Unk.	Bristol	1693–1739
Sandford, Samuel	1669–1710	Unk.	Accomac	1694–1702
Saunders, Jonathan	1670–1701	Unk.	Lynnhaven	1695–1701
Smith, Patrick	16xx–16xx	Unk.	Southwark	1690–91
Wallace, James	1667–1712	Unk.	Elizabeth City	1691–1712d.
Ware, Jacob	16xx–1709	Unk.	St Peter's, Henrico	1690–1709d.
Yates, Robert, Sr.	1673–17xx	Unk.	Christ Church	1699–1703
Young, George	16xx–17xx	Unk.	Petsworth	1699–1700

Appendix III. Universities and colleges attended by seventeenth century Virginia clergymen

University of Aberdeen, King's College
    Allardes, Thomas
    Fordyce, Francis
    Keith, George
    Leslie, Robert
    Moray, Alexander

Edinburgh College
    Blair, James
    Cant, Andrew
    Gray, Samuel
    Mackie, Josias
    Young, George

Glasgow College
    Anderson, Charles

St Andrews
    Robertson, George

University of Cambridge
    Christ's College
        Bolton, John
        Carr, John
    Clare College
        Bargrave, Thomas
        Towers, William
    Corpus Christi College
        Lette, William
        Pendleton, Nathaniel
    Emmanuel College
        Lawrence, John
    Gonville and Caius College
        Bucke, Richard
        Maycocke, Samuel
        Rosier, John
    Jesus College
        Bennett, William
        Glover, Nicholas
        Holt, Joseph

Mitton, Roger
Pretty, Henry
King's College
Bolton, Francis
Magdalene College
Housden, William
Hudson, George
Lake, Thomas
Pembroke College
Gorsuch, John
St Catharine's College
Green, Roger
Key, Isaac
Wright, John
St John's College
Bowker, James
Doggett, Benjamin
Eburne, Samuel
Sidney Sussex College
Butler, Almeric
Butler, William
Harrison, Thomas
Trinity College
Bennett, Thomas
Eaton, Nathaniel
Pead, Deuel
Sandys, David
Whitaker, Alexander
Trinity Hall
Lansdale, Peter

University of Oxford
Brasenose College
Stockton, Jonas
Tompson, William
Watson, Ralph
White, Thomas
Yates, Robert, Sr.
Broadgates Hall
White, George
Christ Church
Godwin, Morgan
Rodgers, John
Wadding, James
Corpus Christi College
Hampton, Thomas
James, Richard
Exeter College
Alford, George

Hart Hall
    Ball, John
    Bracewell, Robert
    Folliott, Edward
    Williams, William
Magdalen College
    Banister, John
    Lidford, Matthew
    Lyford, John
Magdalen Hall
    Clack, James
    Finney, Thomas
    Hunt, Robert
    Wood, John
Merton College
    Clayton, John
    D'Oyle, Cope
    Jones, Rowland
New College
    Farnifold, John
New Inn Hall
    Gwynn, John
Pembroke College
    Sandford, Samuel
    Sellake, William
Queen's College
    Wyatt, Hawte
St Edmund Hall
    Calvert, Simpson
    Dudley, Samuel
    Sclater, James
St Mary's Hall
    Mallory, Philip
Wadham College
    Saunders, Jonathan
    Shepard, John

Harvard College
    Tompson, William

Leyden
    Fouace, Stephen

Appendix IV. A list of early Virginia parishes and seventeenth-century ministers

Abington, ca. 1652, Gloucester County

Gwynn, John	1674–88
Gregg, Stephen	1691–95

Accomack Parish, 1634–43, Accomack County, 1634–43

Bolton, Francis	1621–30
Teackle, Thomas	1658–95
Parke, Henry	1666
Sandford, Samuel	1694–1702

Accomack Parish, 1663–, Accomack County, 1663–
Albemarle Parish, 1738–, Surry County, 1738–53, Sussex County, 1754–
Antrim Parish, 1752–, Halifax County, 1752
Appomattox Parish, ca. 1653–64, Westmoreland County
                Machodick Parish, ca. 1653–64
Bath Parish, 1742–, Dinwiddie County, 1752–
Beckford Parish – 1769–, Frederick County, 1769–72; Dunmore County, 1772–78; Shenandoah County, 1778–
Berkeley Parish – 1770, Spotsylvania County, 1770–
Bermuda Hundred Parish – 1643–1725, Charles City County
Blisland Parish, 1653–, York County, 1653–54, New Kent County, 1654–, James City County, 1767–

Taylor, Thomas	1680–81

Boutracey Parish – no records survive that indicate that this parish was ever formed.

Farnifold, John	1690–1702

Bristol Parish, 1643–1735, Henrico County, 1643–1735
Bromfield Parish – 1752–, Culpeper County, 1752–93
Brunswick Parish – 1732, King George County, 1732–
Bruton Parish, 1674–, York County, 1674–, James City County, 1674–

Jones, Rowland	1674–88
Eburne, Samuel	1688–95
D'Oyley, Cope	1697–1702

Camden Parish, 1767–, Pittslyvania County, 1767–
Cameron Parish, 1749–, Fairfax County, 1749–57; Loudoun County, 1757–

Charles Parish, 1692–, formerly **New Poquoson Parish**, 1635–92, Charles River, 1634–43, York County 1643–

Finney, Thomas	1686–87

Charles City Parish, ca. 1613 – Charles City Corporation, 1618–34, Charles City County, 1634–88

Leslie, Robert	1654–59
Doughty, Francis	1659–62
Hill, Matthew	1669–79
Banister, John	1678–92

Chickacoan Parish, 1645–64, Northumberland County, 1645 – the neck of land between the Rappahannock and Potomac rivers

Taylor, John	1668–70

Chickahominy Parish, 1632–43, **Wallingford Parish**, 1643– to about -72, James City Corporation, 1632–34; James City County, 1634–1721
Chippokes (or **Chippoaks**) **Parish**, 1643–47, James City County, 1643–47
Chishiack (or **Chiskiack**) **Parish**, 1640–43, **Hampton Parish**, 1643–1707, York County, 1640–1707

Keith, George	1628–37
Panton, Anthony	1637–40

Christ Church Parish – 1666, South Side of Rappahannock River; Lancaster County, 1666–69; Middlesex County, 1669–

Cooke, Alexander	1652–57
Armourier, John	1653–54
Cole, Samuel	1657–59
Morris, Richard	1663–66
Shephard, John	1668–82
Doggett, Benjamin	1669–82
Davis, Superior	1682–83
Gray, Samuel	1690–98
Lidford, Matthew	1691–93
Pead, Deuel	1683–90
Yates, Robert, Sr	1699–1703
Jackson, Andrew	1701–10 – a Presbyterian

Cople Parish – ca. 1664, Westmoreland County

Rosier, John	1653–60
Folliot, Edward	1673
Kenyon, Abraham	1684–85
Scrimgeour, John	1687–91
Bolton, John	1693–98
Gray, Samuel	1698–1708

Cornwall Parish, 1757–, Halifax County, 1757–65, Charlotte County, 1765–

Cumberland Parish, 1746–, Lunenburg County, 1746–
Dale Parish, 1735–, Henrico County, 1735–49, Chesterfield County, 1749–
Denbigh Parish, ca. 1635–1725, Warwick County, 1635–1725

White, George	1635
Lawrence, John	1680–84

Dettingen Parish – 1745, Prince William County, 1745–

D'Oyley, Cope	1688–96

Drysdale Parish – 1723–, King and Queen County, 1723–28, King and Queen Caroline Counties, 1728–1780, King and Queen County, 1780–
Elizabeth City Parish – Elizabeth City County

Mease, William	1619–20
Bolton, Francis	1621–23
Fenton, Mr.	1624
Keith, George	1624–26
Stockton, Jonas	1627–28
Graeme, Rowland	1628–16xx
White, Thomas	1622–24
Doughty, Francis	1659–62
Taylor, Jeremiah	1667–68
Aylmer, Justinian	– 1671
Page, John	1677–88
D'Oyley, Cope	1687–88
Wallace, James	1691–1712

Elizabeth River Parish, 1636–1895, Lower Norfolk County, 1637–91, Princess Anne County, 1691–1963

Wilson, John	1637–40
Harrison, Thomas	1640–48
Calvert Simpson	1649
Wern, William	1680
Mackie, Josias	1684–91 – a Presbyterian

Fairfax Parish – 1765, Fairfax County, 1765–1846
Fairfield Parish – 1664–98, Northumberland County, 1645,

Taylor, John	1668–70

Farnham Parish – 1656–83, Rappahannock County, known as the **Upper Parish**

Gordon, Thomas	1671

Fluvanna Parish – 1777–1849, Fluvanna County, 1777–1849
Fredericksville Parish – 1742–, Louisa County, 1742–57; Albemarle and Louisa counties, 1757–1845
Frederick Parish – 1738, Frederick County, 1738–
Hamilton Parish – 1730, Stafford County, 1730–32; Prince William County, 1732–59; Prince William and Fauquier Counties, 1759–70; Fauquier County, 1770–

Hampton Parish, 1643–1707, formerly **Chiskiack Parish**, 1640–43, York County, 1640–1707

Hopkins, George	1643–45
Culverius, Mr	1644
Hampton, Thomas	1645–58

Hanover Parish – 1714–, Richmond County, 1714–20; King George County, 1720–
Harrop Parish, 1645–58, James City County, 1645–58
Henrico Parish, 1611, Henrico Corporation, 1618–34; Henrico County, 1634–

Whitaker, Alexander	1611–17
Wickham, William	1616–22
Bargrave, Thomas	1619–21
Stockton, Jonas	1621–28
Martin, Lazarus	1629
Ball, John	1679–89
Ware, Jacob	c. 1690–1709

Hog Island Parish, ca. 1624, James City Corporation, 1624–34, James City County, 1634–?

Sandys, David	1624–25

Hungar's Parish, 1643, Northampton County, 1643–91–

Bolton, Francis	1623–30
Cotton, William	1632–45
Eaton, Nathaniel	1639–46
Rosier, John	1644–53
Palmer, Thomas	1647–48
Armourier, John	1651–54
Higby, Thomas	1651–54
Doughty, Francis	1655
Rodgers, John	1664
Richardson, Daniel (David?)	16xx–76
Key, Isaac	1676–78
Monroe, John	1692–1723
Palmer, Samuel	1695–1702

Isle of Wight– 1637, Isle of Wight County

Dunster, Robert	1651–56
Bracewell, Robert	1653–58

James City Parish, 1607– James City Corporation, 1618–34, James City County, 1634–1712

Hunt, Robert	1607–08
Bucke, Richard	1610–23
Glover, Nicholas	1611
Poole, John	1611

Wyatt, Hawte	1621–25
Ferrers, Nicholas	1626–37
Hampton, Thomas	1640–81
Green, Roger	1656–71
Lansdale, Peter	1658–60
Mallory, Philip	1657–61
Godwyn, Morgan	1665–60
Aylmer, Justinian	1671
Jones, Samuel	1671
Clough, James	1676–81
Jones, Rowland	1680
Wadding, Jones	1672
Clayton, John	1684–86
Blair, James	1694–1710

Jordan's Journey Parish, 1618–88, Charles City Corporation, 1618–34, Charles City County, 1634–88
Kecoughtan Parish, 1610–19, **Elizabeth City Parish**, 1619–34 Elizabeth City Corporation 1619–35, Elizabeth City County, 1634–1952
King William Parish, 1700–, Henrico County, 1700–28; Goochland and Henrico Counties, 1728–49; Cumberland County, 1749–77; Powhatan County, 1777–
Kingston Parish – ca. 1652, Gloucester County, 1652–1791

Zyperius, Michael	1680–87
Bowker, James	1690–91

Lancaster Parish – 1657–66, Lancaster County, 1657–66

Sax, Thomas	1650–54
Gorsuch, John	1654–57
Morris, Richard	1663–66

Lawne's Creek Parish, 1640–1738, James City County, 1634–52, Surry County, 1652–1738

Tompson, William	1664–65
Wayre, John	1680
Cant Andrew	1696

Leeds Parish – 1770, Fauquier County, 1770–
Littleton Parish, 1772–1912, Cumberland County, 1912
Lower Parish, 1643–91, Northampton County, 1643–91
Lower Parish – ca. 1664–ca. 1680, Stafford County, 1664–77; King George County, 1777–

Choptank Parish – ca. 1680–ca 1702
St Paul's Parish – ca. 1702

Lunenburg Parish – 1732, Richmond County, 1732
Lynnhaven Parish, 1643–, Lower Norfolk County, 1637–91, Princess Anne County, 1691–1963

Wilkerson, William   1635–37
Powis, Robert   1645–52
Mallory, Phillip   1657
Alford, George   1658
Porter, James   1678–83
Saunders, Jonathan   1695–1701

Manchester Parish, 1772–, Chesterfield County, 1772–
Marston Parish, 1654–74, York County, 1654–74

Godwyn, Morgan   1665–66

Martin's Brandon Parish, 1618–, Charles City Corporation, 1618–34, Charles City Corporation, 1634–1703, Prince George County, 1703–

Paulett, Robert   1619–21
Williams, Paul   1680

Martin's Hundred Parish, 1618–1712, James City Corporation, 1618–34, James City County, 1634–1712

Paulett, Robert   1619–21
Lyford, John   1628–29
Mynnard, Mr.   1628
Pooley, Greville   1628–29
Jones, Rowland   1650–55
Bushnell, James   1696–1702
Fouace, Stephen   1702–

Meherrin Parish, 1754, Brunswick County, 1754–81, Greensville County, 1781–
Middle Plantation Parish, 1633–58, Charles River County, 1634–43, York County, 1643–58
Middletown Parish, 1658–74, York County, 1658–74
Mulberry Island Parish, 1634–1725, Warwick River County, 1634–43, Warwick County, 1643–1725

Heyley, Willis   1634–35
Lawrence, John   1680–84

Nansemond Parish, 1636 Nansemond County

Tompson, William   1642-43
Bennett, Thomas   1648

New Poquoson Parish, 1635–92, Charles River, 1634–43, York County 1643–

Wright, John   1680
Davis, Jonathan   1680–81

Newport Parish, 1643–, Isle of Wight County

Housden, William   1680

Nomini Parish – 1653–ca. 1668, Northumberland County, May–July 1653; Westmoreland County, 1653–ca. 1668

Northampton Parish, 1643–63, formerly **Accomack Parish**, 1634–43, Accomack County, 1634–43

Doughty, Francis 1662–65

North Farnham Parish, 1683, Rappahannock County, 1683–92; Richmond County, 1692–
Nottoway Parish, 1748–55, **St Patrick's Parish**, 1755–, Prince Edward County, 1755–
Occohannock Parish, 1652–63, Northampton County, 1652–63
Old Fairfield, Northumberland County

Farnifold, John 1670–72

Overwharton Stafford County

Waugh, John 1680–1706

Petsworth Parish – ca. 1652, Gloucester County, 1652–

Vicaris, Thomas 1666–96
Wadding, James 1672
Holt, Joseph 1697–1700
Young, George 1699–1700

Pianketant Parish – 1657–66, Lancaster County, 1657–66; divided and reunited as Christ Church, Lancaster County

Cole, Samuel 1657–59
Morris, Richard 1663–66

Portsmouth Parish, 1761–, Norfolk County, 1761–
Potomac Parish – ca. 1653, Westmoreland County, 1653–64; Stafford County, 1664–
Raleigh Parish, 1735–, Amelia County, 1735–
St Andrew's Parish, 1720–, Brunswick County, 1720–
St Anne's Parish – 1704, Essex County, 1704–
St Anne's Parish, 1744–, Albemarle County, 1744–
St Asaph's Parish, 1780–, Caroline County, 1780–
St Bride's Parish, 1761, Norfolk County, 1761–
St David's Parish – 1745, King William County, 1745–
St George's Parish – 1714, Essex County, 1714–21; Spotsylvania County, 1721–

Parke, Henry 1666–87

St George's Parish, 1763–, Accomack County, 1763–
St James' Parish – 1720–44, Henrico County, 1720–28; Goochland County, 1728–44
St James-Northam Parish – 1744–, Goochland County, 1744–
St James Parish, 1761–, Lunenburg County, 1761–65, Mecklenburg County, 1765–
St John's Parish – 1680, New Kent County, 1680–91; King and Queen County, 1691–1701; King William County, 1701–

St Luke's Parish, 1762–, Southampton County
St Margaret's Parish– 1721, King William County, 1721–28; Caroline County, 1728–
St Mark's Parish – 1730, Spotsylvania County, 1730–34; Orange County, 1734–49; Culpeper County, 1749–
St Martin's Parish – 1727, Hanover County, 1727–
St Mary's Parish – 1677, Rappahannock County, 1677–92; Richmond County, 1692–1714; Essex County, 1692–1727; Caroline County, 1727–
St Mary's Whitechapel, Lancaster County

    Jackson, Andrew   1683–1710

St Paul's Parish – 1680, Stafford County, 1680–1776; King George County, 1776–
St Paul's Parish – 1704–, New Kent County, 1704–20; Hanover County, 1720–
St Peter's Parish – 1679, New Kent County, 1679

Sellake, William	1680–82
Carr, John	1684–85
Ball, John	1685–89
Page, John	1687–88
Boisseau, James	1690–17xx
Ware, Jacob,	1690–96
Gordon, John	1695
Moreau, Nicholas	1696–16xx
Bowker, James	1698–1703

St Peter's Parish – 1679, New Kent County, 1679–
St Stephen's Parish – ca 1674–, New Kent County, 1674–91, King and Queen County, 1691–
St Stephen's Parish – 1698–, Northumberland County, 1645–
St Thomas' Parish – 1740, Orange County, 1740–
Shelburne Parish – 1770–, Loudoun County, 1770–
Sittenbourne Parish – 1661–1732, Rappahannock County, 1661–92; Essex County, 1692–1704; Richmond County, 1692–1732

Doughty, Francis	1665–69
Butler, Almeric	1671–78
Perkins, Thomas	1684
Dudley, Samuel	1680–84
Alexander, John	1696–1704

Smith's Hundred – 1617–19, Charles City Corporation
South Farnham Parish – 1683, Rappahannock County, 1683–92, Essex County 1692–

Dudley, Samuel	1684–85

Southam Parish, 1744–, Goochland County, 1744–49, Cumberland County, 1749–77, Powhatan County, 1777–
Southhampton Parish – 1619–22, Charles City Corporation, 1618–34
Southern Shore

Powis, Robert	1640–45

Southwark Parish, 1647, James City County, 1647–52, Surry County, 1652–

Lake, Thomas	1655
Tompson, William	1664–65
Clough, James	1684
Smith, Patrick	1690–91
Fordyce, Francis	1696–99

Stanley Hundred Parish, 1627–34
Mulberry Island Parish, 1634–1725
Stratton-Major – 1655–, New Kent County, 1655–91, King and Queen County, 1691–

Munro, John	1650–55
Carr, Robert	1680–86
Holt, Joseph	1696–1700

Tillotson Parish, 1757–, Albemarle County, 1757–61, Buckingham County, 1761–
Trinity Parish – 1762, Louisa County, 1762–
Truro Parish – 1732–, Prince William County, 1732–42; Fairfax County, 1742–
Upper Parish, 1643–91, Northampton County, 1643–91, also known as **Nuswattocks Parish,** and later as **Hungar's Parish**
Varina Parish, 1680–1714, Henrico County, 1680–1714
Wallingford Parish – 1643–1720, Charles City County

Hampton, Thomas	1680–81
Vary, Isaac	1682–85 at least

Ware Parish – ca. 1652, Gloucester County, 1651–

Moray, Alexander	1653–72
Gwynn, John	1672–74
Clack, James	1695–1723

Warwick Parish, 1725–, Warwick County, 1724–1952
Warwisquesake Parish, ca. 1629, (**Upper Parish** after 1643), Warwisquesake County, 1634–37, Isle of Wight County, 1637–
Waters Creek Parish, 1629–1643, **Nutmeg Quarter Parish,** 1643–56, Corporation of Elizabeth City, 1629–34, Warwick County, 1634–56
Washington Parish – 1664–, Westmoreland County
          Washington King George County

Butler, William	1671–81
Paris, William	1682–86

West and Shirley Parish – 1613–22, Charles City Corporation, 1618–34;

Green, Roger	1653–71
Housden, William	1680

Westbury Parish – 1665–ca. 1680, Westmoreland County
Westover Parish, 1618–1721, Charles City Corporation, 1618–34, Charles City County, 1634–1703, Prince George County, 1703–21

Anderson, Charles	1693–1718

Weyanoke Parish, 1618–1721, Charles City Corporation, 1618–34, Charles City County, 1634–1703, Prince George County, 1703–21

Paulett, Robert	1621–22
Pooley, Greville	1622–29
Parks, Robert c.	1680
Williams, Paul c.	1680
Palmer, Samuel	1695–1702

Wicomico Parish – 1648, Northumberland County

Armourier, John	1653–63
Lindsay, David	1655–77
Towers, William	1672
Owens, John	1673–75
Davies, Charles	1680–83

Wilmington Parish, 1658–1725, James City County, 1658–1725

Hampton, Thomas	1680–81
Gordon, John	1695–1702

York County 1634 York County

Watson, Ralph	1645
Mallory, Phillip	1658–61
Johnson, Edward	1664–65

York Parish, ca. 1638–1707, Charles River County, 1634–43, York County, 1643–1707

Panton, Anthony	1637–40
Rosier, John	1640–44
Folliott, Edward	1652–90
White, William	1658
Temple, Peter	1686–87
Flowers, Ralph	1690–91

Yorkhampton Parish, 1707–, James City County, 1712–
Unknown

Maycocke, Samuel	1618–22
James, Richard	1628–29
Leete (Leate), William	1622
Pendleton, Nathaniel	1674
Semple, William	1689
Allardes, Thomas	1699–1701
Davis, William	1697d.
Wood, John	1684–85
Gregory, John	1691
Mitton, Roger ca.	1698
Pretty, Henry	1696

Notes

Prologue

1. Alan Ford, *The Protestant Reformation in Ireland, 1590–1641* (Dublin, 1997): 156–64; Alan Ford, *James Ussher, Theology, History, and Politics in Early Modern Ireland and England* (Oxford, 2007): 85–107.
2. George Maclaren Brydon, *Virginia's Mother Church and the Political Conditions under which it Grew* (Richmond, Philadelphia, 1947, 1952) 2 vols.; John K. Nelson, *A Blessed Company: Parishes, Parson's and Parishioners in Anglican Virginia, 1690–1776* (Chapel Hill, 2001); Rhys Isaac, *The Transformation of Virginia, 1740–1790* (Chapel Hill, 1982).
3. For example it remained outside the scope of Nathan O. Hatch's admirable study, *The Democratization of American Christianity* (New Haven, 1989).
4. John F. Woolverton, 'Philadelphia's William White: Episcopalian Distinctiveness and Accommodation in the Post-Revolutionary Period', *H.M.P.E.C.* 43 (1974) 279–96.
5. William B. Willcox, *The Papers of Benjamin Franklin* (New Haven, 1973) 17: 246; *ibid.* (New Haven, 1975) 19: 246; Nuxall, Elizabeth M. and Mary Gallagher, eds., *The Papers of Robert Morris* (Pittsburgh, 1999) 9: 711, 729, 747, 785, 805, 823, 839.
6. William White, *The Case of the Episcopal Churches in the United States of America* (Philadelphia, 1782): 4.
7. *Ibid.* 5–6.
8. *Ibid.* 6.
9. *Ibid.* 7.
10. *Ibid.* 10–13.
11. *Ibid.* 11.
12. Adams, Charles Francis, *The Works of John Adams, second president of the United States: with a life of the author, notes, and illustrations* (Boston, 1853) Vol. 8: 333–35, 349–50.

Chapter 1: England's Early Imperial Interests: Ireland and Virginia

1. Bede, *The Ecclesiastical History of the English People: The Greater Chronicle: Bede's Letter to Egbert*, Judith McClue and Roger Collins, eds. (Oxford, 1994): 221.
2. Graeme J. White, *Restoration and Reform, 1153–1165: Recovery from Civil War in England* (Cambridge, 2000): 4–5, 8.
3. *Ibid.* 17–18. Bulls are papal letters or edicts, the name of which derives from the Latin *bulla*, or leaden seal, which most often sealed the documents. Donations were gifts or endowments of lands. The most famous was the

Donation of Constantine, which stated that the Roman Emperor gave Italian lands to Sylvester, bishop of Rome. Roman Catholic popes frequently cited the donation in order to give longer and more sturdy and lofty origins to papal territorial claims, but Lorenzo Valla (*ca.* 1407–57), an Italian humanist, showed it to be a forgery of the eighth century.

4. Edmund Curtis and R. B. McDowell, eds., *Irish Historical Documents, 1172– 1922* (London, 1968): 19–22.

5. Donald Barr Chidsey, *Sir Humphrey Gilbert, Elizabeth's Racketeer* (New York, 1932): 78–84, 111–19, 158–95; Raleigh Trevelyan, *Sir Walter Raleigh* (London, 2002): 60–65; Peter C. Mancall, Hakluyt's Promise: An Elizabethan's Obsession for an English America (New Haven, 2007): 69–71, 93–101.

6. Richard Hakluyt, 'A discourse Concerning Western Planting Written in the Year 1584', *Collections of the Maine Historical Society* (Cambridge, Mass., 1877) Second series, Vol. 2: 45–63.

7. *Ibid.*, 7–12.

8. Richard Hakluyt, *Principal Navigations, Voyages, Traffiques & Discoveries of the English Nation made by sea or overland to the remote & farthest distant quarters of the earth at any time within the compasse of these 1600 years* (London, 1589, 1907 edition) VI: 50–8.

9. Hakluyt, *Discourse*: 12; Anthony Pagden, *Lords of all the World: Ideologies of Empire in Spain, Britain and France, c. 1500–c. 1800* (New Haven, 1995): 88.

10. Klaus E. Knorr, *British Colonial Theories, 1570–1850* (Toronto, 1944): 28–9; Pagden, *Lords of all the World*: 35–6; John Frederick Woolverton, *Colonial Anglicans in North America* (Detroit, 1984): 48–9; David Armitage, *The Ideological Origins of the British Empire* (Cambridge, 2000): 62–6.

11. Anthony McFarlane, *The British in the Americas: 1480–1815* (London, 1994): 24–31.

12. E. M. Carus-Wilson, *Medieval Merchant Venturers*. Second edition (London, 1967): 142–3.

13. R. H.Tawney, *Religion and the Rise of Capitalism: A Historical Study* (New York, 1954): 63–72; Christopher Hill, *Change and Continuity in 17th-Century England*, Revised edition (London, 1991): 81–102.

14. Philip Lawson, *The East India Company: A History* (London, 1993): 1–17; John Keay, *The Honourable Company: A History of the English East India Company* (London, 1993): 9, 13; K. N. Chaudhuri, *The English East India Company* (New York, 1965): 10–14; Rudolph Robert, *Chartered Companies and their Role in the Development of Overseas Trade* (London, 1969): 65–7.

15. Wallace MacCaffrey, *Elizabeth I* (London, 1983): 420.

16. R. H. Tawney, *Religion and the Rise of Capitalism: A Historical Study* (New York, 1954).

17. MacCulloch, *Thomas Cranmer*; Thomas F. Mayer, *Reginald Pole: Prince and Prophet* (Cambridge, 2000); V. J. K. Brook, *A Life of Archbishop Parker* (Oxford, 1962); Patrick Collinson, *Archbishop Grindal, 1519–1583* (London, 1979); John Strype, *The Life and Acts of John Whitgift, D.D.: The Third and Last Lord Archbishop of Canterbury in the Reign of Queen Elizabeth* (Oxford, 1822).

18. Colm Lennon and Ciaran Diamond, 'The Ministry of the Church of Ireland, 1536–1636' write that 'The ministry of the first and second generations, that is from 1536 to approximately 1600, was characterized largely by continuity from the Reformation era, and the implications of this continuum bear

scrutiny in the light of the slow progress of the reform before the seventeenth century', in T. C. Barnard and W. G. Neely, eds., *The Clergy of the Church of Ireland, 1000–2000: Messengers, Watchmen and Stewards* (Dublin. 2006): 44.

19. A comparative study of salaries in England is Claire Cross, "The incomes of provincial clergy, 1520–1645', in Rosemary O'Day and Felicity Heal, eds., *Princes and Paupers in the English Church, 1500–1800* (Leicester, 1981): 65–89; Michael L. Zell, 'Economic problems of the parochial clergy in the sixteenth century', in O'Day and Heal, *Princes and Paupers*: 19–43.

20. 'Clergy of the Church of England Database, 1540–1835', www.theclergy database.org.uk (accessed 14 February 2013); and 'The Colonial American Clergy of the Church of England, 1607–1783 Database', www.JamesBBell. com (accessed 14 February 2013).

Chapter 2: The Virginia Company of London and England's Second Colonial Venture: Virginia, 1606–24

1. Charles M. Andrews, *The Colonial Period of American History* (New Haven, 1934), I: 31–40, 82–9, 295. The Charters of each colony may be conveniently found at www.law.Yale.edu at the Law School Library in The Avalon Project, Documents in Law, History, and Diplomacy.

2. Council for New England (1620) was a closed corporation of forty members chartered as a reorganized branch of the Plymouth Company (1606) comprised a group of nobles and landed gentry chiefly interested in developing manors rather than trade. They obtained the 'New England' area between the latitudes 40° and 48° (roughly from southern Pennsylvania to northern Maine), which they planned to grant as fiefs. The attempts of the Council generally failed but its small grants to two non-member groups proved unexpectedly successful: Plymouth Colony survived, and the Massachusetts Bay Company attracted Puritans in large numbers.

3. George D. Langdon, *Pilgrim Colony: A History of New Plymouth, 1620–1691* (New Haven, 1966): 2, 8–9; Andrews, *Colonial Period of American History*, I: 294–96.

4. Andrews, *Colonial Period of American History*, I: 322–5, 344–53; Frances Rose-Troup, *The Massachusetts Bay Company and its Predecessors* (New York, 1930).

5. Andrews, *Colonial Period of American History* I: 344–74.

6. William Waller Hening, *The Statutes at Large being a Collection of all the Laws of Virginia from the First Session of the Legislature in the Year 1619* (Charlottesville, 1969 edition), I: 68–9.

7. Andrews, *Colonial Period of American History*, I: 369.

8. A copy of the charter may be found at www.law.Yale.edu at the Law School Library in The Avalon Project, Documents in Law, History, and Diplomacy.

9. John Winthrop's sermon is conveniently available in the *Winthrop Papers* (Boston, 1931), 2: 282–95. See, too, Francis J. Bremer, *John Winthrop, America's Forgotten Founding Father* (New York, 2003): 173–84; Susan Hardman Moore, 'Popery, Purity and Providence: Deciphering the New England Experiment', in Anthony Fletcher and Peter Roberts, *Religion, Culture and Society in Early Modern Britain* (Cambridge, 1994): 257–89.

10. Samuel Eliot Morison, ed., *Of Plymouth Plantation, 1620–1647* (New York, 1952); Richard S. Dunn, James Savage, and Laetitia Yeandle, *The Journal of John Winthrop, 1630–1649* (Cambridge, 1996).
11. James B. Bell, *The Imperial Origins of the King's Church in Early America, 1607–1783* (London, 2004): 3–5.
12. Susan Myra Kingsbury, ed., *The Records of the Virginia Company of London* (Washington, DC, 1933), 3: 4–5.
13. Bell, *Imperial Origins of the King's Church*: 3–6.
14. Kingsbury, *Records of the Virginia Company*, 3: 1–3.
15. Hening, *Statutes at Large*, I: 68–9. The requirement was refined and repeated by the subsequent sessions of the Assembly on 5 March 1623/24, 24 March 1629/30, 21 February 1631/32: 121, 149, 155.
16. George MacLaren Brydon, *Virginia's Mother Church and the Political Conditions under which it Grew* (Richmond, 1947), I: 16–18; Bernard Bailyn, *The Barbarous Years: The Conflict of Civilization*, (New York, 2012): 49–77, 81–96.
17. Kingsbury, *Records of the Virginia Company*, 3: 93.
18. *Ibid.* 172.
19. *Ibid.*
20. David H. Flaherty ed., *For the colony in Virginia Britannia: Lawes Divine, Morall and Martiall etc.*, compiled by William Strachey (Charlottesville, 1969): xxi–xxii; Richard L. Morton, *Colonial Virginia: The Tidewater Period, 1607–1710* (Chapel Hill, 1960), I: 32.
21. Brydon, *Virginia's Mother Church*, I: 16–18. Flaherty, *Lawes Diuine, Morall and Martiall*: xxii–xxiv.
22. Flaherty, *Lawes Divine, Morall and Martiall*: 10–11.
23. *Ibid.*: 11.
24. *Ibid.*: 11.
25. *Ibid.*: 11–12.
26. *Ibid.*
27. *Ibid.*: 12, *Constitution and Canons Ecclesiastical 1604*, with notes by J. V. Bullard (London, 1934): 72–4.
28. Morton, *Colonial Virginia*, I: 57.
29. Kingsbury, *Records of the Virginia Company*, 3: 102.
30. *Ibid.*
31. See Appendix II.
32. Brydon, *Virginia's Mother Church*, I: 61–9.
33. Warren M. Billings, *A Little Parliament: The Virginia General Assembly in the Seventeenth Century* (Richmond, 2004): 5–10.
34. *Constitution and Canons Ecclesiastical 1604*, 2, 12, Canons 1 and 14; Kingsbury, *Records of the Virginia Company*, 3: 172.
35. *Ibid.*: 171. Apparently the keeping of the Register was an irregular practice by the mid-1680s, perhaps earlier. On 6 July 1686 Governor Francis Howard issued a 'Proclamation concerning parish registers'. He noted that the statutory obligations had not been duly observed in the parishes. Howard required that the vestry, minister, or reader of every parish maintain the record and submit it on 6 April each year to the Secretary of the province. He empowered the Justices of the Peace to inquire of the Grand Jury of their counties whether any minister, reader, or master of a family has been negligent in fulfilling their duties in reporting the details as required

under the law. Billings, *The Papers of Francis Lord Howard of Effingham*: 261–3.

36. *Constitution and Canons Ecclesiastical 1604*: 72–74, Canon 70.
37. Church attendance was viewed as a means of maintaining moral conduct in the community. The General Assembly during the seventeenth century enacted from time to time legislation governing appropriate Sabbath Day observance. A violation of the statutes, such as not attending church, gaming, or fishing, carried punishments and fines. The clergymen and churchwardens were charged by law with monitoring such behaviour and were responsible for upholding the law and presenting violators to the authorities for review and discipline. See Winton U. Solberg, *Redeem the Time: The Puritan Sabbath, in Early America* (Cambridge, 1977): 85–93, 99–103. Anecdotal evidence provides isolated examples of persons who violated the laws and the discipline imposed. A comprehensive analysis of the problem in the seventeenth century would be helpful. A useful comparative work of the situation in England at the time is Christopher Haigh, 'The Clergy and Parish Discipline in England, 1570–1640' in Bridget Heal and Ole Peter Grell, eds., *The Impact of the European Reformation: Princes, Clergy and People* (Aldershot, 2008): 124–41.
38. Kingsbury, *Virginia Company Records*, I: 516.
39. *Ibid.*
40. Hening, *Statutes at Large*, 5 March 1623/24, I: 122–3.
41. *Ibid.*: 123. Nicholas Canny, 'England's New World and the Old, 1480s–1630s' in Nicholas Canny, ed., *The Origins of Empire: British Overseas Enterprise to the Close of the Seventeenth Century* (Oxford, 1998), I: 164. Peter C. Mancall, 'Native Americans and Europeans in English America, 1500–1700' in Canny, ed., *The Origins of Empire*, I: 337–8.
42. Christopher Haigh, *English Reformations: Religion, Politics, and society under the Tudors* (Oxford, 1993) Diarmaid MacCulloch, *The Later Reformation in England, 1547–1603* (Basingstoke, 1990).
43. Keith Wrightson, *English Society, 1580–1680* (London, 1982): 200.
44. Haigh, *English Reformations*: 285–95.
45. For an excellent account of the mission of the leaders and churches of the New England colonies see David A. Weir, *Early New England: A Covenanted Society* (Grand Rapids, 2005): chapters 1 and 2.

Chapter 3: Virginia and Royal Jurisdiction: Laws, Governors, and Church: 1624–60

1. Bernard Bailyn, *The Barbarous Years: The Conflict of Civilization, 1600–1675* (New York, 2012): 77–80.
2. Robert M. Bliss, *Revolution and Empire: English Politics and the American Colonies in the Seventeenth Century* (Manchester, 1990): 17–44.
3. The two clergymen were Richard Bucke (1584–1623), a graduate of Gonville and Caius College at Cambridge University who served the church at Jamestown from 1610 to 1623, and William Mease (1574–16xx) who served the congregation at Elizabeth City from 1610 to 1620. For biographical

details see 'The Colonial American Clergy of the Church of England' at www. jamesbbell.com.

4. R. G. Marsden, 'A Virginian Minister's Library, 1635', *American Historical Review*, 11, 2 (1906): 330.
5. George Abbot, *A Briefe Description of the Whole World* (London, 1599).
6. *Acts of the Privy Council of England, 1628 July–1629 April* (London, 1958): 30; *A.P.C.E. Col. Ser., 1613–1680*, I: 127.
7. *Ibid.*: 82.
8. Hugh Trevor-Roper, *Archbishop Laud, 1573–1645*, second edition (London, 1988): 258.
9. William W. Hening, *The Statutes at Large being a Collection of all the Laws of Virginia from the First Session of the Legislature in the Year 1619* (Charlottesville, 1969 edition), 21 February 1631–32, I: 155–61, 14 September 1632, I: 180–3, 1 February 1632/33, I: 202–8.
10. *Ibid.*: 155.
11. *Ibid.*: 156.
12. *Ibid.*: 158.
13. *Ibid.*: 156–7; *Constitutions and Canons Ecclesiastical 1604*, 66, 62.
14. Hening, *Statutes at Large*, I: 160.
15. *Ibid.*: 159.
16. *Calendar of State Papers Domestic Series of the Reign of Charles I, 1633–1634*, John Bruce, ed. (London, 1863): 225. The Order read: 'The company of Merchant Adventurers should not hereafter receive any minister into their churches in foreign parts without his Majesty's approbation of the person; the Liturgy and discipline used in the Church of England should be received there, and in all things concerning their church government they should be under the jurisdiction of the Bishop of London.' Issued only to the Merchant Adventurers on the continent, the order was not applied to the officials governing royal colonies in America.
17. *Calendar of State Papers, Colonial Series, I, 1574–1660*, 28 April 1634. A similar grant was issued by the Privy Council on 10 April 1636.
18. Alfred Lyon Cross, *The Anglican Episcopate and the American Colonies* (New York, 1902): 18–22.
19. Oliver M. Dickerson, *American Colonial Government 1696–1765: A Study of the British Board of Trade in its Relation to the American Colonies Political, Industrial, Administrative* (Cleveland, 1912): 17.
20. Trevor-Roper, *Laud*: 258.
21. Warren H. Billings, *Sir William Berkeley and the Forging of Colonial Virginia* (Baton Rouge, 2004): 12–28.
22. *Ibid.*: 38; Bailyn, *The Barbarous Years*: 180–6.
23. George MacLaren Brydon, *Virginia's Mother Church and The Political Conditions Under which It Grew* (Richmond, 1947), I: 445. For the 1641 Act see *V.M.H.B.*, IX (1902): 50. See Hening, *Statutes at Large*, I: 311–12 for the March 1645/46 Act that continued the terms of the 1641 and 1644 statutes, and Brydon, *Virginia's Mother Church*, I: 448–9 for the 1647 Act.
24. Hening, *Statutes at Large*, 2 March 1642/43, I: 240.
25. *Ibid. Constitution and Canons Ecclesiastical 1604*: 124–8, Canons 119, 120, and 121.
26. Brydon, *Virginia's Mother Church*, I: 437.

27. Hening, *Statues at Large*, I: 241–2.
28. Warren M. Billings, ed., 'Some Acts Not in Hening's Statutes The Acts of Assembly', April 1652, November 1652 and July 1653, *V.M.H.B.* 83 (1975): 31–2.
29. See Appendix II for a list of the men and congregations.
30. Doughty took the oath of allegiance to Charles II in 1660 and served congregations in Virginia until his death in 1669. See both men's biographical entries at 'Colonial American Clergy of the Church of England, 1607–1783 Database', at www.jamesbbell.com.
31. Hening, *Statutes at Large*, I: 418. The law was reenacted on 13 March 1657/58 as Act CVII, *Ibid.*: 481.
32. Bliss, *Revolution and Empire*: 103–31.
33. Hening, *Statutes at Large*, II: 25–37, 44–55.
34. *Ibid.*, II: 30, Act XXXIII.
35. See Appendix II for a list of the men.
36. Hening, *Virginia Statutes at Large*, II: 30–1. Act XXXV.
37. *Ibid.*: 34.
38. Roger Green, *Virginia's Cure, or an Advise Narrative Concerning Virginia Discovering the True Ground of the Church's Unhappiness, and the only true Remedy. As it was presented to the Right Reverend Father in God Guilbert Lord Bishop of London [Anglican], September 2, 1661. Now publish'd to further the Welfare of that and the like Plantations* (London, 1662).
39. Green's suggestion regarding the need for the development of towns in the province was included in the Royal Instructions to Governor Francis Howard in 1683; Warren M. Billings, ed., *The Papers of Francis Howard, Baron Howard of Effingham, 1643–1695* (Richmond, 1989): 26.
40. The idea for the fellowship program was embraced by the General Assembly in Act XXXV of 23 March 1660/61, Hening, *Statutes at Large*, II: 30–1.

Chapter 4: Churches and Worship

1. Keith Wrightson, *English Society, 1580–1680* (London, 1982): 200.
2. Christopher Haigh, *English Reformations: Religion, Politics, and Society under the Tudors* (Oxford, 1993): 285–95.
3. James B. Bell, *The Imperial Origins of the King's Church, in Early America, 1607–1783* (Basingstoke, 2004): 10–25.
4. Dell Upton, *Holy Things and Profane: Anglican Parish Churches in Colonial Virginia* (Cambridge, 1986).
5. Horton Davies, *Worship and Theology in England: From Cranmer to Hooker, 1534–1613* (Grand Rapids, 1996 edition), I: 356–65; II, *Andrewes to Baxter, 1603–90*: 31–56; Nigel Yates, *Buildings, Faith, and Worship: The Liturgical Arrangement of Anglican Churches, 1600–1900* (Oxford, revised edition, 2000): xvii–xviii, 23–43; Eamon Duffy, *The Stripping of the Altars: Traditional Religion in England c. 1400–c. 1580*, second edition (New Haven, 2005): 377–593.
6. Babette M. Levy, 'Early Puritanism in the Southern and Island Colonies' in *P.A.A.S.* (1960), 70: 107–11.
7. Davies, *Worship and Theology*, II: 329–404.
8. *Ibid.*: 286, for practice in England during the period.

9. *Ibid.*: 215–52.
10. For an account of the religious practices of English families of the period see Christopher Hill, *Society and Puritanism in Pre-Revolutionary England* (London, 1964): 443–79.
11. *Constitution and Canons Ecclesiastical 1604*, with notes by J. V. Bullard (London, 1934): 84–6, Canons, 81, 82.
12. George Yule, 'James VI and I: Furnishing the Churches in His Two Kingdoms' in Anthony Fletcher and Peter Roberts, *Religion, Culture and Society in Early Modern Britain* (Cambridge, 1994): 182–208.For an excellent study of the situation in England see Kenneth Fincham and Nicholas Tyacke, *Altars Restored: The Changing Face of English Religious Worship, 1547–c. 1700* (Oxford, 2007); Peter Lake, "The Laudian Style: Order, Uniformity and the Pursuit of Beauty of Holiness in the 1630s' in Kenneth Fincham, ed., *The Early Stuart Church, 1603–1642* (Basingstoke, 1988): 115–37; Louise Durning and Clare Tilbury, 'Looking unto Jesus' Image and Belief in a Seventeenth-Century English Chancel', *J. Eccl. Hist.* 60 (2009): 491–513.
13. Fincham and Tyacke, *Altars Restored:* 126–352.
14. *Ibid.*: 108–47.
15. Addleshaw and Echtells, *Architectural Setting of Anglican Worship*, 64–107.
16. Jon Butler, ed., 'Two 1642 Letters from Virginia Puritans' *M.H.S.P.* Vol. 84 (Boston, 1973): 99.
17. John Smith, *Captain John Smith, Writings with other Narratives of Roanoke, Jamestown and the First English Settlement of America* (New York, 2007, Library of America edition): 808–9; Philip Alexander Bruce, *Institutional History of Virginia in the Seventeenth Century: An inquiry into the religious, moral educational, legal, military, and political condition of the people there based on original and contemporaneous records* (New York, 1910), I: 94.
18. Smith, *Captain John Smith, Writings*: 44.
19. Bruce, *Institutional History*, I: 94–5; Smith, *Captain John Smith, Writings*: 54; Robert Hunt lost all of his library and possessions except the clothes on his back in the fire.
20. Smith, *Captain John Smith, Writings*: 56, 329.
21. *Ibid.*: 95. See www.preservationvirginia.org for recent details regarding the excavation of James Fort (1607–24) and the possible foundation of the first substantial church built at Jamestown in 1608.
22. Susan Myra Kingsbury, ed., *The Records of the Virginia Company of London* (Washington, DC, 1933), 3: 14, 17.
23. Smith, *Captain John Smith, Writings*: 95–6; Alexander Brown's *Genesis of United States* (New York, 1890), I: 492.
24. Bruce, *Institutional History*, I: 97; Edward Arber, ed., *Works of Captain John Smith* (London, 1895), II: 535.
25. Bruce, *Institutional History*, I: 97–8.
26. *Ibid.*: 101.
27. Duffy, *Stripping of the Altars*: 11–376; Marcus Wiffen, *Stuart and Georgian Churches: The Architecture of the Church of England outside London, 1603–1837* (London, 1947): 9–27; G.W.O. Addleshaw and Frederick Echtells, *The Architectural Setting of Anglican Worship* (London, 1948): 15–173.
28. William Walter Hening, *The Statutes at Large, being a Collection of all of the Laws of Virginia from the First Session of the Legislature in the Year 1619*

(Charlottesville, 1969 edition), 21 February, 1631/32, I: 160–1; Upton, *Holy Things and Profane*, xv.

29. Horton Davies, *The Worship of the Puritans, 1629–1730* (New York, 1990): 233–5, 287–92.

30. Upton, *Holy Things and Profane*: 11–13; Peter Benes, *Meetinghouses of Early New England* (Amherst, 2012): 77–117.

31. *Ibid.*: 8, 12.

32. For a summary account of the central civil and ecclesiastical role played by the parish in England during the period see Mark Kishlansky, *A Monarchy Transformed: Britain, 1603–1714* (London, 1996): 7–8.

33. *Historical Statistics of the United States: Colonial Times to 1970*, Part 2 (Washington, DC, 1975): 1168, 1171.

34. Smith, *Writings*: 329.

35. *Ibid.*: 421–2, 1141, 1180.

36. David S. Katz, *God's Last Words: Reading the English Bible from the Reformation to Fundamentalism* (London, 2004): 44–5.

37. I have not found in a public collection a copy of the *Book of Common Prayer* or the Bible with a reliable provenance of use in a parish or by an individual in seventeenth-century Virginia.

38. The *Geneva Bible* of Governor William Bradford of Plymouth Plantation is deposited in the Collections of the Pilgrim Hall Museum in Plymouth, Massachusetts.

39. Christopher Hill, *The English Bible and the Seventeenth-Century Revolution* (London, 1993): 57.

40. *Ibid.*: 47–66; Katz, *God's Last Words*: 44–5; Hill, *The English Bible*: 57–8.

41. Kingsbury, *Virginia Company Records*, 3: 178.

42. *Ibid.*

43. *Ibid.*

44. *Constitution and Canons Ecclesiastical, 1604*: 84.

45. Francis Procter and Walter Howard Frere, *A New History of the Book of Common Prayer* (London, 1902): 136–43.

46. *Ibid.*: 91–115.

47. Judith Maltby, *Prayer Book and People in Elizabethan and Early Stuart England* (Cambridge, 1998): 24.

48. *Ibid.*: 24–5.

49. *Ibid.*: 25.

50. *Ibid.*: 135.

51. *Ibid.*: 26. Richard Beale Davis in his useful work *Intellectual Life in the Colonial South, 1585–1763* (Knoxville, 1979), II: 580, speculates that 'The small libraries of the humbler or poorer literate colonists were likely to contain, first of all, one or more editions of the Bible, next, the Book of Common Prayer and Anglican catechisms, and third, the pious book of Anglican devotions, called *The Whole duty of Man*.' But the subject of ownership and distribution of the Bible and Book of Common Prayer in Virginia is in need of further study and validation.

52. For a comparative study of English usage see Maltby, *Prayer Book and People*: 24–30. Christopher Hill writes that the 'vernacular Bible became an institution in Tudor England – foundation of monarchical authority, of England's protestant independence, the text-book of morality and social

subordination'. The Bible was central to all art, science, and literature in the sixteenth and seventeenth centuries and was omnipresent in all English houses; *The English Bible*: 4, 31, 39. It remains unknown if the pattern of ownership was similar in Virginia or if more or fewer residents owned a Bible.

53. Hill, *The English Bible*: 7.
54. David Cressy, *Literacy and the Social Order: Reading and Writing in Tudor and Stuart England* (Cambridge, 1980); Jonathan Barry, 'Literacy and Literature in Popular Culture: Reading and Writing in Historical Perspective' in Tim Harris, ed., *Popular Culture in England, c. 1500–1850* (New York, 1995): 69–94.
55. Cressy, *Literacy and the Social Order*: 42–61, 72, 176.
56. *Ibid.*: 145.
57. Kenneth Lockridge, *Literacy in Colonial New England: An Enquiry in the Context of Literacy in the Early Modern West* (New York, 1974): 17, 38–42.
58. Arthur Dent, *The Plain Mans Path-Way to Heaven. Wherein every man may clearly see, whether he shall be saved or damned. Set forth Dialogue-wise, for the better understanding of the simple* (Amsterdam, 1974 edition). I have benefited from Christopher Haigh's illuminating analysis of Dent's comprehensive guide to the Christian life and his comparative description of how ordinary people saw and practised their own religion in his *The Plain Man's Pathways to Heaven: Kinds of Christianity in Post-Reformation England, 1570–1640* (Oxford, 2007).
59. Peter Laslett, *The World We Have Lost: Further Explored*, third edition (London, 1983).

Chapter 5: A Social Profile Of Virginia's Ministers, 1607–1700

1. See Appendix I for a list of the men. Biographical details for the men are drawn from James B. Bell, 'The Colonial American Clergy of the Church of England, 1607–1783 Database', www.jamesbbell.com. For a list of the parishes and the names of the ministers and years of service see Appendix IV.
2. It would be helpful for historians and other researchers to have available a database compilation of the men who served as Church of Ireland ministers for the period between about 1536 and 1800, a resource similar to the databases for clergymen of the period in England and America.
3. James B. Bell, *The Imperial Origins of the King's Church in Early America, 1607–1783* (Basingstoke, 2004): 5–9.
4. Horton Davies, *The Worship of Puritans, 1629–1730* (New York, 1990): 6.
5. *Historical Statistics of the United States: Colonial Times to 1970* (Washington, DC, 1975): 1168.
6. *Ibid.*
7. Mattie E. E. Parker, *North Carolina Charters and Constitutions, 1578–1698* (Raleigh, 1963): 16, 21–2, 46–7, 72. See Perry Miller, *Errand into the Wilderness* (Cambridge, 1956): 99–140, and Edward L. Bond's *Damned Souls in a Tobacco Colony: Religion in Seventeenth Century Virginia* (Macon, GA, 2000) for

studies of the religious impulse supporting the extension and experiences of the church in the province.

8. Bell, *Imperial Origins of the King's Church*: 14–15.
9. Alexander Brown, *The First Republic in America* (Boston, 1898): 386. King was Dean of Christ Church and vice-chancellor of the University of Oxford and subsequently became Bishop of London (1611–21); George MacLauren Brydon, *Virginia's Mother Church and the Political Conditions under which It Grew* (Richmond, 1947), I: 419–21. For Wriothesley's career and wealth see Lawrence Stone, *Family and Fortune: Studies in Aristocratic Finance in the Sixteenth and Seventeenth Centuries* (Oxford, 1973): 214–30.
10. John Darley, *The Glory of Chelsey Colledge Revived* (London, 1662): 18. D. E. Kennedy, 'King James I's College of Controversial Divinity at Chelsea', in D. E. Kennedy, Diana Robertson and Alexandra Walsham, *Grounds of Controversy* (Melbourne, 1989): 99–126.
11. On the Calvinist nature of the early seventeenth-century church, see Nicholas Tyacke, 'Puritainism, Arminianism and Counter Revolution' in Conrad Russell, ed., *The Origins of the English Civil War* (London, 1973): 119–43. For Abbot, see Susan Holland, 'Archbishop Abbot and the Problem of Puritanism', *The Historical Journal* 37 (1994): 23–43; S. M. Holland, 'George Abbot: The Wanted Archbishop', *Church History* 56 (1987): 173; Kenneth Fincham, 'Prelacy and Politics: Archbishop Abbot's Defense of Protestant Orthodoxy', *Historical Research* 61 (1988): 36–64; Kenneth Fincham and Peter Lake, 'The Ecclesiastical Policy of King James I', *Journal of British Studies* 24 (1985): 182–5; Kenneth Fincham, *Prelate as Pastor: the Episcopate of James I* (Oxford, 1990): 39, 46–8, 253–64, 269–70; C. M. Dent, *Protestant Reformers in Elizabethan Oxford* (Oxford, 1983): 100–1, 191–2, 218–22, 228–9, 231–2, 237. Sutcliffe expressed early interests in New England and became a member of the Council of New England on 3 November 1620 and was a supporter of Captain John Smith's *General Historie* (1624). He was one of the commissioners appointed to wind up the affairs of the Virginia Company in 1624.
12. Babette M. Levy, 'Early Puritanism in the Southern and Island Colonies', *P.A.A.S.* 70 (1960): 92–113.
13. Capt. Edward-Maria Wingfield, 'A Discourse of Virginia', *Archaelogia Americana: Transactions and Collections of the American Antiquarian Society*, IV (1860): 102.
14. Susan Myra Kingsbury, ed., *The Records of the Virginia Company of London* (Washington, DC, 1933), 3: 469.
15. Edmund S. Morgan, *American Slavery, American Freedom: The Ordeal of Virginia* (New York, 19750: 149–50; Aubrey C. Land, *Colonial Maryland: A History* (Millwood, NY, 1981): 49–50.
16. Hening, *Virginia Statutes at Large*, I: 241.
17. The men included in this group are as follows: John Alexander (1665–?); Thomas Bennett (1605–?); John Bolton (1635–?); Richard Bucke (1584–1623); James Bushnell (16xx–?); Robert Carr (16xx–?); Samuel Cole, 16xx–59); Alexander Cooke (16xx–?); Patrick Copeland (1579–1651); Charles Davies (16xx–?); Jonathan Davis (16xx–?); Superior Davis (16xx–?); Francis Doughty (1616–69); Nathaniel Eaton (1609–74); Thomas Harrison (1619–82); Matthew Hill (1633–79); Robert Hunt (1568–1608); John

Lawrence (1633–84); John Lyford (1576–1634); Richard Morris (16xx–?); William Paris (16xx–?); Henry Parke (1638–87); William Tompson (1633–65); and Alexander Whitaker (1585–1617). For biographical details of each man see 'The Colonial American Clergy of the Church of England, 1607–1783 Database', www.jamesbbell.com.

18. See Appendix III for a list of the men and the colleges and universities attended.
19. H. C. Porter, *Reformation and Reaction in Tudor Cambridge* (Cambridge, 1958).
20. *Ibid.*: 67–8.
21. *Ibid.*: 174–8.
22. *Ibid.*: 227.
23. *Ibid.*: 241–60.
24. Nicholas Tyacke, *The History of the University of Oxford, Seventeenth Century* (Oxford, 1997) 4: 569.
25. See Appendix II.
26. See Appendix I and the individual biographies for each man at 'Colonial American Clergy of the Church of England Database', at www.james bbell.com.
27. Bell, *Imperial Origins of the King's Church*: 10–19.
28. The information has been derived from the biographical resources included in 'The Clergy of the Church of England Database, 1540–1835', at www. theclergydatabase.org.uk. It is an invaluable resource for the study of an English professional class. While the project remains incomplete the compilers are regularly expanding the number of entries. A number of English dioceses are yet to be partially or entirely included in the database.
29. My evidence on the matter has been gleaned from each man's personal record in the 'Colonial American Clergy of the Church of England Database 1607–1783' at www.jamesbbell.com.
30. See Appendix II. For the refinement of this biographical information I am indebted to the excellent reference work, 'Clergy of the Church of England Database, 1540–1835' compiled under the direction of Arthur Burns, Kenneth Fincham, and Stephen J. C. Taylor. More than 130,000 persons comprise the database as of December 2011.
31. See Appendix II.
32. *Ibid.* See, too, Leonel L. Mitchell, 'Episcopal Ordinations in the Church of Scotland, 1610–1688', *H.M.P.E.C.* 31 (1962): 143–59.
33. See Appendix II.
34. *Ibid.* See, too, the 'Colonial American Clergy of the Church of England Database, 1607–1783 at www.jamesbbell.com.
35. Bell, *Imperial Origins of the King's Church*: 14–18.
36. John Clement, compiler, 'Clergymen Licensed Overseas by the Bishops of London, 1696–1710 and 1715–1760', *H.M.P.E.C.* XVI (1947): 318–49; John Clement, compiler, 'Anglican Clergymen Licensed to the American Colonies, 1710–1744', *Ibid.* XVII (1948): 207–50; George Woodward Lamb, compiler, 'Clergymen Licensed to the American Colonies by the Bishops of London, 1745–1781', *Ibid.* XIII (1944): 128–43.
37. Bell, *Imperial Origins of the King's Church*: 16–17.
38. Kenneth Fincham, Stephen J. C. Taylor, Arthur Burns, 'The Clergy of the Church of England Database, 1540–1835', www.theclergydatabase.org.uk;

James B. Bell, 'The Colonial American Clergy of the Church of England Database', www.jamesbbell.com.
39. David D. Hall, *The Faithful Shepherd: A History of the New England Ministry in the Seventeenth Century* (Chapel Hill, 1972).

Chapter 6: Salaries and Discipline of Seventeenth-Century Ministers

1. See Appendix II for the social origins of each man.
2. For John Goodbourne see R. G. Marsden, 'A Virginian Minister's Library, 1635', *American Historical Review*, 11, 2 (1906): 328–32. For Thomas Teackle's books see, Jon Butler, 'Thomas Teackle's 333 Books: A Great Library in Virginia's Eastern Shore, 1697', *W.M.Q.*, Third Series, 49 (1992): 462–91.
3. James B. Bell, *The Imperial Origins of the King's Church in Early America, 1607–1783* (London, 2004): 110–13; Warren M. Billings, ed., *The Papers of Francis Howard, Baron Howard of Effingham, 1643–1695* (Richmond, 1989): 458.
4. William W. Hening, *The Statutes at Large being a Collection of all the Laws of Virginia from the First Session of the Legislature in the Year 1619* (Charlottesville, 1969 edition), I: 68–9. The East India Company was responsible for the recruitment, transportation and financial support of English clergymen appointed to posts in India during the seventeenth-century. See Eyre Chatterton, *A History of the Church of England in India Since the Early Days of the East India Company* (London, 1924): Chapters 1 and 2.
5. George MacLaren Brydon, *Virginia's Mother Church and The Political Conditions Under Which It Grew* (Richmond, 1947), I: 15.
6. See Appendix II, Bell, *Imperial Origins of the King's Church*: note 23, 221; Brydon, *Virginia's Mother Church*, I: 20–9.
7. Brydon, *Virginia's Mother Church*, I: 47–9.
8. See his entry in The Colonial American Clergy of the Church of England Database, www.jamesbbell.com.
9. Lyon Gardiner Tyler, *Encyclopedia of Virginia Biography* (New York, 1915), 1: 95; Susan Myra Kingsbury, *The Records of the Virginia Company of London* (Washington, 1933), 3: 73–4. Sir Dudley Digges (1582/3–1639) was a politician and diplomat and a graduate of University College, Oxford, in 1601. In 1602, the master of the college and later the Archbishop of Canterbury, George Abbot, introduced Digges to Sir Robert Cecil, who may have provided the young man with his introduction to political life.
10. Bell, *Imperial Origins of the King's Church*, 5–6.
11. Kingsbury, *Records of the Virginia Company*, 3: 92.
12. Jean Kennedy, *Isle of Devils, Bermuda under the Somers Island Company, 1609–1685* (London, 1971): 87–90.
13. Carl Bridenbaugh, *Myths and Realities: Societies of the Colonial South* (Baton Rouge, 1952): 30–2; William Wilson Manross, *A History of the American Episcopal Church* (New York, 1935): 56–61; William Kidder Meade, *Old Churches, Ministers and Families of Virginia* (Baltimore, 1969 reprint).
14. Joan Rezner Gunderson, *The Anglican Ministry in Virginia, 1723–1766, A Study of a Social Class* (New York, 1989); John K. Nelson, *A Blessed Company:*

Parishes, Parsons, and Parishioners in Anglican Virginia, 1690–1776 (Chapel Hill, 2001).

15. Nelson, *A Blessed Company*: 145–62.
16. James B. Bell, *A War of Religion: Dissenters, Anglicans and the American Revolution* (London, 2008).
17. Hening, ed., *Virginia Statutes at Large*, I: 240–3.
18. *V.M.H.B.* 25 (1917): 38–42; Gunderson, *Anglican Ministry*: 119–47.
19. Meade, *Old Churches, Ministers*, 1: 254.
20. *Ibid.*, 1: 230–1.
21. *Ibid.*, 1: 323–4.
22. Bell, 'Colonial American Clergymen of the Church of England Database', www.jamesbbell.com.
23. Brydon, *Virginia's Mother Church*, I: 235–6. See also his entry in 'Colonial American Clergymen of the Church of England Database', www.jamesbbell. com. John Gordon (1674–17xx) served Wilmington Parish (1695–1702) and was the son of Patrick, regent of King's College in Aberdeen, Scotland, and the brother of Alexander, Professor of Humanity, and George, Professor of Oriental Languages at the same institution.
24. H. R. McIlwaine, ed., *Executive Journals of the Council of Virginia* (Richmond, 1925) I: 465.
25. The schoolmasters were Nathaniel Eaton (1639–46), Samuel Gray (1690–1709), and George Robertson (1693–1739); the physicians were Joseph Holt (1696–1700), Robert Pawlett (1619–22), Thomas Teackle (1656–95), and James Wallace (1691–1712); and the lawyer was Robert Powis (1640–52). See the summary account for each man in Appendix I and II and their biographical details in my 'Colonial American Clergymen of the Church of England, 1607–1783 Database' www.jamesbbell.com.

Chapter 7: Divisions in the Virginia Pulpits: Anglicans, Puritans and Nonconformists

1. George Herbert, *A Priest to the Temple, or the Country Parson His Character and Rule of Holy Life in The Works of George Herbert*, F. E. Hutchinson, ed. (Oxford, 1941): 221–90; *The Diary of Ralph Josselin, 1616–1683*, Alan Macfarlane, ed. (London, 1976); James Woodforde, *The Diary of a Country Parson, the Reverend James Woodforde, 1758–1781*, James Beresford, ed. 5 vols. (London, 1924–31).
2. See the men's individual biographical account at the 'Colonial Clergy of the Church of England, 1607–1783 Database' at www.jamesbbell.com.
3. Robert Hunt (1568–1608), born Heathfield, Sussex, Oxford, Magdalen Hall, B.A., 1592, Jamestown.
4. Richard Bucke (1584–1623), born Wymondham, Norfolk, Cambridge, admitted Gonville and Caius, 1600, came to Virginia with Sir Thomas Gates, 1610, James City Parish.
5. Nathaniel Eaton (1609–1674), Cambridge, matriculated, Trinity College, 1629, ordained, curate at Sidington, Cheshire, arrived at Boston, 1637, schoolmaster, Cambridge, discredited, to Virginia, 1639–46, frequent problems with indebtedness, died in London, King's Bench prison, 1674, Hungar's Parish.

6. Samuel Cole (16xx–59), Pianketant, Christ Church Parish.
7. Henry Parke (1638–87), St George's, Accomac parishes.
8. John Alexander (1665–17xx), Sittingbourne Parish.
9. Alexander Whitaker (1585–1617), Cambridge, Trinity College, B.A., 1605, came to Virginia with his friend Sir Thomas Dale, Henrico.
10. Patrick Copeland (1579–1651), born Aberdeen, attended Marischal College, Chaplain East India Company, accepted post as head of proposed Virginia College but did not travel to the colony, in Bermuda, 1625–51, renounced Anglican ministry and became a Congregational parson.
11. Thomas Harrison (1619–1682), born Kingston-upon-Hull, Yorkshire, Cambridge, Sidney Sussex, B.A., 1638, married niece of Governor John Winthrop, Elizabeth River Parish.
12. John Bolton (1635–16xx), Cople Parish.
13. Thomas Bennett (1605–16xx), Cambridge, matriculated, Trinity College, 1621, ordained by Bishop of Peterborough, head of independent congregation, banished from colony by Governor Berkeley, 1648, Nansemond Parish.
14. Philip Mallory (1617–61), born Mobberley, Cheshire, father a clergyman, Oxford, St Mary's Hall, B.A., 1637, Lynnhaven, James City parishes and York County.
15. Matthew Hill (1633–79), born Yorkshire, Cambridge, Magdalene, B.A., 1652/53.
16. Josias Mackie (16xx–1716), born St Johnstone, Donegal, Ireland, Edinburgh, A.M., 1681, Presbyterian, Elizabeth River Parish.
17. William Tompson (1598–1666), born Winwick, Lancashire, Oxford, Brasenose, B.A., 1621/22, ordained, curate at Makefield Chapel, Diocese of Chester, arrived in New England, 1637, York, Maine, 1637–39, Quincy, Mass., 1639–59, missionary to Virginia, 1642–43, Nansemond, Upper Norfolk County, Anglican convert to Congregational Church.
18. Francis Doughty (1616–69), born Bristol, in Virginia, Hungar's, Elizabeth City, Northampton County, Sittingbourne parishes.
19. Daniel Richardson (16xx–16xx), not ordained, Hungar's Parish.
20. Andrew Jackson (1656–1710), Presbyterian, St Mary's Whitechapel, Christ Church parishes.
21. Matthew Hill (1633–79), born Yorkshire, Cambridge, Magdalene, B.A., 1652/53.
22. Superior Davis (16xx–16xx), Christ Church Parish.
23. James Bushnell (16xx–17xx), Martin's Hundred Parish.
24. Alexander Cooke (16xx–16xx), Christ Church Parish.
25. Morgan Godwyn (1640–85), born Bicknor, Gloucestershire, father an Anglican minister, Oxford, Christ Church College, B.A., 1664/65, ordained, Marston-York, James City parishes.
26. Jonathan Davis (16xx–16xx), New Poquoson Parish.
27. John Lawrence (1633–84), born Wormly, Herefordshire, Cambridge, Emmanuel, B.A., 1654, Mulberry Island Parish.
28. Richard Morris (16xx–16xx), Pianketant Parish.
29. Robert Carr (16xx–16xx), Stratton-Major Parish.
30. William Paris (16xx–16xx), Washington Parish.
31. Charles Davies (16xx–16xx), Wicomico, Old Farnham parishes.

32. William Waller Hening, *The Statutes at Large being a Collection of all the Laws of Virginia from the First Session of the Legislature in the Year 1619* (Charlottesville, 1969 edition) I: 58.
33. *Ibid.*: 68–9. The Second Charter issued by the crown to the Virginia Company for the American settlement, on 23 May 1609, does not mention religion but notes in Article XVI that all issues mentioned in former Patents and Charters and 'not revoked, altered, changed, or abridged' but remain in force. *Ibid.*: 122–3.
34. H. R. McIlwaine, ed., *Journals of the House of Burgesses of Virginia, 1619–1658/59* (Richmond, 1915) I: 13.
35. *Ibid.*: 13–14.
36. *Ibid.*: 10.
37. *O.D.N.B.*
38. *Ibid.*
39. Hening, *Statutes at Large*, I: 122–3.
40. *Ibid.*: 149.
41. *Ibid.*: 155–61, 180–5.
42. *Ibid.*: 241; Judith Maltby, *Prayer Book and People in Elizabethan and Early Stuart England* (Cambridge, 1998): 24–30.
43. See Appendix II for a list of the men who were serving in the province during the 1640s.
44. See the biographical entries for each man at the 'Clergy for the Church of England in Colonial America, 1607–1783 Database', wwwjamesbbell.com.
45. *Historical Statistics of the United States Colonial Times to 1970*, Part 2 (Washington, DC, 1975): 1168.
46. See the men's individual biographical account at the 'Colonial Clergy of the Church of England, 1607–1783 Database' at www.jamesbbell.com.
47. For a differing account of the New England Puritan ministers who served in Virginia see April Lee Hatfield, *Atlantic Virginia: Intercolonial Relations in the Seventeenth Century* (Philadelphia, 2004): 93, 104–5, 110–21.
48. George D. Langdon, Jr., *Pilgrim Colony: A History of New Plymouth, 1620–1691* (New Haven, 1966): 20–6; Bernard Bailyn, *The Barbarous Years: The Conflict of Civilization* (New York, 2012): 342–4.
49. William Bradford, *Of Plymouth Plantation, 1620–1647*, Samuel Eliot Morison, ed. (New York, 1952): 147–69.
50. *A.N.B.*
51. 'The Clergy of the Church of England Database, 1540–1835' at www.theclergydatabase.org.uk.
52. Samuel Eliot Morison, *The Founding of Harvard College* (Cambridge, 1995 edition): 202–9.
53. *Ibid.*: 199–204, 228, 237–9.
54. *Ibid.*: 238–9. See, too, James R. Perry, *The Formation of a Society on Virginia's Eastern Shore, 1615–1655* (Chapel Hill, 1990): 183–7.
55. Eaton's shifting religious practices are overshadowed by his longstanding personal problems. Frequently in debt, a factor that may have prompted his removal from Massachusetts to Virginia, he returned to England and between 1646 and 1661 there is little trace of him. He attended the University of Padua in Italy in the late 1640s and presumably his clerical career was suspended during the Interregnum in England. In 1661, at the Restoration of

the Church of England he conformed and reappears as Vicar of Bishop's Castle in Shropshire and in that year his work *De Fastis Anglicis, sive Calendarium Sacrum (The Holy Calendar)* was published. In 1669 the Earl of Bath secured for him the rectory of Bideford in Devon. Yet, his irregular ways continued and he was arrested in 1665 and 1674 for debt. After holding at least two parish posts, he died a debtor in the King's Bench Prison in Southwark, London in 1674. *A.N.B.*

56. Hening, *Statutes at Large*, I: 277.
57. *Ibid.*: 341–2.
58. See his entry in the 'Colonial American Clergy of the Church of England, 1607–1783, Database' at www.jamesbbell.com.
59. Robert Lee Morton, *Colonial Virginia* (Chapel Hill, 1960), I: 153.
60. *The Directory for the Public Worship of God throughout the three kingdoms of England, Scotland, and Ireland: Together with an ordinance of Parliament for the taking away of the Book of common-prayer: and for establishing and observing of the present directory throughout the kingdom of England, and dominion of Wales, Die Jovis, 13 Marti, 1644. Ordered by the Lords and Commons assembled in Parliament, that this ordinance and directory bee forthwith printed and published. John Brown, Clerc. Parliamentarian. H Elsynge, Cler. Parl. D. Com. Printed London, 1644* [i.e. 1645?]; the *Directory for Public Worship* is conveniently found in David Cressy and Lori Anne Ferrell, eds., *Religion and Society in Early Modern England: A Sourcebook* (London, 1996): 186–92; Judith Maltby, 'Suffering and Surviving: The Civil Wars, the Commonwealth and the Formation of "Anglicanism", 1642–1660' in Cressy and Ferrell, *Religion and Society*: 158–80; John Morrill, 'The Church in England, 1642–1649' in his *The Nature of the English Revolution* (London, 1993): 148–75.
61. James B. Bell, *The Imperial Origins of the King's Church in Early America, 1607–1783* (London, 2004): 43–73.
62. John Anderson Brayton, 'The Ancestry of the Rev. Francis Doughty', *The American Genealogist*, 77 (2002): 1.
63. Leonard J. Trinterud, *The Forming of an American Tradition: A Re-examination of Colonial Presbyterianism* (Philadelphia, 1949): 22.
64. Bayard Tuckerman, *Peter Stuyvesant, Director-General for the West India Company in New Netherland* (New York, 1893): 30; Brayton, 'Francis Doughty': 127.
65. Old Rappahannock County Record Book, 1656–65: 256; Record Book, 1668–72: 110; Richard Beale Davis, *Intellectual Life in the Colonial South, 1585–1763* (Knoxville, 1978): 658.
66. Warren M. Billings, ed., *The Papers of Sir William Berkeley* (Richmond, 2007): 338–9.
67. The letter is conveniently reproduced in Warren M. Billings, ed., *The Old Dominion in the Seventeenth Century: A Documentary History of Virginia, 1606–1689* (Chapel Hill, 1975): 319.
68. Bell, *Imperial Origins of the King's Church*: 30–1; Frederic Lewis Weis, 'The Colonial Clergy of the Middle Colonies: New York, New Jersey, and Pennsylvania, 1628–1776', *P.A.A.S.* 66 (1956): 276; Patricia Law Hatcher and Edward H. L. Smith, III, 'Reexamining the Family of the Rev. John Moore of Newtown, Long Island', *New York Genealogical and Biographical Record*, 137 (2006): 258–63.

69. John Langdon Sibley, *Biographical Sketches of Graduates of Harvard University, in Cambridge, Massachusetts* (Cambridge, 1873), I: 354–57.
70. Everett Emerson, *John Cotton*, revised edition (Boston, 1990): 6.
71. See the entry for each man at the 'Clergy for the Church of England in Colonial America, 1607–1783 Database' at wwwjamesbbell.com.
72. Landon C. Bell, *Charles Parish York County, Virginia: History and Registers* (Richmond, 1932): 21–2.
73. Bell, *Imperial Origins of the King's Church*: 47–52.
74. Frederic Lewis Weis, *The Colonial Clergy of Virginia, North Carolina and South Carolina* (Boston, 1955): 33–4.
75. Meade, *Old Churches, Ministers*, 2: 123; Weis, *Colonial Clergy of Virginia*: 27.
76. Warren M. Billings, ed., *The Papers of Francis Howard, Baron Howard of Effingham, 1643–1695* (Richmond, 1989): 274.
77. Billings, *Papers of Francis Howard*: 458. Thomas Finney was born in 1659, the son of William of Penzance, Cornwall and matriculated at Exeter College, Oxford, 25 June 1675, aged 16. He migrated to Magdalen Hall and received his B.A. on 26 March 1680. He received his King's Bounty for Virginia on 12 December 1684 but did not arrive in the colony and take a position at Charles Parish until 1686. He served one year before his death in 1687, aged 28 years. James B. Bell, 'Colonial American Clergymen of the Church of England, 1607–1783 Database' at www.jamesbbell.com.
78. Billings, *Papers of Francis Howard*: 458.
79. *Ibid.*
80. 'Clergy of the Church of England Database, 1540–1835', compiled under the direction of Arthur Burns, Kenneth Fincham, and Stephen J. C. Taylor at www.theclergydatabase.org.uk.
81. For Key's biographical details see my 'Colonial American Clergy of the Church of England, 1607–1783 Database' at www.jamesbbell.com; William Meade, *Old Churches, Ministers, and Families of Virginia* (Baltimore, 1966 edition), 2: 257–8.
82. Lyon Gardiner Tyler, *Encyclopedia of Virginia Biography* (New York, 1915), 1: 215.
83. Meade, *Old Churches, Ministers*, 2: 127.
84. See Appendixes I and II.
85. 'Clergy of the Church of England Database, 1540–1835' at www.theclergydatabase.org.uk.
86. During the 1640s ten men arrived in the colony and during the next decade, 21. See Appendix II.

Chapter 8: The Libraries of Two Seventeenth-Century Ministers

1. The number of known personal libraries of colonial Anglican clergymen by region and colony: New England Colonies: Connecticut and Massachusetts, 4 each; Rhode Island, 1, Total, 9. Middle Colonies: New Jersey, 4, New York, 2, Pennsylvania, 3, Total, 9. Chesapeake Colonies: Maryland, 22, Virginia, 63, Total, 85. Southern Colonies: North Carolina, 3, South Carolina, 20, Total, 23. Grand total, 126. The information has been extracted from the

biographical entries in my 'Colonial American Clergy of the Church of England, 1607–1783 Database', at www.jamesbbell.com.

2. To date his record does not appear in 'The Clergy of the Church of England Database 1540–1835', at www.theclergydatabse.org.uk.

3. A land grant for the plantation was issued for the site in 1635 to William Barker, a wealthy London merchant and the ship owner of the *Globe*, and to merchants Richard Quiney and John Sadler. The property was patented three years later but a church was not established until 1657.

4. Thomas Harrison Montgomery, *A Genealogical History of the Family of Montgomery, including the Montgomery Pedigree* (Philadelphia, 1863). At the Family History Library in Salt Lake City, the publicly available database of persons whose genealogical information has been filed at the library embraces the family historical tradition that Teackle was born about 1624, but erroneously notes his place of birth as Northampton County in Virginia, and not Gloucestershire, England.

5. Christopher Hill, *The Century of Revolution, 1603–1714* (New York, 1961): 27. David Rollinson's *The Local Origins of Modern Society: Gloucestershire 1500–1800* (London, 1992) provides useful information about the world in which Teackle grew up.

6. Jon Butler, 'Thomas Teackle's 333 Books: A Great Library in Virginia's Eastern Shore, 1697', *W.M.Q.*, Third Series, 49 (1992): 452.

7. See Thomas Teackle at www.familysearch.org. and my 'Colonial American Clergymen of the Church of England, 1607–1783 Database, at www.jamesbbell.com. A son, John, was born on 2 September 1693, and married Susanna Upshur on some unknown date, a resident of Upshur's Neck, Accomack County, in Virginia. He died 3 December 1721 and his wife in 1738 in Accomack County. A descendant of Susanna Upshur, Anne Floyd Upshur, was a compiler, with Ralph T. Whitelaw, of 'Library of the Rev. Thomas Teackle,' *W.M.Q.*, Second Series, 23 (1943): 298–308.

8. Anne Floyd Upshur and Ralph T. Whitelaw, 'Library of the Rev. Thomas Teackle,' *W.M.Q.*, Second Series, 23 (1943): 298–303; Butler, 'Thomas Teackle's 333 Books: 462–91.

9. Aubrey C. Land, *Colonial Maryland: A History* (Millwood, 1981): 49–50.

10. See Appendix IV for a list of the parishes and the names of the men who served the congregations between 1607 and 1700. During the seventeenth century several men serving congregations identified as Accomac, Northampton County, and Hungar's Parish are identified as Anglican-Puritans, Puritans with a New England association, and Presbyterian. The Eastern Shore was originally one county, Accomac. In 1643 it was renamed Northampton County, retaining the name until the division peninsula into two counties, Northampton and Accomac, in 1663. Ministers serving Accomac Parish were Francis Bolton (1621–30) and Thomas Teackle (1658–95). By 1653 there were two parishes established on the Eastern Shore, Accomac and Hungar's Parish in Northampton County. Serving the latter congregation were Francis Bolton (1623–30), William Cotton (1632–45), Nathaniel Eaton (1639–45), John Rosier (1644–53), Thomas Palmer (1647–48), John Armourier (1651–54), Thomas Higby (1651–54), Francis Doughty (1655), John Rodgers (1664), Daniel Richardson (16xx–76),

Isaac Key (1676–78), and Henry Parke (1678–87). For the organization of the counties see James R. Perry, *The formation of a Society on Virginia's Eastern Shore, 1615–1855* (Chapel Hill, 1990): 40, 236. For the clergymen serving the churches in the region see 'Colonial American Clergy of the Church of England in Colonial America, 1607–1783 Database', at www.james bbell.com.

11. Warren M. Billings, ed., *The Papers of Francis Howard, Baron Howard of Effingham, 1643–1695* (Richmond, 1989): 458.
12. James Blair was born in 1659 in Banffshire, Scotland and graduated from Edinburgh College, A.M. in 1673. He was appointed in 1685 to a post in Virginia and four years later became the bishop of London's commissary in the colony, serving in the post until his death in 1743. He was the founder of the College of William and Mary in 1693 and president until 1743. John Clayton was born in Preston, in Lancashire, England, in 1657 and graduated from Merton College, in Oxford University, in 1677/78. He was a distinguished naturalist and writer, demonstrating a wide range of scientific interests, and served the James City Parish between 1684 and 1686. He was a Fellow of the Royal Society. John Banister was born in 1650 at Twigworth in Gloucestershire, and graduated from Magdalene College in Oxford University in 1671. A distinguished botanist with scientific interests shared with Bishop of London Henry Compton, he was appointed by the prelate to a Virginia post in 1674/75. He served as minister of the Charles City Parish from 1678 until his death in 1692. Butler, 'Thomas Teackle's 333 Books': 456.
13. See Thomas Teackle, in 'The Clergy of the Church of England Database, 1540–1835', at www.the clergydatabase.org.uk.
14. An inventory of Goodbourne's library is found in the *American Historical Review*, XI (1905–06): 328–32.
15. *Ibid.* and for Teackle see Butler, 'Thomas Teackle's 333 Books': 449–91.
16. Charles T. Laugher, *Thomas Bray's Grand Design: Libraries of the Church of England in America, 1695–1785* (Chicago, 1973): 17–54; Joseph Towne Wheeler, 'Thomas Bray and the Maryland Parochial Libraries', *Maryland Historical Magazine*. 38 (1943): 245–65.
17. Butler, 'Thomas Teackle's 333 Books', 452. It should be noted that unlike the Goodbourne library the inventory of Teackle's collection does not note either the cost or value of the books. The comparative historical value of the books and estate of Goodbourne and Teackle has been drawn from the statistical database compiled by Lawrence H. Officer and Samuel H. Williamson, 'Purchasing Power of British Pounds from 1245 to the Present' database at www.measuringworth.com/ppoweruk. The sums were determined by the use of the index of average earnings.
18. E. S. Leedham-Green, *Books in Cambridge Inventories: Book Lists from the Vice-Chancellor's Court Probate Inventories in the Tudor and Stuart Periods* (Cambridge, 1986).
19. *Ibid.* II: 541–93.
20. *Ibid.* 559–64, 567–72.
21. Leedham-Green, *Books in Cambridge Inventories*: 541–93.
22. Julius Herbert Tuttle, 'The Libraries of the Mathers', *P. A. A. S.* 20 (1911): 268–356; William Prynne, *Sixteen Quaeres Proposed to our Lord Prelates* (Amsterdam, 1637); [David Calderwood]. *The Pastor and Prelate, or*

Reformation and Conformitie Shortly compared by the Word of God, by Antiquity and the Proceedings of the Ancient Kirk (Leyden, 1628), and also his *The Presbyterian Government is Divine; Reasons to Prove that it is Unlawful to hear the Ministers of England; and That King may Abrogate Prelacy Without any Violation of his Oath.* (Leyden, 1628); James B. Bell, *A War of Religion: Dissenters, Anglicans and the American Revolution* (London, 2008): 9.

23. Leonard Woods Labaree, *Royal Instructions to British Colonial Governors, 1670–1776* (New York, 1935) II: 484–85.
24. 'The Clergy of the Church of England Database, 1540–1835'at www. theclergydatabse.org.uk.

Chapter 9: An Age of New Imperial Policies: Church and State, 1660–1713

1. Mark Goldie, 'Danby, the Bishops and the Whigs', in Tim Harris, Paul Seaward and Mark Goldie, eds., *The Politics of Religion in Restoration England* (Oxford, 1990): 75–105; Robert M. Bliss, *Revolution and Empire: English Politics and the American Colonies in the Seventeenth Century* (Manchester, 1990): 103–31.
2. Oliver Morton Dickerson, *American Colonial Government, 1695–1765: A Study of the British Board of Trade in relation to the American Colonies Political, Industrial, Administration* (Cleveland, 1912): 17–79.
3. *Ibid.* 19; James B. Bell, *The Imperial Origins of the King's Church in Early America, 1607–1783* (London, 2004): 15–16; Michael J. Braddick, 'The English Government, War, Trade, and Settlement, 1625–1688', in Nicholas Canny, ed., *The Origins of Empire: British Overseas Enterprise to the Close of the Seventeenth Century* (Oxford, 1998) I: 298–300.
4. Braddick, 'The English Government, War, Trade, and Settlement, in Canny, ed., *The Origins of Empire*, I: 294–97; Bliss, *Revolution and Empire*: 161–89.
5. *Historical Statistics of the United States: Colonial Times to 1970, Part 2* (Washington, DC, 1975): 1168.
6. See Appendix II for a list of the men and their estimated years of service.
7. Edward Carpenter, *The Protestant Bishop: being the life of Henry Compton, 1632–1713, Bishop of London* (London, 1956): 25–51.
8. Cal.S.P. Col. Ser., 1677–1680: 117–18; Darret B. Rutman, 'The Evolution of Religious Life in Early Virginia', *Lex et Scientia. The International Journal of Law and Science* 14 (1978): 197; Darret B. and Anita H. Rutman, *A Place in Time: Middlesex County, Virginia, 1650–1750* (New York, 1984): 24–5.
9. The document is conveniently reprinted in Hugh Hastings, ed. E.R.S.N.Y. I: 693–94; Rutman and Rutman, *A Place in Time*: 56–7, 125–27.
10. F.P.P., XI: 1–2, Article 2 of the Instructions to Governor Sir George Yardley, 19 April 1626.
11. F.P.P., XI: 3–4, Instructions to Sir Thomas Wyatt and Sir William Berkeley.
12. This body was subsequently known as the Council of Trade and Plantations and the Board of Trade and Plantations.
13. Bell, *Imperial Origins of the King's Church*: chapter 2.
14. *Ibid.* 18.

15. Carpenter, *The Protestant Bishop*: 5–8, 29–30.
16. *Ibid.* 256; Andrew Browning, *Thomas Osborne, Earl of Danby and Duke of Leeds, 1632–1712* (Glasgow, 1951), I: 195.
17. Ronald Hutton, *Charles the Second, King of England, Scotland, and Ireland* (Oxford, 1991): 326–28; Browning, *Thomas Osborne*, I: 146–84; Bell, *Imperial Origins of the King's Church*: 17–18.
18. *Ibid.* 12–13; Roger Green, *Virginia's Cure: or An Advisive Narrative Concerning Virginia. Discovering the True Ground of that Churches Unhappiness and the only true Remedy. As it was presented to the Right Reverend Father in God Guilbert (Sheldon) Lord Bishop of London, September 2, 1661* (London, 1662).
19. Bell, *Imperial Origins of the King's Church*: 13–14.
20. *Ibid.* 14; Cal. S.P. Col. Ser., 1675–76: 435–36. Cal. S.P. Col. Ser., 1677–1680: 121–22.
21. F.P.P., XI: 7–10, John Banister to Robert Morison, *The Falls*, 6 April 1679. In the Sloane MSS at the British Library are two manuscript books from Banister to Compton describing Virginia plants. Banister compiled a catalogue of plants published by John Ray in his influential *Historia Plantarum* of 1686 (*Philosophical Transactions*, 17 (1693), 667–72, *Ibid.* (1700), 807–14; A.N.B. Brooke Hindle, *The Pursuit of Science in Revolutionary America, 1735–1789* (Chapel Hill, 1956): 16.
22. For Clayton (1657–1725) see, Edmund Berkeley and Dorothy Smith Berkeley, eds., *The Rev. John Clayton, a parson with a scientific mind; his writings and other related papers* (Charlottesville, 1965). For a biographical account of Pead (1647–1727) and a list of his published sermons see his entry at 'Colonial American Clergy of the Church of England, 1607–1783 Database', at www.jamesbbell.com.
23. Leonard Woods Labaree, *Royal Instructions to British Colonial Governors, 1670–1776* (New Haven, 1935), II: 482–85.
24. Cal.S.P. Col. Ser., 1710–1711: 560. J.C.T.P., February 1708/9 to March 1714/5: 284, 378.
25. Bell, *Imperial Origins of the King's Church*: 18–25.
26. *Ibid.* 58–73.
27. Leonard Woods Labaree, *Royal Government in America: A Study of the British Colonial System before 1783* (New Haven, 1930): 8–18.
28. *Ibid.* 95.
29. *Ibid.* 115–18.
30. Labaree, *Royal Instructions.* II: 482–83.
31. *Ibid.*
32. *Ibid.* 484–85.
33. *Ibid.*
34. Billings, *Papers of Francis Howard*: 260–61.
35. Bell, *Imperial Origins of the King's Church*: 19, 126.
36. Labaree, *Royal Instructions.* II: 486.
37. Hening, *Virginia Statutes at Large*: I: 155–61, 240–42.
38. The instructions were omitted for all the governors of dissenting Massachusetts and from those to the governors of New Hampshire before 1761. The clause in the commission conferring the right of collating to benefices was omitted from all Massachusetts commissions and from those for New Hampshire before 1715.

39. Labaree, *Royal Instructions*, II: 489–90. See also F.P.P. 36: 48, Bishop of London Henry Compton to Francis Howard, Baron Howard of Effingham, London, 14 September [1685].
40. Labaree, *Royal Instructions*, II: 487.
41. *Ibid*. 487–88.
42. Both documents are conveniently available in Billings, *Papers of Francis Howard*. The Commission was issued 28 September 1653, at 9.15, and the Instructions followed on 24 October 1683, at 16.30.
43. *Ibid*. 12.
44. *Ibid*. 20.
45. *Ibid*. 20–21.
46. *Ibid*. 21.
47. *Ibid*. 24. According to Canon XCIX, the Table of Marriages were required to be hung in each church. *Constitution and Canons Ecclesiastical 1604, with notes by J. V. Bullard* (London, 1934): 106.
48. Labaree, *Royal Instructions*, I: 7, 9.
49. *Ibid*.
50. Bell, *Imperial Origins of the King's Church*: 16.
51. The members of the court of ecclesiastical commission were Nathaniel Crew (1633–1721), third Baron Crewe Bishop of Durham, a close friend of the king and a member of the Privy Council; Thomas Sprat (1635–1713), bishop of Rochester, historian of the Royal Society, and loyal servant of James II; and Thomas White (1628–98), bishop of Peterborough and chaplain to James II's protestant daughter, Anne.
52. John Evelyn noted in his dairy, '8th September [1686] Dr. Compton, Bishop of London was on Monday suspended, on pretence of not silencing Dr. Sharp of St. Giles's, for something of a sermon in which he zealously reproved the doctrine of the Roman Catholics. The Bishop having consulted the civilians, they told him he could not by any law proceed against Dr. Sharp without producing witnesses, and impleading according to form, but it was overruled by my Lord Chancellor, and the Bishop sentenced without so much as being heard to any purpose. This was thought a very extraordinary way of proceeding, and was universally resented, and so much the rather for that two bishops, Durham and Rochester, sitting in the Commission and giving their suffrages, the Archbishop of Canterbury [William Sancroft] refused to sit amongst them. He was only suspended *ab officio*, and then that was soon taken off'. Austin Dobson, *The Diary of John Evelyn* (London, 1906) III: 209–10.
53. Carpenter, *The Protestant Bishop*: 71–103.
54. Carpenter, *Henry Compton*: 125, 145–46. The origin of the office of commissary is a legacy of the medieval English church's diocesan ecclesiastical administration: a position that took recognized form in the diocese of Canterbury by the late thirteenth century and about 1350 in the diocese of Lincoln.[4] Following the English Reformation, Archbishop Thomas Cranmer issued in 1547 a commissarial commission that allowed jurisdiction in all causes, including marriage and divorce. It further granted power to the appointee to sequester fruits, induct to benefices, issue dispensations for marriages without banns published, inquire and punish those charged with blasphemy and perjury, and hold testamentary jurisdiction over men

dying within the diocese. Appointment to the office was for life. By 1575 the commissaries were allowed to visit clergy and parishes. By tradition the post was held by a priest, an equal in the ministerial office of those over whom he had jurisdiction. As an office rooted in the diocesan administrative practices of the medieval church, it was passing from usage in England in the seventeenth and eighteenth centuries. Norman Sykes, *From Sheldon to Secker, aspects of English Church History, 1660–1768* (Cambridge, 1959): 19. Bell, *Imperial Origins of the King's Church*: 65–66.

55. Bell, *Imperial Origins of the King's Church*: 44–45, 58–59.
56. *Ibid.*
57. *Ibid.* 59–60.
58. Labaree, *Royal Government*: 9, 126, 373, and his *Royal Instructions.* II: 482–90.
59. Bell, *Imperial Origins of the King's Church*: 19.
60. *O.D.N.B.* Parke Rouse, Jr., *James Blair of Virginia* (Chapel Hill, 1971): 5–7.
61. *Ibid.* 8–15. The 1685 meeting of the ministers is the first known session of the clergy in the colony that I have found. The next sessions were convened by Commissary Blair in July 1690 and on 25 June 1696 at James City. Rouse, *James Blair*, 141, *Cal.S.P.Col.Ser. 15 May 1696–31 October 1697*, J. W. R. Fortescue, ed., (London, 1904): 24–5.
62. Rouse, *James Blair*: 15–16.
63. *O.D.N.B.*
64. Rouse, *James Blair*, 17–20. *O.D.N.B.*
65. Rouse, *James Blair*, 20–21.
66. Bell, *Imperial Origins of the King's Church*: 60.
67. *Ibid.*
68. Labaree, *Royal Instructions.* II: 490.
69. Bell, *Imperial Origins of the King's Church*: 60.

Chapter 10: The Peace Disturbed: Salaries and Controversies, 1696–1777

1. Rosemary O'Day 'The reformation of the ministry, 1558–1642', in Rosemary O'Day and Felicity Heal, *Continuity and Change: Personnel and administration of the Church of England, 1500–1642* (Leicester, 1976): 57; Michael L. Zell, 'Economic problems of the parochial clergy in the sixteenth century', in Rosemary O'Day and Felicity Heal, *Princes and Paupers in the English Church, 1500–1800* (Leicester, 1981): 19–43; Felicity Heal and Rosemary O'Day, eds., *Church and Society in England: Henry VIII to James I* (London, 1977): 99–118.
2. Geoffrey F. A. Best, *Temporal Pillars: Queen Anne's Bounty, the Ecclesiastical Commission and the Church of England* (Cambridge, 1964): 11–34; Alan Savidge, *The Foundation and Early Years of Queen Anne's Bounty* (London, 1955): 1–70.
3. Best, *Temporal Pillars*: 21–28; Savidge, *Queen Anne's Bounty*: 4–15.
4. Best, *Temporal Pillars*: 28–34; Savidge, *Queen Anne's Bounty*: 16–26.
5. Christopher J. Fauske, *Jonathan Swift and the Church of Ireland, 1720–1724* (Dublin, 2002): 27–35; Irvin Ehrenpreis, *Swift: The Man, His Works, and the*

Age (London, 1967) II: 225–29, 323–26, 394–405; John Middleton Murry, *Jonathan Swift: A Critical Biography* (London, 1954): 128–30, 165–67. Denis Johnston, *In Search of Swift* (Dublin, 1959): 138.

6. Wesley Frank Craven notes that the Bermuda Company paid ministers on a contract basis in his *The Southern Colonies in the Seventeenth Century, 1607–1689* (Baton Rouge, 1949): 130.

7. Susan Myra Kingsbury, The Records of the Virginia Company of London (Washington, 1933) 3: 401–402.

8. Evarts B. Greene and Virginia D. Harrington, *American Population before the Federal Census of 1790* (New York, 1932): 135. Appendix II.

9. Martin's Hundred Plantation was probably chartered by the Virginia Company in 1618 for a group of investors known as the Society for Martin's Hundred. Granted 20,000 acres the Society could administer the plantation as they pleased to attempt to make a profit on their investment. In 1619 about 220 men and women arrived and settled at the plantation. The Anglo-Native American War (Massacre) of 1622 killed 78 of the 140 inhabitants and the remaining 62 persons were captured or fled seeking safety in Jamestown. By 1623 about 50 settlers returned to the plantation but nearly half of the group had died of disease by February 1625. See Ivor Noel Hume, *Martin's Hundred* (New York, 1982): 62–83.

10. Among the men, two were not ordained Anglican clergymen. See Appendix II.

11. Christopher Hill, *Economic Problems of the Church from Archbishop Whitgift to the Long Parliament* (Oxford, 1956): 77–8; Clara Ann Bowler, 'The Litigious Career of William Cotton, Minister', *V.M.H.B.* 86 (1978): 282–94.

12. Hening, *Virginia Statutes at Large*, I: 159–60.

13. *Ibid.* 220.

14. *Minutes of the Council and General Court of Colonial Virginia, 1622–1632, 1670–1676, with notes and excerpts from original Council and General Court Records, into 1683, now lost.* H. R. McIlwaine, ed. (Richmond, 1924): 472.

15. Hening, *Virginia Statutes at Large*, I: 240–3.

16. *Ibid.* 328; Bell, *Imperial Origins of the King's Church*: 76.

17. Greene and Harrington, *American Population*: 136. Appendix II; Hening, *Virginia Statutes at Large*, II: 45.

18. Greene and Harrington, *American Population*: 137. Appendix II.

19. Hening, *Virginia Statutes at Large*, III: 151–53.

20. *Journals of the House of Burgesses of Virginia 1695–1696, 1696–1697, 1698, 1699, 1700–1702*, H. R. McIlwaine, ed. (Richmond, 1913): 94, 98–9, 100–102. Hening, Virginia Statutes at Large, III: 151–53.

21. For a discussion of the use of tithes in England during the sixteenth and seventeenth centuries see Christopher Hill, *Economic Problems of the Church: From Archbishop Whitgift to the Long Parliament* (Oxford, 1956): 77–131.

22. *Journals of the House of Burgesses of Virginia, 1727–1734, 1736–1740*, H, R. McIlwaine, ed. (Richmond, 1910): 28, 29, 34, 35, 37, 40, 52.

23. Kingsbury, *Records of the Virginia Company*, 3: 443–44, 460–61.

24. *Ibid.* 3: 401–402.

25. Ivor Noel Hume, *Martin's Hundred* (New York, 1982): 65.

26. Susan M. Ames, ed., *American Legal Records, Vol. 7, County Court Records of Accomac-Northampton, Virginia, 1632–1640* (Washington, DC, 1954): 10–11, 15, 24–6, 39, 45, 64, 76–7, 101, 158.
27. F.P.P., XI: 305–08, the Rev. Alexander Forbes to Lt. Gov. Hugh Drysdale, Virginia, 9 May 1723.
28. *Journals of the House of Burgesses of Virginia, 1717–1734, 1736–1740*: 28, 29, 34, 35, 37, 40, 52.
29. F.P.P., XII: 188–9, Lt. Gov. William Gooch to Bishop Edmund Gibson, Williamsburg, 12 August 1732.
30. During the colonial era at least 66 Virginia parsons served as schoolmasters and in the Old Dominion an additional 23 men served as tutors to the children of prominent families. James B. Bell, 'The Colonial American Clergy of the Church of England, 1607–1783 Database', at www.jamesbbell.com.
31. Greene and Harrington, *American Population*: 140.
32. Leonard J. Trinterud, *The Forming of an American Tradition* (Philadelphia, 1949): 129–30; Bill J. Leonard, *Baptists in America* (New York, 2005): 15–16.
33. Richard L. Morton, *Colonial Virginia* (Chapel Hill, 1960), II: 751–819; Bernhard Knollenberg, *Origins of the American Revolution, 1759–1766* (New York, 1960): 53–64; Rhys Isaac, 'Religion and Authority: Problems of the Anglican Establishment in Virginia in the Era of the Great Awakening and the Parson's Cause', *W.M.Q.*, Third series. XXX (1973): 3–36; Bernard Bailyn, *Pamphlets of the American Revolution, 1750–1776* (Cambridge, 1965), I: 293–99; Bell, *Imperial Origins of the King's Church*: 77–81.
34. Thad W. Tate, 'The Coming of the Revolution in Virginia: Britain's Challenge to Virginia's Ruling Class, 1763–1776', *W.M.Q.* Third series. XIX (1962): 333–43.
35. F.P.P., XIII: 210–11. Clergy comments on a Bill which passed both Houses of Virginia Assembly, 29 November 1755.
36. F.P.P., XIII: 202–09, A Deputation of Seven Clergymen to the Bishop of London, Virginia, 29 November 1755.
37. John K. Nelson, *A Blessed Company: Parishes, Parson, and Parishioners in Anglican Virginia, 1690–1776* (Chapel Hill 2001): 48–56.
38. A clergyman's salary probably represented at least 80 to 85 per cent of his annual income. The balance would comprise the value of his parsonage, income from the produce raised and sold from his glebe holding, and fees for performing such ceremonies as baptisms, marriages, and burials. A census and description of seventeenth- and eighteenth-century accommodations for ministers and of the size, productivity, and value of parish glebes is needed.

    Parsonages have loomed large in English history and literature particularly during the eighteenth and nineteenth centuries. But as Alan Savidge has noted in his detailed work, *The Parsonage in England* (London, 1964) very few ministers lived in either thatched cottages or Georgian-style rectories. He provides a valuable historical analysis of the accommodations of English clergymen from the fourteenth to the mid-twentieth centuries (see especially 78–112). For Virginia such resources as vestry records, land records, and other papers should be systematically consulted. A useful model would be Dell

Upton's admirable study of the colonial churches, *Holy Things and Profane: Anglican Parish Churches in Colonial Virginia* (Cambridge, 1986). A number of questions should be considered including the dates of construction and use, the style of the house, the number of rooms, outbuildings, if any, and the number of acres of land and any additions or sales to the property.

39. Morton, *Colonial Virginia*, II: 756–57. For a useful and detailed analysis of Kay's case, see Rhys Isaac, 'Religion and Authority', 8–9. George MacLaren Brydon, *Virginia's Mother Church and the Political Conditions under which it Grew* (Philadelphia, 1952), II: 263–65.

40. Morton, *Colonial Virginia*, II: 756–764. Brydon, *Virginia's Mother Church*, II: 278; Isaac, 'Religion and Authority', 13–14.

41. Morton, *Colonial Virginia*, II: 786.

42. F.P.P., XIII 202–209, A Deputation of Seven Clergymen to the Bishop of London, Virginia, 29 November 1755; *Ibid.* XIII, 210–11, Clergy comments on a bill which passed both Houses of Virginia Assembly, November 1755.

43. Morton, *Colonial Virginia*, II: 784–86. Brydon, *Virginia's Mother Church*, II: 296–97.

44. Morton, *Colonial Virginia*, II: 786–88. Brydon, *Virginia's Mother Church*, II: 301.

45. *Journal of the Commissioners of Trade and Plantations, 1759–1763* (London, 1935); 66: 39. Robert G. Ingram, *Religion, Reform and Modernity in the Eighteenth Century: Thomas Secker and the Church of England* (Woodbridge, 2007): 218–20.

46. *Journal of the Commissioners of Trade and Plantations, 1759–1763* (London, 1935) 66: 39.

47. Richard Bland, *A Letter to the Clergy of Virginia, in which the Conduct of the General-Assembly is vindicated, Against the Reflexions contained in a Letter to the Lords of Trade and Plantations, from the Lord Bishop of London* (Williamsburg, 1760): iii–iv. *Journal of the Commissioners of Trade and Plantations, 1759–1763*, 66:46.

48. *Journal of the Commissioners of Trade and Plantations, 1759–1763.* 66: 46, 47.

49. *Ibid.* 56.

50. Morton, *Colonial Virginia*, II: 756–97. Brydon, *Virginia's Mother Church*, II: 301–302.

51. Landon Carter, *A Letter to the Right Reverend Father in God the Lord Bishop of L[ondo]n. Occasioned by the Letter of his Lordship's to the L[ord]ds of Trade, on the Subject of the Act of Assembly passed in the Year 1758, intituled, An Act to enable the Inhabitants of this Colony to discharge their publick Dues &c. in Money for ensuing Year. From Virginia* (Williamsburg, 1759?); Isaac, 'Religion and Authority': 12–16.

52. Richard Bland, *A Letter to the Clergy of Virginia* (Williamsburg, 1760).

53. John Camm, *A Single and Distinct View of the Act, Vulgarly entituled, The Two penny Act: Containing An Account of its beneficial and wholesome Effects in York Hampton Parish* (Annapolis, 1763).

54. Landon Carter, *The Rector Detected: Being a Just Defence of the Twopenny Act, Against the Misrepresentation of the Reverend John Camm, Rector of York-Hampton, in his Single and Distinct View. Containing also a plain Confutation of his several Hints, as a Specimen of the Justice and Charity of Colonel Landon*

Carter (Williamsburg, 1764); John Camm, *A Review of the Rector Detected or the Colonel Reconnoitred* (Williamsburg, 1764).

55. [Richard Bland] *Colonel Dismounted: or the Rector Vindicated. In a Letter addressed to His Reverence. Containing a Dissertation upon the Constitution of the Colony. By Common Sense* (Williamsburg, 1764); John Camm, *Critical Remarks on a Letter ascribed to Common Sense containing an attempt to prove that the said Letter is an Imposition on Common Sense. With a Dissertation on Drowsiness, as the Cruel Cause of the Imposition* (Williamsburg, 1765).

56. Morton, *Colonial Virginia*, II: 807–14; Brydon, *Virginia's Mother Church*, II: 302,309–10; Isaac, 'Religion and Authority': 19–21.

57. Brydon, *Virginia's Mother Church*. II: 373–86.

58. James B. Bell, 'Colonial American Clergy of the Church of England, 1607–1783', Database', at www.jamesbbell.com.

59. *The Papers of James Madison*, William T. Hutchinson and William M. E. Rachal, eds. (Chicago, 1962) I: 111–14.

60. Brydon, *Virginia's Mother Church*. II: 373–86.

61. James B. Bell, *The Imperial Origins of the King's Church in Early America, 1607–1783* (London, 2004): 189.

62. *Ibid.* 190.

Chapter 11: Virginia's Favoured Anglican Church Faces an Unknown Future, 1776

1. Richard L. Bushman, *The Age of Refinement of America: Persons, Houses, Cities* (New York, 1992): x. The *Oxford English Dictionary* notes that the phrase 'to anglicize' first appeared in use about 1710.

2. Harry S. Stout, *The New England Soul: Preaching and Religious Culture in Colonial New England* (New York, 1986): 127–28.

3. James B. Bell, *The Imperial Origins of the King's Church in Early America, 1607–1783* (London, 2004): 43–57.

4. *Ibid.* 189–209. James B. Bell, *A War of Religion: Dissenters, Anglicans and the American Revolution* (Basingstoke, 2008): 195–221.

5. My definition of a primary church is one that conducted weekly worship services and had a minister in residence. A secondary church was maintained by a lay reader and it was common for the clergyman of the closest parish to visit and conduct services and the sacraments no more frequently that once a month, or quarterly, or less often.

   Throughout the colonies there were 235 primary and an estimated 258 secondary churches. The number of congregations was most numerous in the Chesapeake colonies at the beginning of the War for Independence, where the church had been long favoured by legal establishment. See Bell, *A War of Religion*: 198–200.

6. *Ibid.* 203–209.

7. *Ibid.* 205. Only a handful of sermons survive to indicate the political attitudes of the men and in each instance they were Patriots and chaplains in the Continental Army. No printed sermons survive to illustrate the sympathies of the parsons loyal to the English crown. I am indebted to the admirable and extensive published essays of Professor Otto Lohrenz on the political

sentiments of the colony's Anglican clergymen at the outbreak of the War for Independence.

8. Bell, *War of Religion*: 205.
9. C. G. Chamberlayne, ed., *The Vestry Book of St. Paul's Parish, Hanover County, Virginia, 1706–1786* (Richmond, 1940: 569–70; C. G. Chamberlayne, ed., *The Vestry Book of Stratton Major Parish, King and Queen County, Virginia, 1729–1783* (Richmond, 1931): 219–23, 229.
10. Landon C. Bell, *Cumberland Parish, Lunenburg County Virginia, 1746–1816, Vestry Book, 1746–1816* (Richmond, 1930): 444–50; C. G. Chamberlayne, *The Vestry Book of Kingston Parish, Mathews County (until May 1 1791, Gloucester County), 1679–1796* (Richmond, 1929): 113–14; Churchill Gibson Chamberlayne, ed., *The Vestry Book and Register of Bristol Parish, Virginia, 1720–1789* (Richmond, 1898): 255–65, 269; C. G. Chamberlayne, ed., *The Vestry book of Stratton Major Parish, King and Queen County, Virginia, 1729–1783* (Richmond, 1931): 209–10, 218–22; C. G. Chamberlayne, ed., *The Vestry Book of Petsworth Parish, Gloucester County, Virginia, 1677–1793* (Richmond, 1933): 363–68. 370–73. C. G., Chamberlayne, ed., *The Vestry Book of St. Paul's Parish, Hanover County, Virginia, 1706–1786* (Richmond, 1940): 534–6, 564–6, 569–74; C. G. Chamberlayne, ed., *The Vestry Book of Blisland (Blissland) Parish, New Kent and James City Counties, Virginia, 1721–1786* (Richmond, 1935): 213–15; George Carrington Mason, ed., *The Colonial Vestry Book of Lynnhaven Parish, Princess Anne County, Virginia, 1723–1786* (Newport News, 1949): 109–10.
11. Selby, *Revolution in Virginia*: 204–26.
12. *Ibid.* 286–309.
13. John K. Nelson, *A Blessed Company: Parishes, Parsons, and Parishioners in Anglican Virginia, 1690–1776* (Chapel Hill, 2001): 35–7.
14. Alice Granbery Walter, ed., *Vestry Book of Elizabeth River Parish, 1749–1761* (New York, 1961): 14; Bell, *Imperial Origins of the King's Church*: 128–29; for the text of the oaths see C. G. Chamberlayne, ed., *The Vestry Book and Register of St. Peter's Parish, New Kent, and James City Counties, Virginia, 1684–1786* (Richmond, 1937): 502–504, and C. G. Chamberlayne, ed., *The Vestry Book of Blisland (Blissland) Parish, New Kent and James City Counties, Virginia, 1721–1786* (Richmond, 1935): 65.
15. William Waller Hening, *The Statutes at Large. Being a Collection of all the Laws of Virginia from the First Session of the Legislature in the year 1619* (Richmond, 1821) 9: 97–8.
16. *Ibid.* 9: 317–19, 439, 442–43; 10: 366; 11: 73, 130, 279, 537–38.
17. *Ibid.* 9: 424, 525–27; 10: 209–10; *The Papers of Thomas Jefferson*, Julian P. Boyd, ed (Princeton, 1950) II: 112–13; C. G. Chamberlayne, ed., *The Vestry Book of Stratton Major Parish, King and Queen County, Virginia, 1729–1783* (Richmond, 1931): xii; C. G. Chamberlayne, ed., *The Vestry Book of St. Paul's Parish, Hanover County, Virginia, 1706–1786* (Richmond, 1940): 538–40.
18. Nelson, *A Blessed Company*: 39.
19. Jonathan Boucher, *A View of the Causes and Consequences of the American Revolution; in Thirteen Discourses, Preached in North America between the years 1763 and 1775* (London, 1797): 296.
20. *Maryl.Hist.Mag.* 8 (1913): 44. Jonathan Boucher to the Rev. John James, 25 July 1769.

21. Boucher, *A View of the Causes*: 232.
22. Jonathan Bouchier, ed. *Reminiscences of an American Loyalist, 1738–1789. Being the Autobiography of the Revd. Jonathan Boucher, Rector of Annapolis in Maryland and afterwards Vicar of Epsom, Surrey, England* (Boston, 1925): 102.
23. Boucher, *A View of the Causes*: xliv.
24. *Ibid*. xlix.
25. *Ibid*. 232.
26. *Ibid*.
27. A major general in the French expeditionary forces led by General Comte de Rochambeau, Chastellaux (1734–88) was the principal liaison officer between the French Commander-in-chief and General George Washington.
28. Howard C. Rice, Jr., ed., *Travels in North America in 1780, 1781, and 1782 by the Marquis de Chastellaux* (Chapel Hill, 1963) II: 442.
29. Bell, *Imperial Origins of the King's Church*: 203–204.
30. *Ibid*. 204.
31. Isaac Weld, *Travels Through the States of North America* (1807, 1968 edition) I: 177.
32. *Ibid*. 206–207.
33. William Stevens Perry, ed., *Journals of General Conventions of the Protestant Episcopal Church in the United States, 1785–1835* (Claremont, 1874) I: 416–18.
34. J. Hector St. John de Crevecoeur, Letters From an American Farmer and Sketches of 18th Century America, Albert E. Stone, ed. (New York, 1981): 250–53.
35. Bell, *A War of Religion*: 206.
36. *Ibid*. 207–208.
37. Frederick V. Mills, Sr., *Bishops by Ballot: An Eighteenth-Century Ecclesiastical Revolution* (New York, 1978): 182–208.
38. Bell, *A War of Religion*: 204.

Chapter 12: The College of William and Mary Faces an Unknown Future, 1776

1. Parke Rouse, Jr., *James Blair of Virginia* (Chapel Hill, 1971): 43–4; Susan B. Godson, *The College of William and Mary: A History* (Williamsburg, 1993) I: 3–39; *Cal. S.P. Col. Ser., 1689–1692*, J. W. Fortescue, ed. (London, 1901): 297; *W.M.Q.*, Second series, 10 (1930): 239–42, Letter of James Blair to Governor Francis Nicholson, London, 3 December 1691.
2. *W.M.Q.*, Second series, 10 (1930): 239–42, Letter of James Blair to Governor Francis Nicholson, London, 3 December 1691.
3. Rouse, *James Blair*: 63–79. *W.M.Q.* Second series, 10 (1930): 242–44. James Blair to Francis Nicholson, London, 27 February 1691/92. A copy of the charter is conveniently found in Henry Hartwell, James Blair, Edward Chilton, *The Present State of Virginia and the College* (Williamsburg, 1940): 65–72. Godson, *College of William and Mary*: 3–21.
4. Rouse, *James Blair*: 69–72. Godson, *College of William and Mary*. I: 7–15.
5. Serving as Chancellors of the college from 1693 to the War of Independence were the following: Henry Compton, Bishop of London (1693–1700), Thomas Tenison, Archbishop of Canterbury (1700–07), Henry Compton

(1707–13), John Robinson, Bishop of London (1714–23), William Wake, Archbishop of Canterbury (1723–29), Edmund Gibson, Bishop of London (1736–37), William Wake (1736–37), Edmund Gibson (1737–48), Thomas Sherlock, Bishop of London (1749–61), Thomas Hayter, Bishop of London (1762), Charles Wyndham, second Earl of Egremont, Secretary of State (1762–63), Philip Yorke, the first earl of Hardwicke, Lord Chancellor of England (1764), Richard Terrick, Bishop of London (1764–76) and succeeded in 1788 by George Washington, who served until his death in 1799.

6. R. B. McDowell and D. A. Webb, *Trinity College Dublin, 1592–1952: An academic history* (Cambridge, 1982): 1–2. J. V. Luce, *Trinity College Dublin: The First 400 Years* (Dublin, 1992): 1–4.

7. McDowell and Webb, *Trinity College Dublin*: 2–3.

8. *Ibid.* 4–5.

9. J. V. Luce, *Trinity College Dublin*: 6. On the strength and influence of the Church of England's Puritan faction see H. C. Porter, *Reformation and Reaction in Tudor Cambridge* (Cambridge, 1958) 7.

10. Susan Myra Kingsbury, ed., *The Records of the Virginia Company of London* (Washington, DC, 1933), 3: 102.

11. H. R. McIlwaine, *Journals of the House of Burgesses of Virginia, 1619–1658/59.* (Richmond, 1915) I: 8.

12. *Ibid.* 101, 671.

13. *W.M.Q.*, Second Series, 18 (1938): 475–76, Robert Henry Land, 'Henrico and its College'.

14. *Ibid.* 483–84.

15. William Waller Hening, *The Statutes at Large being a Collection of all the Laws of Virginia from the First Session of the Legislature in the Year 1619* (Charlottesville, 1969 edition) II: 25, 37, 56.

16. *Ibid.* II: 25.

17. *Ibid.* 30–31.

18. *Ibid.* 37.

19. George MacLaren Brydon, *Virginia's Mother Church and the Political Conditions under which It Grew* (Richmond, 1947) I: 289–91. Cal. S.P. Col. Ser., 1689–1692: 452–54; Godson, *College of William and Mary*: 4, 7–15.

20. Rouse, *James Blair*: 88. Godson, *College of William and Mary*. I: 29–30.

21. Rouse, *James Blair*: 88. Document Relating to the Early History of the College of William and Mary and the Church in Virginia', Herbert L. Ganter, contributor, *W.M.Q.*, Second series. 19 (1939): 346. *Ibid.* 10 (1930): 248. Godson, *College of William and Mary*: 24–9.

22. *Cal. S.P. Col. Ser., America and West Indies, 15 May, 1696–31 Oct. 1697*, J. W. Fortescue, ed. (London, 1904): 457; *W.M.Q.*, Second series, 19 (1939): 351; *Ibid.* 8 (1928): 220–24.

23. *W.M.Q.*, Second series, 20 (1940): 118. It was not until after 1695 and the Surveyor General's death that it would prove possible for the college to begin to collect the fees from issuing surveyor's licences. Godson, *College of William and Mary*. I: 26

24. Godson, *College of William and Mary*: 26.

25. Luce, *Trinity College Dublin*: 5–6.

26. Brydon, *Virginia's Mother Church*. I: 304.

27. Hartwell, Blair, Chilton, *The Present State of Virginia*: 69–70.

28. *W.M.Q.*, Second Series, 10 (1930): 248. For accounts of the income receipts and construction costs for the first college building see *W.M.Q.*, Second series, 8 (1928): 220–25. The name Mungo Inglis suggests Scottish origins: mungo means 'the dear one' and Glasgow's patron saint is St Mungo.
29. Lambeth Palace Library, File CFS F/3, fos. 77–8, Letters and Papers, Bishop of London Henry Compton, Grant by Queen Anne for rebuilding the college building destroyed by fire in 1705; Bell, *The Imperial Origins of the King's Church*: 91; James B. Bell, *A War of Religion: Dissenters, Anglicans, and the American Revolution* (London, 2008): 31, 213.
30. Godson, *College of William and Mary*. I: 50–51.
31. Bell, *Imperial Origins of the King's Church*: 71–2.
32. Rouse, *James Blair*: 92–116; Hartwell, Blair, Chilton, *The Present State of Virginia*: 65–72.
33. Bell, *Imperial Origins of the King's Church*: 71–2.
34. *Ibid.* 72–3.
35. Godson, *College of William and Mary*. I: 35–47.
36. Bell, *Imperial Origins of the King's Church*: 72–3.
37. F.P.P., XI: 170–71, Clergy of Virginia to Bishop Compton, 25 Aug. 1703. Rouse, *James Blair*: 136, 148–51.
38. Rouse, *James Blair*: 152–74; Brydon, *Virginia's Mother Church*, I: 294–97.
39. Bell, *Imperial Origins of the King's Church*: 119; Rouse, *James Blair*: 192–208.; Godson, *College of William and Mary*; I: 58–62.
40. Bell, *Imperial Origins of the King's Church*: 71, 119, 133.
41. F.P.P., XII: 318–19. Governor Hugh Drysdale to Bishop Edmund Gibson, Williamsburgh, 26 November 1723.
42. *W.M.Q.*, First series, 21 (1911): 256–57. F.P.P., XII: 21–4, James Blair to Bishop Edmund Gibson, Williamsburg, 17 July 1724.
43. *W.M.Q.*, Second series, 20 (122), James Blair to Bishop Edmund Gibson, Williamsburg, 15 January 1734/35.
44. *Ibid.*
45. *Ibid.*
46. *W.M.Q.*, Second series, 20 (1940): 123–25. James Blair to Bishop Edmund Gibson, Williamsburg, 18 September 1735.
47. *Ibid.*
48. *Ibid.* 126–27.
49. *O.D.N.B.* Norman Sykes, *Edmund Gibson, Bishop of London, 1669–1748: A Study in Politics & Religion in the Eighteenth Century* (Oxford, 1926): 83–122.
50. Godson, *College of William and Mary*: 167–68. The College was not the only colonial collegiate institution in such financial circumstances, for it was a common experience among all of the colleges. See Beverly McAnear, 'The Raising of Funds by the Colonial Colleges', *The Mississippi Valley Historical Review*. 38 (1951): 591–612. For the desperate financial conditions at Harvard see Samuel Eliot Morison, *Three Centuries of Harvard, 1636–1936* (Cambridge, 1936): 153–60.
51. *W.M.Q.*, First series, 1 (1892–93): 72.
52. *Ibid.*
53. Godson, *College of William and Mary*. I: 53–7.
54. W.M.Q. First Series, 21 (1911): 237–39; *Ibid.* 237–39; *Ibid.* First Series, 1 (1892–93): 79; *Ibid.* Second series, 20 (1940): 119.

55. Ann D. Gordon, *The College of Philadelphia, 1749–1779: Impact of an Institution* (New York, 1989); Edward Potts Cheney, *History of the University of Pennsylvania, 1740–1840* (Philadelphia, 1940); Albert Frank Gegenheimer, *William Smith, Educator and Churchman, 1727–1803* (Philadelphia, 1943). William Smith (1727–1803) was born in Aberdeen, Scotland and graduated from King's College, Aberdeen, A.B., 1744. He was the founder and first president of the College of Philadelphia (1754–79).
56. David C. Humphrey, *From King's College to Columbia, 1746–1800* (New York, 1976); Robert A. McCaughey, *A History of Columbia University in the City of New York, 1754–2004* (New York, 2003).
57. Rouse, *James Blair*: 214–19.
58. Godson, *College of William and Mary*: 64–72.
59. *Ibid*. 65.
60. *Ibid*. 68–70.
61. *Ibid*. 67.
62. *Ibid*. 71.
63. Bell, *A War of Religion*: 204–206.
64. The five governments in succession were led by the Earl of Bath (1746–54), Duke of Newcastle (1754–56), Duke of Devonshire (1756), Duke of Newcastle (1757–62), and the Earl of Bute (1762).
65. Following Blair as President of the College were: William Dawson (1743–52), William Stith (1752–55), Thomas Dawson (1755–60), William Yates (1761–64), James Horrocks (1764–71), John Camm (1771–76), and James Madison (1776–1812).
66. Bell, *A War of Religion*: 115–20.
67. Godson, *College of William and Mary*: 112–19. For problems of student discipline at Yale in the 1760s see Brooks Mather Kelley, *Yale, A History* (New Haven, 1974): 66–7.
68. Godson, *College of William and Mary*: 101–108.
69. *Ibid*. 94–108.
70. Samuel Eliot Morison, *Three Centuries of Harvard, 1636–1936* (Cambridge, 1936): 108.
71. *Ibid*.
72. Morison, *Three Centuries of Harvard*: 102.
73. James McLachlin, *Princetonians, 1748–1768: A Biographical Dictionary* (Princeton, 1976): 666. Richard A. Harrison, *Princetonians, 1769–1775: A Biographical Dictionary* (Princeton, 1980): *Ibid*. *Princetonians, 1776–1783: A Biographical Dictionary* (Princeton, 1981): 460–63, 543.
74. Conrad Edick Wright, *Revolutionary Generation: Harvard Men and the Consequences of Independence* (Amherst, 2005).
75. *The Writings of George Washington*, John C. Fitzpatrick, ed. (Washington, DC, 1940) 37: 497–98. Douglas Southall Freeman, *George Washington: A Biography* (New York, 1951) 3: 272–73, 312–323.
76. *Ibid*. 498.
77. *Ibid*. 272–73.
78. *The Papers of George Washington*, Dorothy Twohig, ed., *Retirement Series*, W. W. Abbott, ed. (Charlottesville, 1998) 2: 37–8.
79. *Ibid*. 220.
80. Godson, *College of William and Mary*: 121–22.

81. *Ibid.* 165–240.
82. *Ibid.* 263–66.
83. *Ibid.* 267–90.
84. *Ibid.* 287–88.
85. *Ibid.* 334–56.
86. *Ibid.* 357–79.
87. *Ibid.* 381–411.

Chapter 13: Epilogue: A New Age: Breaks with the Past

1. In 1597/98 James I was the author of the works *The True Law of Free Monarchs* (1597/98) and *A Speech to the Lords and Commons of the Parliament at White-Hall* (1610) in which he argued a theological basis for monarchy. Conveniently found in David Wooton, ed., *Divine Right and Democracy* (London, 1986): 99–109.
2. James B. Bell, *The Imperial Origins of the King's Church in Early America, 1607–1783* London, 2004): 11–18, 43–57.
3. *Ibid.* 26–40.
4. Ray A. Billington, *The Protestant Crusade, 1800–1860: A Study of the Origins of American Nativism* (New York, 1938): 380–89; 407–30; Sean Wilentz, *The Rise of American Democracy: Jefferson to Lincoln* (New York, 2005): 682–85, 693–97.
5. Thomas Paine, *Common Sense* (New York, 1976); Harvey J. Kaye, *Thomas Paine and the Promise of America* (New York, 2005): 43–56.
6. It remains for an inquiring researcher to undertake a census of the churches in each new state to determine if they closed during the years of the War for Independence and if so for how long, one, two, three, or more years? With the accompanying decline of the number of active clergymen following the War did the churches re-open, if so, how many and in which states, or was the local congregation a victim of the shifting course of social, religious, and political events?
7. Frederick V. Mills, Sr., *Bishops by Ballot: An Eighteenth-Century Ecclesiastical Revolution* (New York, 1978).
8. Bell, *Imperial Origins*: 204.
9. *Ibid.* 207–208.
10. *Ibid.* 205–208.
11. William Stevens Perry, ed., *Journals of the General Conventions of the Protestant Episcopal Church in the United States, 1785–1835* (Claremont, 1874) I: 416–18.
12. Bell, *Imperial Origins of the King's Church*: 208.
13. J. C. D. Clark, *English Society, 1660–1832: Religion, Ideology and Politics during the Ancien Regime* Second edition (Cambridge, 2000): 64–7.
14. Carl H. Esbeck, 'Dissent and Disestablishment: The Church–State Settlement in the Early American Republic', *Brigham Young University Law Review* (Provo, 2004): 1386–1592; John F. Wilson and Donald L. Drakeman, *Church and State in American History* Third edition. (Boulder, 2003): 1–10.

Select Bibliography

Abbreviations

A.N.B.	*American National Biography*
A.P.C.E.Col.Ser.	*Acts of the Privy Council of England Colonial Series*
Cal.S.P.Col.Ser.	*Calendar of State Papers Colonial Series*
E.R.S.N.Y.	*Ecclesiastical Records of the State of New York*
F.P.P.	Fulham Palace Papers
H.M.P.E.C.	*Historical Magazine of the Protestant Episcopal Church*
J,A.Hist.	*Journal of American History*
J.Eccl.Hist.	*Journal of Ecclesiastical History*
Maryl.Hist.Mag.	*Maryland Historical Magazine*
Mass.Hist.Soc.P.	*Massachusetts Historical Society Proceedings*
O.D.N.B.	*Oxford Dictionary of National Biography*
P.A.A.S.	*Proceedings of the American Antiquarian Society*
S.P.G.	*Society for the Propagation of the Gospel in Foreign Parts*
V.M.H.B.	*Virginia Magazine of History and Biography*
W.M.Q.	*William and Mary Quarterly*

Abbot, George, *A Briefe Description of the Whole World*. London, 1599

Acts of the Privy Council of England, 1628 July–1629 April. London, 1958

Acts of the Privy Council of England, Colonial Series, 1613–1680. London, 1908

Adams, Henry *History of the United States of America during the First Administration of Thomas Jefferson*. New York, 1921

Addleshaw, G. W. O. and Frederick Echtells, *The Architectural Setting of Anglican Worship*. London, 1948

Ahlstrom, Sydney E. *A Religious History of the American People*. New Haven, 1972

Albright, Raymond W. *A History of the Protestant Episcopal Church*. New York, 1964

Ames, Susan M., ed., *American Legal Records, Vol. 7, County Court Records of Accomac-Northampton, Virginia, 1632–1640*. Washington, D.C., 1954

Andrews, Charles M., *The Colonial Period of American History*. New Haven, 1934

Anesko, Michael. 'So Discreet a Zeal: Slavery and the Anglican Church in Virginia, 1680–1730'. *V.M.H.B.* 93 (1985)

Arber, Edward, ed., *Works of Captain John Smith*. London, 1895

Armitage, David, *The Ideological Origins of the British Empire*. Cambridge, 2000

Bailyn, Bernard, *Pamphlets of the American Revolution, 1750–1776*. Cambridge, 1965

——*The Ideological Origins of the American Revolution*. Cambridge, 1967

——*Faces of Revolution: Personalities and Themes in the Struggle for American Independence*. New York, 1990

——*The Barbarous Years: The Conflict of Civilization, 1600–1675.* New York, 2012

Banister, John, in John Ray, *Historia Plantarum of 1686 (Philosophical Transactions,* 17 (1693)

Barnard, Leslie W. *Thomas Secker: An Eighteenth Century Primate.* Sussex, 1998

Barry, Jonathan, 'Literacy and Literature in Popular Culture: Reading and Writing in Historical Perspective', in Tim Harris, ed., *Popular Culture in England, c. 1500–1850.* New York, 1995

Bede, *The Ecclesiastical History of the English People The Greater Chronicle Bede's Letter to Egbert,* Judith McClue and Roger Collins, eds. Oxford, 1994

Beers, Donald Chidsey, *Sir Humphrey Gilbert, Elizabeth's Racketeer.* New York, 1932

Bell, James B. 'Anglican Clergy in Colonial America Ordained by Bishops of London'. *P.A.A.S.* 83 (1973)

——*The Imperial Origins of the King's Church in Early America, 1607–1783.* London, 2004

——*A War of Religion: Dissenters, Anglicans and the American Revolution.* London, 2008

Bell, Landon C., *Cumberland Parish, Lunenburg County Virginia, 1746–1816, Vestry Book, 1746–1816.* Richmond, 1930

——*Charles Parish York County, Virginia: History and Registers.* Richmond, 1932

Benes, Peter, *Meetinghouses of Early New England.* Amherst, 2012

Bennett, J. H. 'English Bishops and Imperial Jurisdiction 1660–1725'. *H.M.P.E.C.* 32 (1963)

Berkeley, Edmund, and Dorothy Smith Berkeley, eds., *The Rev. John Clayton, a parson with a scientific mind; his writings and other related papers.* Charlottesville, 1965

Bertie, David M. *Scottish Episcopal Clergy, 1689–2000.* Edinburgh, 2000

Best, Geoffrey F. A., *Temporal Pillars: Queen Anne's Bounty, the Ecclesiastical Commission and the Church of England.* Cambridge, 1964

Billings, Warren M., ed., 'Some Acts Not in Hening's Statutes The Acts of Assembly, April 1652, November 1652 and July 1653, *V.M.H.B.* 83 (1975)

——*The Old Dominion in the Seventeenth Century: A Documentary History of Virginia, 1606–1689.* Chapel Hill, 1975

——*The Papers of Francis Howard, Baron Howard of Effingham, 1643–1695.* Richmond, 1989

——*Sir William Berkeley and the Forging of Colonial Virginia.* Baton Rouge, 2004

——*A Little Parliament: The Virginia General Assembly in the Seventeenth Century.* Richmond, 2004

——*The Papers of Sir William Berkeley.* Richmond, 2007

Billings, Warren M., Selby, John E., Tate Thad W., *Colonial Virginia: A History.* White Plains, 1986

Billington, Ray A., *The Protestant Crusade, 1800–1860: A Study of the Origins of American Nativism.* New York, 1938

Bland, Richard, *A Letter to the Clergy of Virginia, in which the Conduct of the General-Assembly is vindicated, Against the Reflexions contained in a Letter to the Lords of Trade and Plantations, from the Lord Bishop of London.* Williamsburg, 1760

[Bland Richard], *Colonel Dismounted: or the Rector Vindicated. In a Letter addressed to His Reverence. Containing a Dissertation upon the Constitution of the Colony. By Common Sense.* Williamsburg, 1764

Bliss, Robert M., *Revolution and Empire: English Politics and the American Colonies in the Seventeenth Century*. Manchester, 1990

Bond, Edward L., 'Anglican Theology and Devotion in James Blair's Virginia, 1688–1743', *V.M.H.B.* 104 (1996)

——*Damned Souls in a Tobacco Colony: Religion in Seventeenth Century Virginia*. Macon, 2000

——*Spreading the Gospel in Colonial Virginia: Preaching Religion and Community. With Selected sermons and other Primary Documents. Introduction and Notes*. Lanham, Maryland, 2005

Bonomi, Patricia, *Under the Cope of Heaven*. New York, 1986

Boucher, Jonathan, *A View of the Causes and Consequences of the AmericanRevolution; in Thirteen Discourses, Preached in North America between the years 1763 and 1775*. London, 1797

Bouchier, Jonathan, ed., *Reminiscences of an American Loyalist, 1738–1789. Being the Autobiography of the Revd. Jonathan Boucher, Rector of Annapolis in Maryland and afterwards Vicar of Epsom, Surrey, England*. Boston, 1925

Bowler, Clara Ann, 'The Litigious Career of William Cotton, Minister', *V.M.H.B.* 86 (1978)

Boyd, Julian P., ed., *The Papers of Thomas Jefferson*. Princeton, 1950

Braddick, Michael J., 'The English Government, War, Trade, and Settlement, 1625–1688', in Nicholas Canny, ed., *The Origins of Empire: British Overseas Enterprise to the Close of the Seventeenth Century*. Oxford, 1998

Bradford, William, *Of Plymouth Plantation, 1620–1647*, Samuel Eliot Morison, ed. New York, 1952

Bradshaw, Paul F. *The Anglican Ordinal. Its History and Development from the Reformation to the Present Day*. London, 1971

Brayton, John Anderson, 'The Ancestry of the Rev. Francis Doughty', *The American Genealogist*. 77 (2002)

Bremer, Francis J., *John Winthrop, America's Forgotten Founding Father*. New York, 2003

Bridenbaugh, Carl, *Myths and Realities: Societies of the Colonial South*. Baton Rouge, 1952

——*Mitre and Sceptre: Transatlantic Faiths, Ideas, Personalities, and Politics 1689–1775*. New York, 1962

——*Cities in the Wilderness: 1625–1742*. New York, 1964

Brock, Robert A. *The Official Letters of Alexander Spotswood, Lieutenant-Governor of the Colony of Virginia, 1710–1722, New First Printed from the Manuscript in the Collections of the Virginia Historical Society, Collections of the Virginia History Society, new ser.* Richmond, 1882, 1885

Brook, V. J. K., *A Life of Archbishop Parker*. Oxford, 1962

Brown, Alexander, *Genesis of United States*. New York, 1890

——*The First Republic in America*. Boston, 1898

Brown, William Cabell. 'Draft for the Creation of a Bishoprick in Virginia'. *V.M.H.B.* 36 (1928)

Browning, Andrew, *Thomas Osborne, Earl of Danby and Duke of Leeds, 1632–1712*. Glasgow, 1951

Bruce, Philip Alexander, *Institutional History of Virginia in the Seventeenth Century: an inquiry into the religious, moral educational, legal, military, and political condition of the people there based on original and contemporaneous records*. New York, 1910

Brydon, George MacLaren, *Virginia's Mother Church and the Political Conditions under which it Grew*. Richmond, 1947, Philadelphia, 1952
——'The Clergy of the Established Church in Virginia and the Revolution'. *V.M.H.B.* 41 (1933)
——'David Griffith, 1742–1789. First Bishop-Elect of Virginia'. *H.M.P.E.C.* IX (1940)
——'New Light upon the History of the Church in Colonial Virginia'. *H.M.P.E.C.* X (1941)
——'Parson Sclater and His Vestry', *V.M.H.B.* 53 (1945)
Bushman, Richard L. *The Age of Refinement of America: Persons, Houses, Cities*. New York, 1992
Butler, Jon, 'Two 1642 Letters from Virginia Puritans', *M.H.S.P.* (84) 1972
——'Thomas Teackle's 333 Books: A Great Library in Virginia's Eastern Shore, 1697', *W.M.Q.*, Third Series. 49 (1992)
——*Awash in a Sea of Faith: Christianizing the American People*. Cambridge, 1990
[Calderwood, David]. *The Pastor and Prelate, or Reformation and Conformitie Shortly compared by the Word of God, by Antiquity and the Proceedings of the Ancient Kirk*. Leyden, 1628
——*The Presbyterian Government is Divine; Reasons to Prove that it is Unlawful to hear the Ministers of England; and That King may Abrogate Prelacy Without any Violation of his Oath*. Leyden, 1628
Calendar of State Papers, Colonial Series, I, 1574–1660. London, 1860
Calendar of State Papers, Colonial Series, 1675–76. London, 1893
Calendar of State Papers, Colonial Series, 1677–1680. London, 1896
Calendar of State Papers, Colonial Series, 1689–1692. London, 1901
Calendar of State Papers, Colonial Series, 1710–1711. London, 1924
Calendar of State Papers, Colonial Series, 15 May 1696–31 October 1697. London, 1904
Calendar of State Papers, Domestic Series of the Reign of Charles I, 1633–1634. London, 1863
Camm, John, *A Single and Distinct View of the Act, Vulgarly entituled, The Two-penny Act: Containing An Account of its beneficial and wholesome Effects in York*-Hampton Parish. Annapolis, 1763
——*A Review of the Rector Detected or the Colonel Reconnoitred*. Williamsburg, 1764
——*Critical Remarks on a Letter ascribed to Common Sense containing an attempt to prove that the said Letter is an Imposition on Common Sense. With a Dissertation on Drowsiness, as the Cruel Cause of the Imposition*. Williamsburg, 1765
Canny, Nicholas, 'England's New World and the Old, 1480s–1630s', in Nicholas Canny, ed., *The Origins of Empire: British Overseas Enterprise to the Close of the Seventeenth Century*. Oxford, 1998
Carpenter, Edward. *Thomas Sherlock, 1678–1761, Bishop of Bangor, 1728; of Salisbury, 1734; of London, 1748*. London, 1936
——*The Protestant Bishop: being the life of Henry Compton, 1632–1713, Bishop of London*. London, 1956
Carter, Landon, *A Letter to the Right Reverend Father in God the Lord Bishop of L[ondo]n. Occasioned by the Letter of his Lordship's to the L[ord]ds of Trade, on the Subject of the Act of Assembly passed in the Year 1758, intituled, An Act to enable the Inhabitants of this Colony to discharge their publick Dues &c. in Money for ensuing Year. From Virginia*. Williamsburg, 1759

——*The Rector Detected: Being a Just Defence of the Twopenny Act, Against the Mis-representation of the Reverend John Camm, Rector of York-Hampton, in his Single and Distinct View. Containing also a plain Confutation of his several Hints, as a Specimen of the Justice and Charity of Colonel Landon Carter*. Williamsburg, 1764

Carus-Wilson, E. M., *Medieval Merchant Venturers*. Second edition. London, 1967

Chamberlayne, Churchill Gibson, ed., *The Vestry Book and Register of Bristol Parish, Virginia, 1720–1789*. Richmond, 1898

Chamberlayne, Churchill Gibson, *The Vestry Book of Kingston Parish, Mathews County (until May 1 1791, Gloucester County), 1679–1796*. Richmond, 1929

——*The Vestry book of Stratton Major Parish, King and Queen County, Virginia, 1729–1783*. Richmond, 1931

——*The Vestry Book of Petsworth Parish, Gloucester County, Virginia, 1677–1793*. Richmond, 1933

——*The Vestry Book of Blisland (Blissland) Parish, New Kent and James City Counties, Virginia, 1721–1786*. Richmond, 1935

——*The Vestry Book and Register of St. Peter's Parish, New Kent, and James City Counties, Virginia, 1684–1786*. Richmond, 1937

——*The Vestry Book of St. Paul's Parish, Hanover County, Virginia, 1706–1786*. Richmond, 1940

Champion, J. A. I., *The Pillars of Priestcraft Shaken: The Church of England and its Enemies, 1660–1730*. Cambridge, 1992

Chatterton, Eyre, *A History of the Church of England in India Since the Early Days of the East India Company*. London, 1924

Chaudhuri, K. N., *The English East India Company*. New York, 1965

Cheney, Edward Potts, *History of the University of Pennsylvania, 1740–1840*. Philadelphia, 1940

Clark, J.C.D. *Revolution and Rebellion: State and Society in England in the Seventeenth and Eighteenth Centuries*. Cambridge, 1986

——*English Society, 1660–1832: Religion, Ideology, and Political Politics during the Ancien Regime*. Cambridge, 2000

Clarke, Basil F. L. *The Building of the Eighteenth Century Church*. London, 1963

Clement, John, compiler, 'Clergymen Licensed Overseas by the Bishops of London, 1696–1710 and 1715–1760', *H,M.P.E.C.* XVI (1947)

——'Anglican Clergymen Licensed to the American Colonies, 1710–1744'. XVII (1948)

Collier, Jeremy. *An Ecclesiastical History of Great Britain, Chiefly of England: From the First Planting of Christianity in this Island with a Brief Account of the Affairs of Religion in Ireland*. London, 1714

Collinson, Patrick. *The Elizabethan Puritan Movement*. London, 1967

——*Archbishop Grindal, 1519–1583*. London, 1979

——*From Cranmer to Sancroft*. London, 2006

Constitution and Canons Ecclesiastical 1604, with notes by J. V. Bullard. London, 1934

Craven, Wesley Frank, *The Southern Colonies in the Seventeenth Century, 1607–1689*. Baton Rouge, 1949

Cremin, Lawrence A., *American Education: The Colonial Experience, 1607–1783*. New York, 1970

Cressy, David, *Literacy and the Social Order: Reading and Writing in Tudor and Stuart England*. Cambridge, 1980

Cressy, David and Lori Anne Ferrell, eds., *Religion and Society in Early Modern England: A Sourcebook.* London, 1996

Cross, Alfred Lyon, *The Anglican Episcopate and the American Colonies.* New York, 1902

Cross, Clare, 'The incomes of provincial clergy, 1520–1645', in Rosemary O'Day and Felicity Heal, eds., *Princes and Paupers in the English Church, 1500–1800.* Leicester, 1981

Curtis, Edmund and R. B. McDowell, eds., *Irish Historical Documents, 1172–1922.* London, 1968

Curtis, Mark H., *Oxford and Cambridge in Transition, 1558–1642: An Essay on Changing Relations between the English University and English Society.* Oxford, 1959

Darley, John, *The Glory of Chelsey Colledge Revived.* London, 1662

Davidson, Philip. *Propaganda and the American Revolution, 1763–1783.* Chapel Hill, 1941

Davies, Horton *Worship and Theology in England: From Cranmer to Hooker, 1534–1613.* Grand Rapids, 1996

——*Worship and Theology in England: Andrewes to Baxter, 1603–90 — The Worship of the Puritans, 1629–1730.* New York, 1990

Davis, Richard Beale, *Intellectual Life in the Colonial South, 1585–1763.* Knoxville, 1979

Dent, Arthur, *The Plain Mans Path-way to Heaven. Wherein every man may clearly see, whether he shall be saved or damned. Set forth Dialogue-wise, for the better understanding of the simple.* Amsterdam, 1974

Dent, C. M., *Protestant Reformers in Elizabethan Oxford.* Oxford, 1983

Dickerson, Oliver M., *American Colonial Government 1696–1765: A Study of the British Board of Trade in its Relation to the American Colonies Political, Industrial, Administrative.* Cleveland, 1912

Directory of Worship, *The Directory for the Public Worship of God throughout the three kingdoms of England, Scotland, and Ireland: Together with an ordinance of Parliament for the taking away of the Book of common-prayer: and for establishing and observing of the present directory throughout the kingdom of England, and dominion of Wales, Die Jovis, 13 Marti, 1644. Ordered by the Lords and Commons assembled in Parliament, that this ordinance and directory bee forthwith printed and published. John Brown, Clerc. Parliamentarian. H Elsynge, Cler. Parl. D. Com. Printed London, 1644* [i. e. 1645?]

Dobson, Austin, *The Diary of John Evelyn.* London, 1906

Duffy, Eamon, *The Stripping of the Altars: Traditional Religion in England c. 1400–c. 1580,* Second edition. New Haven, 2005

Dunn, Richard S., James Savage, and Laetitia Yeandle, *The Journal of John Winthrop, 1630–1649.* Cambridge, 1996

Durning, Louise, and Clare Tilbury, 'Looking unto Jesus' Image and Belief in a Seventeenth-Century English Chancel', *J. Eccl. Hist.* 60 (2009)

Ehrenpreis, Irvin, *Swift: The Man, His Works, and the Age.* London, 1967

Emerson, Everett, *John Cotton,* Revised edition. Boston, 1990

Fauske, Christopher J., *Jonathan Swift and the Church of Ireland, 1720–1724.* Dublin, 2002

Fincham, Kenneth, 'Prelacy and Politics: Archbishop Abbot's Defense of Protestant Orthodoxy', *Historical Research* 61 (1988)

——*Prelate as Pastor: the Episcopate of James I.* Oxford, 1990
Fincham, Kenneth, and Peter Lake, 'The Ecclesiastical Policy of King James I', *Journal of British Studies* 24 (1985)
Fincham, Kenneth, and Nicholas Tyacke, *Altars Restored: The Changing Face of English Religious Worship, 1547–c. 1700.* Oxford, 2007
Fitzpatrick, John C., ed., *The Writings of George Washington.* Washington, D.C., 1940
Flaherty, David H., ed., *For the colony in Virginia Britannia: Lawes Divine, Morall and Martiall etc., compiled by William Strachey.* Charlottesville, 1969
Ford, Alan, *The Protestant Reformation in Ireland, 1590–1641.* Dublin, 1997
——*James Ussher, Theology, History, and Politics in Early Modern Ireland and England.* Oxford, 2007
Foster, Joseph. *Alumni Oxonienses 1500–1714.* 4 vols. Oxford, 1891–1892; *1715–1886.* 4 vols. London, 1887–1888
Foster, Stephen. *The Long Argument: English Puritanism and the Shaping of New England Culture, 1570–1700.* Chapel Hill, 1991
Freeman, Douglas Southall, *George Washington: A Biography.* New York, 1951
Ganter, Herbert L., Document Relating to the Early History of the College of William and Mary and the Church in Virginia', *W.M.Q.*, Second series. 19 (1939)
Gegenheimer, Albert Frank, *William Smith, Educator and Churchman, 1727–1803.* Philadelphia, 1943
Germann, William. 'The Crisis in the Early Life of General Peter Muhlenberg'. *P.M.H.B* 37 (1913)
Gibson, William. *The Achievement of the Anglican Church, 1689–1800: The Confessional State in Eighteenth-Century England.* Lewiston, N.Y., 1995
Godson, Susan B., *The College of William and Mary: A History.* Williamsburg, 1993
Goldie, Mark, 'Danby, the Bishops and the Whigs', in Tim Harris, Paul Seaward and Mark Goldie, eds., *The Politics of Religion in Restoration England.* Oxford, 1990
Goodwin, Edward Lewis. *The Colonial Church in Virginia and Biographical Sketches of the First Six Bishops of the Diocese of Virginia and Other Historical Papers Together with Brief Biographical Sketches of the Colonial Clergy of Virginia.* Milwaukee, 1927
Gordon, Ann D., *The College of Philadelphia, 1749–1779: Impact of an Institution.* New York, 1989
Green, Roger, *Virginia's Cure, or an Advise Narrative Concerning 'Virginia. Discovering the True Ground of the Church's Unhappiness, and the only true Remedy. As it was presented to the Right Reverend Father in God Guilbert Lord Bishop of London [Anglican], September 2, 1661. Now publish'd to further the Welfare of that and the like Plantations.* London, 1662
Greene, Evarts B. and Virginia D. Harrington, *American Population before the Federal Census of 1790.* New York, 1932
Grisbrooke, W. Jardine. *Anglican Liturgies of the Seventeenth and Eighteenth Centuries.* London, 1958
Gunderson, Joan Rezner, *The Anglican Ministry in Virginia, 1723–1766, A Study of a Social Class.* New York, 1989
Haigh, Christopher, *English reformations: religion, politics, and society under the Tudors.* Oxford, 1993

——*The Plain Man's Pathways to Heaven: Kinds of Christianity in Post-Reformation England, 1570–1640*. Oxford, 2007
——'The Clergy and Parish Discipline in England, 1570–1640' in Bridget Heal and Ole Peter Grell, eds., *The Impact of the European Reformation: Princes, Clergy and People*. Aldershot, 2008
Hakluyt, Richard, 'A discourse Concerning Western Planting Written in the Year 1584', *Collections of the Maine Historical Society*. Second series, Vol. 2. Cambridge, 1877
——*Principal Navigations, Voyages, Traffiques & Discoveries of the English Nation made by sea or overland to the remote & farthest distant quarters of the earth at any time within the compasse of these 1600 years*. London, 1589, 1907 edition
Hall, David D. *The Faithful Shepherd: A History of the New England Ministry in the Seventeenth Century*. Chapel Hill, 1972
Hall, Michael Garibaldi. *Edward Randolph and the American Colonies, 1676–1703*. Chapel Hill, 1960
Harrison, Richard A., *Princetonians, 1769–1775: A Biographical Dictionary*. Princeton, 1980
——*Princetonians, 1776–1783: A Biographical Dictionary*. Princeton, 1981
Hartwell, Henry, James Blair, Edward Chilton, *The Present State of Virginia and the College*. Williamsburg, 1940
Hatcher, Patricia Law and Edward H. L. Smith, III, 'Reexaming the Family of the Rev. John Moore of Newtown, Long Island, *New York Genealogical and Biographical Record*, 137 (2006)
Hatfield, April Lee, *Atlantic Virginia: Intercolonial Relations in the Seventeenth Century*. Philadelphia, 2004
Hawks, Francis L. and Perry, William Stevens. *Historical Notes and Documents*. Claremont, 1874
——*Collections of the Protestant Episcopal Historical Society for the Year 1851*. New York, 1851
Heal, Felicity, and Rosemary O'Day, eds., *Church and Society in England: Henry VIII to James I*. London, 1977
Hempton, David, *Religion and Political Culture in Britain and Ireland: From the Glorious Revolution to the Decline of Empire*. Cambridge, 1996
Hening, William Waller, *The Statutes at Large being a Collection of all the Laws of Virginia from the First Session of the Legislature in the Year 1619*. Charlottesville, 1969 edition
Herbert, George, *A Priest to the Temple, or the Country Parson His Character and Rule of Holy Life in The Works of George Herbert*, F. E. Hutchinson, ed. Oxford, 1941
Heylyn, Peter. *Cyprian us Anglicus or, the History of the Life and Death of the Most Reverend and Renowned Prelate William by Divine Providence, Lord Archbishop of Canterbury*. London, 1671
Hill, Christopher, *Economic Problems of the Church from Archbishop Whitgift to the Long Parliament*. Oxford, 1956
——*Society and Puritanism in Pre-Revolutionary England*. London, 1964
——*Change and Continuity in 17th-Century England*, Revised edition. London, 1991
——*The English Bible and the Seventeenth-Century Revolution*. London, 1993
Hindle, Brooke, *The Pursuit of Science in Revolutionary America, 1735–1789*. Chapel Hill, 1956
Historical Statistics of the United States: Colonial Times to 1970, Part 2. Washington, D.C., 1975

Hocker, Edward W. *The Fighting Parson of the American Revolution; a Biography of General Peter Muhlenberg, Lutheran Clergyman, Military Chieftan, and Political Leader.* Philadelphia, 1936

Hoffman, Ronald and Peter J. Albert, eds. *Religion in a Revolutionary Age.* Charlottesville, 1994

Holland, S. M. 'George Abbot: The Wanted Archbishop', *Church History* 56 (1987)

Holland, Susan, 'Archbishop Abbot and the Problem of Puritanism', *The Historical Journal* 37 (1994)

Hooker, Richard. *Of the Laws of Ecclesiastical Polity. Books VI, VII, VIII.* P. G. Stanwood, ed. Cambridge, 1981

Horn, James. *Adapting to a new world: English Society in the Seventeenth Century Chesapeake.* Chapel Hill and London, 1994

Hume, Ivor Noel, *Martin's Hundred.* New York, 1982

Humphrey, David C., *From King's College to Columbia, 1746–1800.* New York, 1976

Hurd, Richard, ed. *The Works of William Warburton.* II. London, 1788–94

Hutchinson, William T. and William M. E. Rachal, eds., *The Papers of James Madison.* Chicago, 1962

Hutton, Ronald. *The Restoration: A Political and Religious History of England and Wales, 1658–1667.* Oxford, 1985

——*Charles the Second, King of England, Scotland, and Ireland.* Oxford, 1991

Ingram, Robert G., *Religion, Reform and Modernity in the Eighteenth Century: Thomas Secker and the Church of England.* Woodbridge, 2007

Isaac, Rhys, 'Religion and Authority: Problems of the Anglican Establishment in Virginia in the Era of the Great Awakening and the Parson's Cause', *W.M.Q.,* Third series. XXX (1973)

——*Transformation of Virginia, 1740–1790.* Chapel Hill, 1982

Jacob, W.M. *Lay People and Religion in the Early Eighteenth Century.* Cambridge, 1996

——*The Clerical Profession in the Long Eighteenth Century, 1680–1840.* Oxford, 2007

Jarratt, Devereux. *The Life of Devereux Jarrett.* Cleveland, 1995, orig. 1806

Johnston, Denis, *In Search of Swift.* Dublin, 1959

Josselin, Ralph, *The Diary of Ralph Josselin, 1616–1683*, Alan Macfarlane, ed. London, 1976

Journal of the Commissioners for Trade and Plantations, April 1704–May 1782. London, 1920–38

Journals of the House of Burgesses of Virginia, 1619–1658/59. H. R. McIlwaine, ed. Richmond, 1915

Journals of the House of Burgesses of Virginia, 1695–1696, 1696–1697, 1698, 1699, 1700–1702, H. R. McIlwaine, ed. Richmond, 1913

Journals of the House of Burgesses of Virginia, 1727–1734, 1736–1740, H, R. McIlwaine, ed. Richmond, 1910

Kaye, Harvey J. *Thomas Paine and The Promise of America.* New York, 2005

Keay, John, *The Honourable Company: A History of the English East India Company.* London, 1993

Keith, George. *A Journal of Travels from New Hampshire to Caratuck, on the Continent of North America.* London, 1706

Kelley, Brooks Mather, *Yale, A History.* New Haven, 1974

Kennedy, D. E., 'King James I's College of Controversial Divinity at Chelsea', in D. E. Kennedy, Diana Robertson and Alexandra Walsham, *Grounds of Controversy.* Melbourne, 1989

Kennedy, Jean, *Isle of Devils, Bermuda under the Somers Island Company, 1609–1685*. London, 1971

Kingsbury, Susan Myra, ed., *The Records of the Virginia Company of London*. Washington, D.C., 1933

Kirby, Ethyn Williams, *George Keith (1638–1716)*. New York, 1942

Kishlansky, Mark, *A Monarchy Transformed: Britain, 1603–1714*. London, 1996

Knollenberg, Bernhard, *Origins of the American Revolution, 1759–1766*. New York, 1960

Knorr, Klaus E., *British Colonial Theories, 1570–1850*. Toronto, 1944

Knox, R. Buick. *James Ussher, Archbishop of Armagh*. Cardiff, 1967

Labaree, Leonard Woods, *Royal Government in America: A Study of the British Colonial System before 1783*. New Haven, 1930

——*Royal Instructions to British Colonial Governors, 1670–1776*. New Haven, 1935

Lake, Peter, *Moderate Puritans and the Elizabethan Church*. Cambridge, 1982

——'The Laudian style: order, uniformity and the pursuit of beauty of holiness in the 1630s', in Kenneth Fincham, ed., *The Early Stuart Church, 1603–1642*. Basingstoke, 1988

——*Anglicans and Puritans? Presbyterianism and English Conformist Thought from Whitgift to Hooker*. London, 1988

Lamb, George Woodward, compiler, 'Clergymen Licensed to the American Colonies by the Bishops of London, 1745–1781', *H.M.P.E.C.* XIII (1944)

Land, Aubrey C. *Colonial Maryland: A History*. Millwood, N.Y., 1981

Land, Robert Henry 'Henrico and its College', *W.M.Q.*, Second Series, XVIII (1938)

Langdon, George D., *Pilgrim Colony: A History of New Plymouth, 1620–1691*. New Haven, 1966

Laslett, Peter, *The World We Have Lost: Further Explored*. Third edition. London, 1983

Laugher, Charles T., *Thomas Bray's Grand Design: Libraries of the Church of England in America, 1695–1785*. Chicago, 1973

Lawson, Philip, *The East India Company: A History*. London, 1993

Leedham-Green, E. S., *Books in Cambridge Inventories: Book Lists from the Vice-Chancellor's Court Probate Inventories in the Tudor and Stuart Periods*. Cambridge, 1986

Lennon, Colm and Ciaran Diamond , in T. C. Barnard and W. G. Neely, eds., *The Clergy of the Church of Ireland, 1000–2000: Messengers Watchmen and Stewards*. Dublin. 2006

Leonard, Bill J., *Baptists in America*. New York, 2005

Levy, Babbette M., 'Early Puritanism in the Southern and Island Colonies', in *P.A.A.S.* 70 (1960)

Lockridge, Kenneth, *Literacy in Colonial New England: An Enquiry in the Context of Literacy in the Early Modern West*. New York, 1974

Lovejoy, David S. *The Glorious Revolution in America*. New York, 1972

Loveland, Clara O. *The Critical Years. The Reconstitution of the Anglican Church in the United States of America: 1780–1789*. Greenwich, 1956

Luce, J. V., *Trinity College Dublin: The First 400 Years*. Dublin, 1992

MacCaffrey, Wallace, *Elizabeth I*. London, 1983

MacCulloch, Diarmaid, *The Later Reformation in England, 1547–1603*. Basingstoke, 1990

——*Thomas Cranmer*. New Haven, 1996

McAnear, Beverly 'The Raising of Funds by the Colonial Colleges', *The Mississippi Valley Historical Review.* 38 (1951)

McCaughey, Robert A., *A History of Columbia University in the City of New York, 1754–2004.* New York, 2003

McDowell, R. B., and D. A. Webb, *Trinity College Dublin, 1592–1952: An academic history.* Cambridge, 1982

McFarlane, Anthony, *The British in the Americas: 1480–1815.* London, 1994

McLachlin, James, *Princetonians, 1748–1768: A Biographical Dictionary.* Princeton, 1976

McLaren, Colin A. *Aberdeen Students, 1600–1860.* Aberdeen, 2005

Mackesy, Piers. *The War for America, 1775–1783.* Lincoln, Neb., 1993

McIlwaine, H. R., ed., *Executive Journals of the Council of Virginia.* Richmond, 1925

Maier, Pauline. *From Resistance to Revolution: Colonial Radicals and the Development of American Opposition to Britain, 1765–1776.* New York, 1974

Maltby, Judith, *Prayer Book and People in Elizabethan and Early Stuart England.* Cambridge, 1998

——'Suffering and Surviving: The Civil Wars, the Commonwealth and the Formation of 'Anglicanism', 1642–1660' in David Cressy and Lori Anne Ferrell, *Religion and Society.* London, 2008

Mancall, Peter C., 'Native Americans and Europeans in English America, 1500–1700', in Nicholas Canny, ed., *The Origins of Empire.* Vol. 1. Oxford, 1998

——*Hakluyt's Promise: An Elizabethan's Obsession for an English America.* New Haven, 2007

Manross, William Wilson. *A History of the American Episcopal Church.* Third edition revised. New York, 1959

Marsden, R. G., 'A Virginian Minister's Library, 1635', *American Historical Review,* 11 , (1905-06)

Mason, George Carrington, ed., *The Colonial Vestry Book of Lynnhaven Parish, Princess Anne County, Virginia, 1723–1786.* Newport News, 1949

Mathews, Donald G., *Religion in the Old South.* Chicago and London, 1977

Mayer, Thomas F., *Reginald Pole: Prince and Prophet.* Cambridge, 2000

Meade, William Kidder, *Old Churches, Ministers and Families of Virginia.* Baltimore, 1969

Miller, Perry, *Errand into the Wilderness.* Cambridge, 1956

Mills, Frederick V. Sr., *Bishops by Ballot: An Eighteenth-Century Ecclesiastical Revolution.* New York, 1978

Minuets of the Council and General Court of Colonial Virginia, 1622–1632, 1670–1676, with notes and excerpts from original Council and General Court Records, into 1683, now lost. H. R. McIlwaine, ed. Richmond, 1924

Mitchell, Leonel, L. 'Episcopal Ordinations in the Church of Scotland, 1610–1688', *H.M.P.E.C.* XXXI (1962)

Montgomery, Thomas Harrison, *A Genealogical History of the Family of Montgomery, including the Montgomery Pedigree.* Philadelphia, 1863

Moore, Susan Hardman, 'Popery, Purity and Providence: Deciphering the New England Experiment', in Anthony Fletcher and Peter Roberts, *Religion, Culture and Society in Early Modern Britain.* Cambridge, 1994

Morgan, Edmund S., *American Slavery, American Freedom: The Ordeal of Virginia.* New York, 1975

——*Inventing the People. The Rise of Popular Sovereignty in England and America.* New York, 1988

Morison, Samuel Eliot, *Three Centuries of Harvard, 1636–1936.* Cambridge, 1936

——*Of Plymouth Plantation, 1620–1647.* New York, 1952

——*The Founding of Harvard College.* Cambridge, 1995 edition

Morrill, John, 'The Attack on the Church of England in the Long Parliament, 1640–1642', in Derek Beales and Geoffrey Best, eds., *History, Society and the Churches: Essays in Honour of Owen Chadwick.* Cambridge, 1985

——'The Church in England, 1642–1649', in his *The Nature of the English Revolution.* London, 1993

Morton, Richard L., *Colonial Virginia: The Tidewater Period, 1607–1710.* Chapel Hill, 1960

Muhlenberg, Henry Augustus. *The Life of Major General Peter Muhlenberg of the Revolutionary Army.* Philadelphia, 1849

Muhlenberg, John Peter Gabriel. 'Orderly Book of General John Peter Gabriel Muhlenberg, March 26–December 20, 1777'. *P.M.H.B.* 33 (1909)

Murry, John Middleton, *Jonathan Swift: A Critical Biography.* London, 1954

Nelson, John K., *A Blessed Company: Parishes, Parsons, and Parishioners in Anglican Virginia, 1690–1776.* Chapel Hill, 2001

Nugent, Nell Marion, *Cavaliers and Pioneers: Abstracts of Virginia Land Patents and Grants, 1623–1666.* Baltimore, 1983

O'Day, Rosemary, 'The reformation of the ministry, 1558–1642', in Rosemary O'Day and Felicity Heal, *Continuity and Change: Personnel and administration of the Church of England, 1500–1642.* Leicester, 1976

Pagden, Anthony, *Lords of all the World: Ideologies of Empire in Spain, Britain and France, c. 1500–c. 1800.* New Haven, 1995

Paine, Thomas, *Common Sense.* New York, 1976

Parker, Mattie E. E., *North Carolina Charters and Constitutions, 1578–1698.* Raleigh, 1963

Pearson, A.F. Scott. *Thomas Cartwright and Elizabethan Puritanism, 1535–1603.* Gloucester, 1966

Perry, James R., *The Formation of a Society on Virginia's Eastern Shore, 1615–1655.* Chapel Hill, 1990

Perry, William Stevens, ed., *Journals of General Conventions of the Protestant Episcopal Church in the United States, 1785–1835.* Claremont, 1874

——*Historical Collections Relating to the American Colonial Church.* Hartford, 1871–78

Phillimore, Robert. *The Ecclesiastical Law of the Church of England.* London. 1873

Porter, H. C., *Reformation and Reaction in Tudor Cambridge.* Cambridge, 1958

Porteus, Beilby. *The Works of Thomas Secker, LL. D., Late Lord Archbishop of Canterbury, to which is prefixed a Review of His Grace's Life and Character.* London, 1811

Procter, Francis, and Walter Howard Frere, *A New History of the Book of Common Prayer.* London, 1902

Prynne. William, *Sixteen Quaeres Proposed to our Lord Prelates.* Amsterdam, 1637

Rappahannock County Record Book, 1656–65; 1668–72

Reese, George, ed. *The Official Papers of Francis Fauquier, Lieutenant Governor of Virginia, 1758–1768.* Charlottesville, 1980–83

Rhoden, Nancy L. *Revolutionary Anglicanism: The Colonial Church of England Clergy during the American Revolution.* Basingstoke, 1999

Rice, Howard C., Jr., ed., *Travels in North America in 1780, 1781, and 1782 by the Marquis de Chastellaux.* Chapel Hill, 1963

Rightmyer, Nelson Waite. 'The Holy Orders of Peter Muhlenberg'. *H.M.P.E.C.* XXX (1961)

Rivers, Isabel. *Reason, Grace, and Sentiment: A Study of the Language of Religion and Ethics in England, 1660–1780.* Cambridge, 1991

Robbins, Caroline. *The Eighteenth-Century Commonwealthman.* Cambridge, 1959

Roche, John F. *The Colonial Colleges in the War for Independence.* Millwood, N.Y., 1986

Rodes, Robert E. Jr. *Law and Modernization in the Church of England: Charles II to the Welfare State.* South Bend, 1991

Rollinson, David, *The Local Origins of Modern Society: Gloucestershire 1500–1800.* London, 1992

Rose-Troup, Frances, *The Massachusetts Bay Company and its Predecessors.* New York, 1930

Rouse, Parke, Jr., *James Blair of Virginia.* Chapel Hill, 1971

Rudolph, Robert, *Chartered Companies and their Role in the Development of Overseas Trade.* London, 1969

Rutman, Darret B., 'The Evolution of Religious Life in Early Virginia', *Lex et Scientia. The International Journal of Law and Science.* 14 (1978)

Rutman, Darret B. and Anita H. Rutman, *A Place in Time: Middlesex County, Virginia, 1650–1750.* New York, 1984

St John de Crevecoeur, J. Hector, *Letters From an American Farmer and Sketches of 18th Century America,* Albert E. Stone, ed. New York, 1981

Savidge, Alan, *The Foundation and Early Years of Queen Anne's Bounty.* London, 1955

Sibley, John Langdon, *Biographical Sketches of Graduates of Harvard University, in Cambridge, Massachusetts.* Cambridge, 1873

Smith, John, *Captain John Smith, Writings with other Narratives of Roanoke, Jamestown and the First English Settlement of America.* New York, 2007

Solberg, Winton U., *Redeem the Time: The Puritan Sabbath, in Early America.* Cambridge, 1977

Spurr, John. *The Restoration of the Church of England, 1646–1689.* New Haven, 1991

Stone, Lawrence, *Family and Fortune: Studies in Aristocratic Finance in the Sixteenth and Seventeenth Centuries.* Oxford, 1973

Stout, Harry S. *The New England Soul: Preaching and Religious Culture in Colonial New England.* New York, 1986

Strype, John, *The Life and Acts of John Whitgift, D.D.: The Third and Last Lord Archbishop of Canterbury in The Reign of Queen Elizabeth.* Oxford, 1822

Sydnor, William. 'Doctor Griffith of Virginia: Emergence of a Church Leader, March 1779–June 3, 1786'. *H.M.P.E.C.* XLV (1976)

——'Doctor Griffith of Virginia: The Breaking of a Church Leader, September 1786–August 3, 1789'. *H.M.P.E.C.* XLIV (1976)

——David Griffith — Chaplain, Surgeon, Patriot'. *H.M.P.E.C.* XLIV (1975)

Sykes, Norman, *Edmund Gibson, Bishop of London, 1669–1748: A Study in Politics & Religion in the Eighteenth Century.* Oxford, 1926

——*Church and State in England in the XVIIIth Century*. Cambridge, 1934
——*From Sheldon to Secker, aspects of English Church History, 1660–1768*. Cambridge, 1959
Tate, Thad W. 'The Coming of the Revolution in Virginia: Britain's Challenge to Virginia's Ruling Class, 1763–1776', *W.M.Q.* Third series. XIX (1962)
——'William Stith and the Virginia Tradition', in Lawrence Leder, ed., *The Colonial Legacy*. New York, 1973
Tawney, R. H., *Religion and the Rise of Capitalism: A Historical Study*. New York, 1954
Taylor, Stephen. 'William Warburton and the Alliance of Church and State'. *J.Eccl.Hist.* 43 (1992)
——'Whigs, Bishops and America: The Politics of Church Reform in Mid-Eighteenth-Century England'. *The Historical Journal* 36 (1993)
Trevelyan, Raleigh, *Sir Walter Raleigh*. London, 2002
Trevor-Roper, Hugh R. *Archbishop Laud, 1573–1645*. Second edition. Hamden, Conn., 1962
Trinterud, Leonard J., *The Forming of an American Tradition: A Re-examination of Colonial Presbyterianism*. Philadelphia, 1949
Tuckerman, Bayard, *Peter Stuyvesant, Director-General for the West India Company in New Netherland*. New York, 1893
Tuttle, Julius Herbert, 'The Libraries of the Mathers', *P. A. A. S.* 20 (1911)
Twohig, Dorothy, ed., *The Papers of George Washington, Retirement Series*, W. W. Abbott, ed. Charlottesville, 1998
Tyacke, Nicholas, 'Puritainism, Arminianism and Counter Revolution', in Conrad Russell, ed., *The Origins of the English Civil War*. London, 1973
——*The History of the University of Oxford, Seventeenth Century*. Oxford, 1997
Tyler, Lyon Gardiner, *Encyclopedia of Virginia Biography*. New York, 1915
Upshur, Anne Floyd and Ralph T. Whitelaw, 'Library of the Rev. Thomas Teackle,' *W.M.Q.*, Second Series, 23 (1943)
Upton, Dell, *Holy Things and Profane: Anglican Parish Churches in Colonial Virginia*. Cambridge, 1986
Van Horne, John C. ed. *Religious Philanthropy and Colonial Slavery: The American Correspondence of the Associates of Dr. Bray, 1717–1777*. Urbana, 1985
Van Tyne, Claude Halstead. *The Loyalists in the American Revolution*. New York, 1902
——*The Causes of the War of Independence*. Boston, 1922
Walsh, James P. "'Black Cotted Rascals:' Anti-Anglican Criticism in Colonial Virginia', *V.M.H.B.* 88 (1980)
Walter, Alice Granbery, ed., *Vestry Book of Elizabeth River Parish, 1749–1761*. New York, 1961
Warburton, William. *Alliance of Church and State*. London, 1736
Washburn, Wilcombe E. *The Governor and the Rebel: A History of Bacon's Rebellion in Virginia*. Chapel Hill, 1957
Webb, Stephen Saunders. 1676, *The End of American Independence*. New York, 1984
——*Lord Churchill's Coup: The Anglo-American Empire and the Glorious Revolution Reconsidered*. Syracuse, 1995
Weir, David A. *Early New England: A Covenanted Society*. Grand Rapids, 2005
Weis, Frederick Lewis. *The Colonial Clergy and the Colonial Churches of New England*. Lancaster, 1938

——*The Colonial Clergy of Virginia, North Carolina and South Carolina.* Boston, 1955

——'The Colonial Clergy of the Middle Colonies: New York, New Jersey, and Pennsylvania, 1628–1776', *P.A.A.S.* 66 (1956)

Wertenbaker, Thomas J. *The Golden Age of Colonial Culture.* New York, 1949

Weston, Edward. *The Englishman Directed in the Choice of his Religion, Reprinted for the Use of English Americans, with a Prefatory Address Vindicating the King's Supremacy and Authority of Parliament, in Matters of Religion, and Thereby Demolishing All the Pleas of Dissenters for Separation, according to the Concessions of the Dissenting Gentleman's Answer to the Rev. Mr. White's Letters. Pages 3, and 53. Being Also a Justification of the Church of England Against the Misrepresentation of that Answer.* Boston, 1748

White, Graeme J., *Restoration and Reform, 1153–1165: Recovery from Civil War in England.* Cambridge, 2000

Whiteman, Anne. 'The Re-Establishment of the Church of England, 1660–1663'. *Transactions of the Royal Historical Society.* Fifth Series. 5 (1955)

——'The Restoration of the Church of England', in *From Uniformity to Unity, 1662–1962.* Geoffrey F. Nuttal and Owen Chadwick, eds. London, 1962

——*The Compton Census of 1676: A Critical Edition.* Oxford, 1986

Whitmore, William Henry, ed. *The Andros Tracts. The Prince Society.* II. Boston, 1870

Wickwire, Franklin B. *British Subministers and Colonial America.* Princeton, 1966

Wiffen, Marcus, *Stuart and Georgian Churches: The Architecture of the Church of England outside London, 1603–1837.* London, 1947

Wilentz, Sean, *The Rise of American Democracy: Jefferson to Lincoln.* New York, 2005

Wilson, John F. and Donald L. Drakeman, *Church and State in American History.* Third edition. Boulder, 2003

Wingfield, Capt. Edward-Maria, 'A Discourse of Virginia', *Archaelogia Americana: Transactions and Collections of the American Antiquarian Society,* IV (1860)

Winthrop Papers. Boston, 1931

Wood, Gordon S. *The Radicalism of the American Revolution.* New York, 1992

Woodforde, James, *The Diary of a Country Parson, the Reverend James Woodforde, 1758–1781,* James Beresford, ed. London, 1924–31

Woolverton, John Frederick, *Colonial Anglicans in North America.* Detroit, 1984

Wooton, David, ed., *Divine Right and Democracy.* London, 1986

Wright, Conrad Edick, *Revolutionary Generation: Harvard Men and the Consequences of Independence.* Amherst, 2005

Wrightson, Keith, *English Society, 1580–1680.* London, 1982

Yates, Nigel, *Buildings, Faith, and Worship: The Liturgical Arrangement of Anglican Churches, 1600–1900.* Revised edition. Oxford, 2000

Young, B. W. *Religion and the Enlightenment in Eighteenth-Century England: Theological Debate from Locke to Burke.* Oxford, 1998

Young, Brian, 'A History of Variations: The Identity of the Eighteenth-Century Church of England', in Tony Claydon and Ian McBride, eds., *Protestantism and National Identity: Britain and Ireland, c. 1650–1850.* Cambridge, 1998

Yule, George, 'James VI and I: Furnishing the Churches in His Two Kingdoms', in Anthony Fletcher and Peter Roberts, *Religion, Culture and Society in Early Modern Britain.* Cambridge, 1994

Zell, Michael L., 'Economic problems of the parochial clergy in the sixteenth century', in Rosemary O'Day and Felicity Heal, eds., *Princes and Paupers in the English Church, 1500–1800*. Leicester, 1981

Zimmer, Anne Young, *Jonathan Boucher, Loyalist in Exile*. Detroit, 1978

Zimmer, Anne Young and Kelly, Alfred H. 'Jonathan Boucher: Constitutional Conservative'. *J.A.Hist.* 58 (1972)

Index

Abbot, George, Archbishop of
Canterbury (1662–1633), 20,
37–8, 54, 62, 75, 81, 83, 86;
Puritan, 38; member of Virginia
Company of London, 38
Abbot, Sir Maurice, merchant
(1565–1642), 86
Aberdeen: Kings's College, 67, 68;
Marischal College, 120
Accomack Parish, 42, 98
Acts of Parliament: Act to Prevent
Frauds and Abuses of 1696, 110;
Act of Toleration, 1689, 5, 167–69,
171, 174; Act of Uniformity, 54
Adams, John (1735–1826), 4, 12, 162
Adams, Samuel (1722–1803), 4, 162
Admiralty, 114
Africa, 25
American Revolution, 12, 128, 158,
159
Americanization, 10, 12, 136–37, 147
Ames, William (1576–1633), 88
Andrewes, Lancelot, bishop
(1555–1626), 167
Andros, Edmund, governor
(1637–1714), 23, 30, 125, 150,
151, 152; relations with James
Blair, 151
Anglicization, 67, 111, 127, 136–37,
147, 148, 152, 155, 168
Anne, Queen (1665–1714), 122, 151;
First Fruits and Tenths, 122–23;
Queen Anne's Bounty, 123
Antwerp, 18
archbishops, bishops, 2–3, 34, 37, 137,
140, 141, 144, 145, 156, 163, 169
archdeacon, 61, 118
Archdioceses, dioceses, 2, 34, 118,
137, 140, 144, 163, 169
Argall, Governor Sir Samuel, governor
(1580–1624), 29–30, 32, 50, 75, 85;

Proclamation, religious and moral
discipline, 29, 30
Arnold, Benedict (1741–1801), 139
Auditor General of the Plantation
Revenues, 114
Aylmer, John, Bishop of London
(1521–94), 56, 78

Bacon's Rebellion, 1676, 24, 111, 114,
149
Bancroft, Richard, Archbishop of
Canterbury (1544–1610), 20
Banister, John (1650–92), 96, 100, 112
Baptists, 133–34, 144, 168, 173;
churches, number of, 166;
ministers, 164
Bargrove, Thomas (1581–1621), 96
Battle of the Boyne, 24
Baxter, Richard (1615–91), 56
Bay Psalm Book, 163
Bayly, Lewis, Bishop of Bangor
(1565–1631), 56
Bede, Venerable (672 or 673–735), 5
Bennett, Richard, governor (1609–75),
23
Bennett, Thomas (1605–????), 87, 89
Berkeley, George, bishop (1685–1753),
3, 22, 167
Berkeley, Sir William, governor
(1605–77), 23, 24, 30, 40, 42, 53,
64, 86, 89, 91, 94, 95, 99, 105,
111–12, 119, 125
Bermuda, 18, 32, 76
Bible: Geneva, 7, 53–4; Bishop's, 7,
53–4; King James I, 7, 54; Great
Bible, 54
Blair, James (1655–1743), 5, 91, 99,
100, 105, 106, 113, 119–21, 127,
128, 147, 148, 149–50, 151, 152,
153, 154–55, 156, 161, 166

CPSIA information can be obtained at www.ICGtesting.com
Printed in the USA
LVOW10*1716070414

380669LV00012B/365/P